CU00828585

Wings
on the
Whirlwind

Wings on the Whirlwind

Compiled and edited
by
Anne Grimshaw

North West Essex and East Hertfordshire Branch
Air Crew Association

For they have sown the wind and they shall reap the whirlwind.
Hosea 8:7.

They have sowed the wind and now they are going to reap the whirlwind.
Sir Arthur 'Bomber' Harris, Chief of Bomber Command, 1942

Compiled and edited by Anne Grimshaw
Copyright: North West Essex and East Hertfordshire Branch of the Air Crew Association
1998

Published by:
Air Crew Association
North West Essex and East Hertfordshire Branch
John Guy (Secretary)
'The Staithe'
43 Farmadine
Saffron Walden
Essex CB11 3HR

ISBN 0 9534486 0 6

Printed by:
Warwick Printing Co. Ltd.,
Theatre St
Warwick C34 4DR

Cover design and photographs: Anne Grimshaw

Contents

Foreword

by

Bill Reid, holder of the Victoria Cross

SOME thirty years after the end of the war, in 1977, the Air Crew Association was formed. It was then that people began to retire from work and had more time on their hands. They wanted to renew old friendships and it was this that assured the new Association's success. We can see today, in its twenty-first year, how it has gone from strength to strength as more members have joined and given of their leisure for the benefit of the Association.

Bill Reid VC, 1997

I have been fortunate to have been associated with the ACA since its inception and enjoyed many meetings with members all over the UK, including Northern Ireland. Some of the branches have been especially active in helping to strengthen the Association. This applies particularly to the North West Essex and East Hertfordshire Branch based at Saffron Walden, Essex, and so when I was asked to write a few lines to add to a book of their members' memoirs I accepted gladly.

I was in the RAF hospital at Ely, Cambridgeshire, when it was announced that I had been awarded the Victoria Cross. That was on 12 December 1943. I left hospital about a week later and picked up my kit from Syerston, Nottinghamshire, as my squadron, 61, had moved to Skellingthorpe,, west of Lincoln. I then went on two weeks' sick leave.

At the end of my sick leave I had to report to Air Vice Marshal Cochrane at Swinderby. After a few preliminaries on the state of my health, he announced that I was to be posted to 617 Squadron at Woodhall Spa, to the south-east of Lincoln.

I was then in the process of forming a new crew, as my flight engineer was still convalescing and my gunners had joined other crews while I had been in hospital. Les Rolton, my bomb aimer, joined me and Dave Luker, wireless operator/air gunner, with whom I had shared a room when instructing at Operational Training Unit, also said he would start his second tour with me. It was then a case of picking up crew as they came available.

Wing Commander Leonard Cheshire was in charge at Woodhall Spa where some of the operations were being filmed by a film crew from London. Thus it was in the first week of February 1944 that they had to get back to London. Most of the squadron had been on ops. the night before and so W/Cdr Cheshire asked me if I would fly them down to Northolt near London. I agreed immediately asking who would crew with me. He said the engineering leader would act as my engineer and, as it was in daylight, I could map read so I wouldn't need a navigator. I also had my wireless operator aboard in case we needed a fix.

Please remember I hadn't flown for three months, had been in hospital for six weeks and had a 'sprog' flight engineer. (I am making all the excuses before the facts are revealed!)

We took off in a spare Lancaster, as I still hadn't been allocated one, and we got down to Northolt all right, although something had made me wonder whether my flight engineer was quite as capable as I'd like. We circled round, did the usual drills and came in to land at this fighter station, then run by a Polish Spitfire squadron. I could feel on approach that I was a bit high and normally would have gone round again. But it was this feeling of uncertainty about my flight engineer's actions if I overshot that made me decide to have a go at landing.

I cut the power, got down to the runway and levelled out but there was a strong cross-wind. I drifted onto the grass as I touched down but I still thought I'd make it all right. However, this being a fighter 'drome, it had all those blast(ed) bunkers erected near the end of the runway. I was rapidly approaching one of them but felt I might manage to swing the nose round at the last minute. I did and avoided colliding with the bunker.

Just as the plane came to a halt, I felt a click as I stopped. The underpart of the tail fin had caught on the top of the banking of the blast bunker—and the tail unit broke off at the joint beside the Elsan chemical toilet: that meant you could look right out of the tail... You can appreciate why we returned to Woodhall Spa by bus... albeit an RAF bus.

When I got back I explained what had happened to the Group Commander who wasn't impressed. Next day, W/Cdr Cheshire spoke to me in his office saying that it was his fault for not checking me out after a long lay-off. I said it wasn't his fault at all and explained that it was the lack of a regular flight engineer as far as I was concerned.

I don't think there are, or have been, many who have been awarded the Victoria Cross on one trip and then, on the next, been given a red endorsement. It could perhaps be worthy of an entry in *The Guinness book of records*!

I congratulate the Saffron Walden-based branch of the Air Crew Association on their enterprise.

Bill Reid VC
61 and 617 Squadrons, Syerston and Woodhall Spa

Introduction

MY only claim to fame in the literature of wartime aviation is a small book, *The last flight of Lancaster LL919 W*. It describes how I researched the crew and events surrounding the shooting down of one ill-fated Lancaster bomber during World War II. This 'project' developed into a slide-talk presentation which I give to various RAF groups, including the North West Essex and East Hertfordshire Branch of the Air Crew Association, as well as 'civilian' groups. However, it was sufficient by way of 'credentials' to be asked if I would like to compile members' memories of their flying days into a book. I wasn't even around during World War II and have no connections with the RAF—my grandfather and father were army men in World Wars I and II. However I have had *one* flying lesson! Consequently, I felt something of a 'sprog' but very honoured to be asked and agreed to take on the task.

Having worked on various books and similar 'projects' before, I knew how time-consuming it would be and, being in full-time employment as well, I knew I wouldn't have many spare moments until it was finished!

Working closely with John Guy, secretary of the above branch of the ACA and whose idea this book was, we compiled a list of potential 'candidates' based on questionnaires John had circulated around members of the branch. The response was gratifying with anecdotes, reminiscences and photographs being sent to me. There were invitations to visit, come for a cup of tea, lunch or a drink and 'interviews' ensued. Several members had already written of their experiences either for publication elsewhere or for their own and families' interest. They kindly allowed me to use chapters from their books.

Others spent hours talking to me, correcting my draft of their 'interview' ("as told to Anne Grimshaw...") or writing their memories in their own words. Even so, it was not possible to use everything that everyone sent to me exactly as it was sent and so some editing had to take place. For example, imaginary dialogue has been used here and there to liven up the narrative and make it more 'immediate'—literary licence—but each chapter has been approved by the contributor before publication.

Consequently, I would like to thank everyone who took the trouble to contribute to this book and answer my questions, either face-to-face or on the telephone. Not only for their time but for all the good wishes and encouragement during the book's production. I really felt that this branch of the ACA had taken me under its wing, so to speak! Indeed, many thanked *me* for taking an interest and giving my time to write their stories. Their thanks are much appreciated but not necessary—it was a pleasure.

Certain themes recur throughout: the aircrews' gratitude to the ground crews, without whom they could not have operated and who did their work in often appalling conditions; the worst thing about aircrews' time in the RAF during the war was losing friends and, amongst the fondest memories, the WAAFs who welcomed them back to base. Perhaps the main 'theme' was a love of flying and aircraft.

Their stories are touching, funny, harrowing, dramatic—but with the wisdom of hindsight these men no longer seek the 'excitement' of war although several say they would not have wanted to miss the experiences it offered at the time. However, war is the last thing they want for their children and grandchildren.

There is no 'line-shooting', no bragging, no derring-do, no heroics; indeed, many men were often casual and dismissive of what they did and it was sometimes difficult to get them to tell me what they did that could be considered 'brave'. Many were unduly modest: "I didn't do anything much... It was pretty dull much of the time... I had a very undistinguished RAF career... Sorry I can't make it more interesting... I was no different from thousands of others... It was my just my job... It's all been written about before..." Maybe it has in general terms or as seen by top brass or military historians, but it has not often been written about from their own individual points of view: that's what makes each man's contribution unique.

Regarding decorations: again came the modest replies, "My DFC? Oh, *that*... I've forgotten what I got it for... Lots of chaps did the same as me but they never got recognised... Oh, I just got it for general good service... I was quite ordinary..." Ordinary? Perhaps, but they did the most extraordinary things in world-shaking circumstances.

Most contributions consist of short anecdotes or incidents although some are long and detailed, for example, describing life as a prisoner of war, what it was like being a pilot on a bombing raid and what kind of career the RAF could offer a post-war pilot during the Cold War.

When I asked how they had felt when they had joined the RAF, or during their training or on ops. with every likelihood of being killed they often replied, "We never thought of tomorrow."

So now, whenever I see a gentleman who looks as though he's passed the Big Seven-O (at least), I wonder what he did. Had he been in the RAF? Perhaps leading a Pathfinder Force marking targets? Had he baled out over enemy territory? Saved colleagues' lives? Extinguished fires in aircraft engines at umpteen thousand feet? Spent long, lonely hours over the sea on anti-submarine patrols? Brought a bomber out of a spin and limped home with all still safely on board? Or done any one of the many extraordinary things written about in this book. I see such men every day in the street, on the train, driving cars, quite 'ordinary' today but fifty years ago they were the heroes of the day.

Now, with our often misplaced political correctness, a luxury that in peacetime we can afford, we forget or even belittle what these men did. Whether they joined the RAF because their pals joined, or because they didn't want to be left out, or because they thought it offered glamour and excitement, or even for the higher ideals of preserving democracy and freedom, does not matter. They took part in one of the momentous events of history and we, the following generations, must never forget what they did for us and should be forever grateful.

The post-war generations often have little idea as to what their fathers and grandfathers actually did, what a tremendous effect those war years had on their lives and how often to them the war "seems like yesterday". In the late 1930s many young men had boring, dead-end jobs with no 'career prospects'. Many had not had the benefit of a good education. They came from all walks of life: shop assistant, clerk, university undergraduate, actor, librarian, factory worker, labourer... They did not travel abroad on holiday as we do today. They did not have the opportunity to indulge in thrilling, 'high risk' activities and sports. They did not have much money. Few had cars. Those joining the RAF all loved aeroplanes and the idea of flying.

Within a few months after joining the RAF many of yesterday's teenagers found themselves in Canada, South Africa or the USA learning to be a member of an aircrew; many trainee pilots had not even had the opportunity to learn to drive a car! They were sent to Commonwealth countries because good weather there meant regular flying and they were safe from enemy air attacks whilst training.

Once in the RAF and undergoing training, the greatest fear of many was that the war would be over before they had had a chance to do their bit. But, for most, it wasn't over and they had their chance.

The ambition to fly overrode everything else and they achieved that ambition at a time when it would have otherwise been impossible for most of them to even set foot inside an aircraft. They were grateful for that chance and for what the RAF offered them but it is we, the generations who followed, who should be grateful to them.

Anne Grimshaw

Acknowledgements

I am indebted to all the contributors for their words and pictures. Thanks also go to John Guy for proof reading and whose idea this book was; Rod Jones former Royal Navy and Royal Naval Reserve but happy to 'help out' the Brylcreem boys(!) by proof reading, and to Ted Wharnsby (former Royal Observer Corps) for drawing the cartoons and laboriously checking miscellaneous details.

After fifty years or more it has not always been possible to trace the copyright holders of some of the pictures. These were supplied for the book in good faith and have been used as they so graphically illustrate the stories; similarly with stories written by now deceased members of this branch of the ACA where it has been virtually impossible to trace family or publisher. However, to anyone who has not been credited, I must extend apologies for any inconvenience caused.

I extend my thanks to everyone who so willingly gave their time to help in the production of this book.

AG

Glossary

AC1, AC2 = Aircraftman First Class/Second Class
ack-ack guns/fire = anti-aircraft guns/fire
AFB = Air Force Base
AFC = Air Force Cross
AOC = Air Officer Commanding
AOS = Air Observer School
AG = Air gunner
ATC = Air Training Corps
Bar = Bar on medal ribbon to indicated the award was given on two separate occasions
BOAC - British Overseas Airways Corporation
Caterpillar Club = Organisation for airmen who parachuted out
CB = Companion of the Order of the Bath
CBE = Compnion of the Order of the British Empire
CFS = Central Flying School
CO = Commanding Officer
Cookie = 4,000lb bomb
DF = Direction finding
DFC = Distinguished Flying Cross
DFM = Distinguisged Flying Medal
DR = distant reading
DSC = Disttinguished Service Cross (Navy)
DSM = Distinguished Service Medal (Navy)
DSO = Distinguished Service Order
EFTS = Elementary Flying Training School
ENSA = Entertainment National Service Association
ETA = Estimated Time of Arrival
FAA = Fleet Air Arm
FIS = Flying Instructors' School
flak = anti-aircraft fire
F/O = Flying Officer
F/Lt = Flight Lieutenant
FU = Ferry Units
G = force of gravity
Gee = Navigational aid using ground transmitters and airborne receiver
Hallybags = Halifax bombers
HCU = Heavy Conversion unit
HFDF = High Frequency Direction Finding
H2S = Experimental airborne radar navigational and target location aid
IFF = Identification Friend or Foe
ITW = Initial Training Wing
Ju88 = Junkers 88 (German fighter)
Kriegies = Prisoners of War
LAC = Leading Aircraftman
Link trainer = early type of flight similator
MBE = Member of the Order of the British Empire

Me109 = Messerschmitt 109 – (German fighter)
Met. = Meteorological
MF = Medium Frequency
MFDF = Medium Frequency Direction Finding (station)
Mozzie = Mosquito bomber
MTU = Mosquito Training Unit
NAAFI = Navy, Army, Air Force Institute (service canteens)
NATO = North Atlantic Treaty organisation
NCO = Non Commissioned Officer
NJG = Nacht Jagdflieger Gruppe
O/C = Officer in Charge
OCU = Operational Conversion Unit
OFU = Operational Ferry Unit
ops. = operations
OTU = Operational Training Unit
PFF = Pathfinder Force
PNB = Pilots, navigators, bomb aimers
P/O = Pilot Officer
POW = Prisoner of War
QDM = code for a means of finding out by wireless the location of an aircraft and directing it to a course
R&R = Rest and recuperation
RAAF = Royal Australian Air Force
RAE = Royal Aircraft Establishment
RAFRO = Royal Air Force Reserve Officers
RAFVR = Royal Air Force Volunteer Reserve
RCAF = Royal Canadian Air Force
Recce = reconnaissance
RNZAF = Royal New Zealand Air Force
R/T = Radio telegraphy/telephony/transmission/transmitter
SD = Special Duties
SFTS = Service Flying Training School
Sgt = Sergeant
S/Ldr = Squadron Leader
SD = Special Duties
SOE = Special Operations Executive
Sprog = new recruit
SWO = Station Warrant Officer
u/s = unserviceable, useless
u/t = under training
TI = Target Indicator
VC = Victoria Cross
WAAF = Women's Auxiliary Air Force
Wimpeys = Wellington bombers
'Wings' = qualification to fly
W/O = Warrant Officer
W/O2 = Warrant Officer 2nd Class
W/OP = Wireless operator
WOP/AG = Wireless operator/Air gunner
WRNS = Women's Royal Naval Service
W/T = Wireless telephony/telegraphy/transmission/transmitter

Mel Bennett

DFC, USA DFC, Star of Brunei

Pilot

30, 34, 47, 88 Squadrons, 240 and 242 OCU, CFS

Mel Bennett during pilot training in Florida 1945

Mel taking the salute on Remembrance Day 1994

Stia Negara Brunei (Star of the State of Brunei) awarded to Mel in 1963 (See story opposite)

Mel Bennett

Mel Bennett entered the RAF in 1943 after two years with the Air Training Corps. He went first to Canada and then to Florida, USA, where he trained as a pilot. He returned to England and in 1949 was involved in the Berlin Airlift. In 1951 he was posted to 88 Squadron (Singapore) after completing a course at RAF Calshot on Sunderland flying boats. While in Singapore the Korean War broke out and Mel flew fifty-six missions over Korea. For his services in Korea he was awarded the Distinguished Flying Cross. He had already been awarded the Queen's Commendation for Valuable Service in the Air—for the first time. Back in England in 1954 he trained on Meteor and Vampire jets and qualified as an instructor with Transport Command Examining Unit. In 1962 he returned to Singapore and undertook a special mission in Borneo for which he was awarded the Star of Brunei and The Queen's Commendation for Valuable Service in the Air—for the second time.

In 1966 he flew the first Hercules aircraft from the USA into the UK. Before leaving the RAF to begin a new career in civil aviation, he formed two new squadrons which were to fly Hercules. During his flying career Mel must surely rank as a founder member of the 'jet set'—it is easier to list where Mel hasn't been in the world, rather than where he has been! His latest 'career' is as Supernumerary Officer with 1824 Squadron Air Training Corps coaching cadets in operational flying and navigation.

Star of Brunei

IN mid 1962, when I was Officer Commanding 34 Squadron at Seletar, Singapore, the Chinese army invaded Assam in north-eastern India. My squadron, flying the big transport planes, Blackburn Beverleys, was moved to Calcutta to evacuate British civilians from the city and also fly Indian troops to the front line—politically, a hush-hush operation.

One day I was told that a Shackleton would collect me as the Air Officer Commanding in Singapore wanted to see me. The result was that my squadron was to move to Borneo for a special mission—an 'emergency' in Brunei.

It was late afternoon on 8 December 1962 when a hundred Ghurkas boarded the Beverley and I took off. It was dark as we were coming into land at an airfield in the jungle but we'd been spotted.

"What are all those blue flashes?" a voice behind me said.

"We're being shot at!" I said.

As soon as we touched down the Ghurkas were out of the aircraft and disappeared into the darkness—just melted into the jungle. With bullets flying about I didn't hang around and I wasn't looking forward to the next trip into the jungle airfield.

It was the first of four such trips that night but by the final trip there was no more gunfire and all was quiet. Within half an hour the Ghurkas had recaptured the airfield that had been taken over by Indonesia rebels. The Ghurkas haven't got their reputation for nothing! We continued our flights, dropping personnel and supplies to the army in the jungle. The Ghurkas maintained control of the

3

airfield until the 'emergency' was over and the whole of Brunei had been recaptured.

The upshot of all this was that the Sultan of Brunei presented me with the Star of Brunei.

The next time I go to Brunei in an official capacity I can have an escort of four pikemen and four swordsmen.

So far, I haven't any plans for a return visit...

A cushy ride to New Zealand?

IT was February 1964 that my crew and I looked forward to a pleasant ride from Singapore to New Zealand in our Beverley XM104. It did have a reputation as a 'rogue' aircraft but I didn't pay too much attention to that notion.

About an hour after take-off all the port side hydraulics 'went'. A return to base showed the problem was a leak in a pipe on the pressure side of the pump on No.1 engine. This was quickly fixed.

"Looks like we've lost a day. Too late to set off again now," I told the crew.

"You're probably right," agreed my co-pilot, Keith Winter, "Cocos Island's pretty tiny and there's a big ocean out there. Don't want to miss it, do we?" So, after twenty-four hours' delay we set off again and arrived on Cocos Island (north west of Australia) nine hours later.

The run to Perth was, fortunately, uneventful but the next leg of the trip, across the Great Australian Bight, was the longest. We were about half way through that leg and somewhere over the Bight when the starboard hydraulics 'went'.

"I don't believe it!" said our engineer, Al Dunbar, after inching down the wing crawl-way to diagnose the fault in No.4 engine. "I just don't believe it!"

"Well, we're an hour's flying time from land and three hours from the nearest airfield—that's Edinburgh Field," said navigator Alf Jones.

"We'll head for Edinburgh Field," I said thinking: if two of the four pipes in the

twohydraulic systems were faulty, what of the other two pipes?

The crew congregated for a 'flight deck committee meeting' and, after listening to Al's report I said,

"OK, we'll feather the two starboard engines, tape the pipe to reduce the spray and refill the system. We'll use the cans in the fly-away pack."

With the two starboard engines feathered, signaller Geordie French put out a PAN (emergency) call. Al and his ground crew worked on the hydraulics and we began a slow descent to the sea. It worked and soon we were back on four engines! We could breathe easily again.

"Cancel the PAN," signalled Geordie to Kalgoorlie Air Traffic Control.

"Thank Christ for that, mate!" came a relieved Aussie voice, "you should have seen the panic you caused down here!"

"Can't have been any worse than the panic up here!" Geordie assured him.

After repairs at Edinburgh Field we completed the rest of our trip to Ohakea on the North Island of New Zealand without further trouble.

Flying display

We were due to take part in a flying display and there was a rehearsal the day before. We had trouble finding Palmerston North, the satellite airfield from where we were to take off for our part in the display. We circled round while Alf frantically tried to make the map fit the ground.

"Hurry up, Alf, we haven't got all day."

"Sorry, but it just doesn't fit—oh—"

"What?"

"I've cocked it up. I applied the variation the wrong way. Forgot we were in the southern hemisphere. Should have been 30 degrees. We've got a track error of 60 degrees. Sorry."

There were groans all round but we got there eventually.

We took part in the rehearsal which went well—we had to drop a 105mm gun and Land Rover for troops on the ground to use in an 'attack'—and the television cameras were there to witness it. On returning to Ohakea we clustered round the TV to watch ourselves on the news. The Beverley trundled across the screen but it wasn't quite right. The gun and the Land Rover left the aircraft all right but appeared to fly skywards!

"What the hell?"

"Some bloody film editor's cut it in upside down!" There were roars of laughter.

On the day of the flying display itself there were no such problems. The weather was fine and the skies clear but fluctuating wind direction was forecast. That was a bit worrying as, for the run-in for our drop, we needed the actual wind velocity from the anemometer in the tower. However, all seemed OK as we did our run-in and prepared to drop the 105mm gun and Land Rover, which were fixed on platforms with parachute cords attached. Meanwhile, paratroopers were dropping from an Argosy and a Hastings and troops were emerging from a RNZAF Bristol Freighter to use the vehicle and gun in the 'attack' on 'enemy lines'.

"You have a head wind of ten knots," we were informed by air traffic control.

"Green on!" said Alf confidently preparing to drop our load into the dropping zone. The loadmaster pulled the release handle,

"Load moving," he called. "Load clear!"

There was the usual lurch after "Load gone!"

There followed an unusual silence. Finally, I couldn't stand it any longer,

"What's happening back there?"

"Can't see the load," reported the loadmaster, "disappeared after it went over the sill. Looks like the 'chutes haven't opened." There was another silence. "I can see them now. The 'chutes have opened. It's landed all right but it's miles away—er—it's pretty near one of the public car parks..." the loadmaster's voice trailed away.

We had had a tail wind of ten knots instead of a head wind of ten knots as we had been told on the run-in. This meant that the load had not only landed in 'enemy' lines but when the 66-foot 'chute had automatically disconnected, one 'chute had hooked itself under the bumper of a parked car and lifted and dragged it sideways into the next car. Another 'chute had been seen chasing two old ladies across a field until it had been 'arrested' by an agile policeman.

That evening Major Roy Royal (47 AD Coy.) gave us the full story:

"I could see what was happening and so I sprinted through 'enemy' lines to get the Land Rover and trailer off the platform—and keep the display going. It was so close to the parked cars I couldn't drive it off using the ramps so I reversed it off the back of the platform. I reckoned I could get it back to the troops to keep the show on the road.

"The Land Rover didn't seem any the worse and I tore off towards the aircraft. I slammed on the brakes as I approached but nothing happened. I pumped them but still nothing. (Turned out the brake pipes had been severed when I'd reversed it off the platform.) So I went sailing straight past the aircraft and the troops, swung round to slow down then came back to them at a snail's pace. Must have looked a bit odd. Just hope the audience thought it was all part of the show!"

The saving grace in all this which prevented our being the butt of jokes in the bar that night was that the crew of the Argosy which was dropping paratroopers outshone our short landing by demolishing a barbed wire boundary fence. Even with their makeshift arrester gear they still had a longer landing run than us!

Unofficial stopover

We were nearing the end of our Australasian trip and I decided we'd have an unofficial stopover in Rotorua.

"Fancy seeing the hot springs, lads?"

"Oh yes! Good idea."

"Sounds terrific."

"OK. Let's go! But don't forget—we aren't supposed to be there. If anyone asks—you've never been to Rotorua, have you?"

"No, skip!" chorused the crew.

We 'buzzed' the town and landed on the airstrip where a group of locals came out to welcome us. They gave us a marvellous time but when it came to leave the old Beverley was up to her tricks again. No.2 engine wouldn't turn. I couldn't report engine trouble in a place we weren't supposed to be!

"We'll have to do it the hard way. Windmill start—demonstration for the locals."

It was hard work and nothing happened at the first attempt. With the second attempt the engine sprang to life. We bade a hasty farewell to the people of Rotorua and headed for Whenuapai for a scheduled overnight stop. I reminded the crew again,

"Don't forget—Rotorua was hush-hush."

By the time we returned to Singapore I'd almost forgotten about our unofficial trip to Rotorua and, true to their promise, none of the crew had said a word. Then I had a telephone call,

"It's the *Rotorua Gazette* on the phone. Wants an interview with you about your Rotorua visit," said a puzzled voice on the switchboard. "I didn't know you'd been to Rotorua..."

Later that night I treated the telephonist to a few drinks in the bar until he had totally forgotten about the telephone call from the *Rotorua Gazette.*

Also based on an account by Mel's co-pilot Keith Winter *Singapore to New Zealand the hard way)*

Sunderland as flown by Mel on the Honeymoon Express *(see story opposite)*

Honeymoon Express?

IT was 23 October 1952 and I was captain on Sunderland flying boats of 88 Squadron ferrying between Singapore and the UK. On one trip I was actually coming home to marry my fiancée, June. Four other crew members were also to be married. (One set off with us with that intention but returned to us still single but engaged to another girl—however, that's another story!)

We had a false start when we lost an engine, had to jettison 1,000 gallons of fuel and underwent an engine change. It wasn't a very auspicious start but after that things went smoothly enough. We put in at Malta for a couple of days then set off on the last leg to the UK confident that all our troubles were behind us.

Over France all four engines iced over. We lost height and dropped to 4,800 feet. Eventually, we made it back up to 8,000 feet but had to divert to Calshot because of bad weather instead of landing at Pembroke Dock—known as PD. We finally got to PD and left again a couple of days later on 20 November for Singapore. We lost an engine and returned to PD. An air test two days later proved OK but we couldn't leave for Malta because of bad weather over France again and the swell was too great for us to land at Gibraltar. We eventually arrived at Gibraltar on 1 December and at Malta the next day. Here, during a taxi test No.3 engine blew up. This couldn't be fixed, there were no spares—nothing—but eventually we were fixed up and left for Fanara in Egypt thirty-five days after landing in Malta.

While we were stuck there I knew the ship taking my wife, June, to Singapore had left the UK and I couldn't help think that, at this rate, she would arrive there before I did!

When the time came to leave Fanara, one of the crew, Sandy Hurt, was in the astrodome on the start-up panel.

"All four fuel warning lights are going on and off!" he said

"What?"

"I tell you all four lights are blinking."

"They can't be."

"Well, they are."

"All four?"

"All four," he confirmed. He pressed all the buttons but nothing changed. They continued to blink. The engineer did the same on his panel. Nothing. We jettisoned fuel again—another 1,000 gallons—and 'splashed'.

Sandy twisted his ankle on a rope in the bottom on the dinghy as he got aboard and had to spend a night in the RAF hospital at Ishmalaya but he was OK to continue with us when we took off on 9 January heading for Bahrain.

At Mauripur we tried to take off from Korangi Creek but the water was flat calm. What little wind there was came from the wrong side. The upshot was that there was not enough airspeed for sufficient rudder control to keep straight down the narrow creek. After a couple of unsuccessful attempts I suggested to my co-pilot, Stuart Holmes, that he try to 'porpoise'.

"It's a bit of a risk but it's worth a try."

'Porpoising' was risky because there was the possibility of an uncontrolled 'porpoise' resulting in total loss of longitudinal control and the aircraft nosing into the water.

"OK, here we go," said Stuart and began the risky manoeuvre. I glanced round and saw the two engineers, Paddy McMurty and Jock Cunningham, adopting the 'crash position' behind the main spar. They knew all about 'porpoising' and I heard Paddy's voice faintly as he spoke to Jock,

"Will you listen to that pair of bloody comedians up front?"

However, it worked and we were airborne.

"You can come out now, you two," I said to

7

Paddy and Jock. "Bahrain next stop."

The remainder of the trip was, I'm glad to say, uneventful and we arrived back in Singapore on 12 January—we'd have done it quicker in a sailing ship!

Everything worked out in the end. I had time to make arrangements and get married quarters set up. We flew out to welcome June as her ship approached Singapore in late February. I couldn't help thinking that it wasn't so much the Honeymoon Express as a slow (flying) boat to China.

(With contributions from Sandy Hurt and Stuart Holmes)

Testing, testing...

IN the mid 1950s I was test flying Meteor jets after their routine maintenance. After maintenance there were always things that needed adjustment or trimming. On one occasion I could find nothing wrong at all—the aircraft flew perfectly. I put it through all the manoeuvres and was about to come into land but the undercarriage wouldn't budge. I tried again. Nothing. I did everything I knew to lower it but to no avail.

I glanced at the fuel gauge. It was a bit low but should be all right. I radioed that I couldn't shift the undercarriage.

"Ditch the ventral tank and come in with no wheels," I was told. The ventral tank was empty of fuel but full of petrol vapour. As such it was more dangerous than petrol itself and could blow up in a trice. There was no way I could land with that underneath.

"Will do," I replied and reached for the lever that would release the ventral tank and drop away. But it didn't. It wouldn't move either. I glanced at the fuel gauge again. It was reading noticeably less than before.

"Can't shift that either," I radioed back wondering how I was going to get down. There was one way but it was a last resort and I might not have enough fuel.

"Go round again and give it another try."

"I'm getting low on fuel."

"You'll be OK." It was all right for them...

This was the last time round. If it didn't work this time I'd have to go up high (or as high as what fuel I had left would allow) and bale out. I was preparing myself for that when a voice in my ear said a trifle apologetically,

"Oh, forgot to tell you—the ventral tank lever now turns through 90 degrees. It's a new adjustment we made. Try it."

I did and the ventral tank fell away. I let out an audible sigh of relief but I still had to get down with no undercarriage. I managed it but I was out of that plane before the blood wagon had reached me. The aircraft was a write-off, though.

Interesting experience...

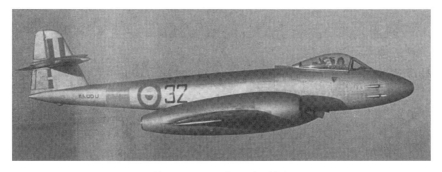

Meteor as test flown by Mel

Geoff Boston

Pilot

61, 88, 254, 295, 297 Squadrons

F/Lt Geoff Boston at work flying a Sunderland flying boat near Saishu, Japan in 1951

Geoff in 1997

Flying over Germany at 100 feet, July 1949 en route from Tegel to Schleswigland during the Berlin airlift (see story opposite)

Geoff Boston

Geoff Boston joined the RAF in April 1945 as an officer cadet after a short course at Durham University. He was awarded his 'Wings' in September 1947 and commissioned two months later. Geoff has flown many different aircraft including, in the late 1940s Oxfords, Hastings and Wellingtons, in the 1950s it was Vampires and Canberras and in the1960s, Comets, Beverleys, Andovers and Meteors. On leaving the RAF Geoff joined the staff of the King Faisal Air Academy in Saudi Arabia teaching Saudi students to fly.

Berlin airlift

MY first operational role was with 297 Squadron as part of the Berlin airlift. At last felt I was doing something useful! Nearly all my flights were into Berlin/Tegel, although a few were into Gatow.

Almost invariably the cargo carried was coal, although occasionally there was a mixed assortment of goods. It was a fascinating job and very worthwhile.

Recreational sorties were made to Eckernforde on the Baltic coast for swimming, drinking, games and 'a bit of the other'—if you were lucky. Currency was mostly coffee, cigarettes or chocolate with taxi rides at one cigarette per mile—not sure what the currency was for 'a bit of the other'!

Flying boats

IN 1950 I went to 235 OCU Calshot for conversion to Sunderland flying boats. They were magic and gave rise to many a funny (and sometimes not-so-funny) incident.

An example of the former was when flying to Manila to pick up the Air Officer Commanding. We asked for landing clearance and were given the land runway. Amused, we pointed out that we were in a Sunderland flying boat. The controller replied, "That's OK, the runway's concrete!"

On another occasion when returning from an all-night sortie in a Sunderland over the China Sea in winter (there was no heating in the flying boat), we were approaching western Japan, all frozen stiff and desperate for a warm bed. It was just about dawn when we suddenly noticed a Mustang fighter on our wing tip. We hastily switched on the radio and heard this exchange between the American radar people and the Mustang regarding an unidentified aircraft (a 'bogey')—us:

Radar: "Do you have that bogey?"
Fighter: "Yeah, I got it."
Radar (in some panic): "Well, what is it?"
Fighter (laconically): "I dunno, but it sure is a big bastard."

This incident was caused by a broken (IFF) Identification Friend or Foe set.

An example of a not-so-funny incident was in Hong Kong in the 1950s with 88 Squadron from which the Station Equipment Officer was to be repatriated to the UK on the ship *Empire Orwell.* He had been a good friend to the squadron so it was decided to give him a lively send-off.

Three Sunderlands got airborne to beat up the ship and drop small smoke bombs nearby.

These were thrown out of a hatch by a crew member on intercom and taking instructions from the captain. On one aircraft, at the critical moment, the intercom became unplugged and the 'bomb aimer' didn't hear the captain's command to stop.

A 'bomb' hit the ship's funnel with disastrous results. The captain was not amused and in due course, the squadron received a very rude letter from him.

The other incident occurred when we were carrying out an exercise in the Pacific with an Australian submarine. We obtained their permission to make a mock depth charge attack and, on flying very low over the sub, we saw the deck littered with sunbathing sailors,

HMS Warrior *as seen from taxying Sunderland in the Pacific, March 1951*

some idly waving.

"It's all right for some, eh?" I commented. "Wouldn't mind a spot of sunbathing myself!"

We made a second run-in low again but this time there was not a soul to be seen.

"Where is everybody?" I said puzzled.

"Everything looks pretty well battened down," added one of the crew. The submarine was as deserted as the *Marie Celeste*.

An explanation was soon forthcoming in no uncertain terms: we had made the first run with the trailing aerial out—it must have slashed across the submarine like a cheese cutter. Seemed funny at the time but it could have been very nasty.

Bombing tactics in Korea... and Suez

DURING the Korean War when I was with 88 Squadron all flights from Iwakuni, Japan, operated under the auspices of the US Navy. We received our flight briefs from them and sometimes (when duty crew) would sleep aboard the USS *Salisbury Sound* in Iwakuni Bay. In the whole war I was shot at only twice—both times by the US Navy. Trigger happy, that was their trouble!

From Seletar, Singapore, most of our ops. were against Communist bandits in Malaya. We carried 358 12.5lb anti-personnel bombs in boxes and, as it was impracticable to use the bomb racks for so many small bombs, all available crew members were summoned to throw the things from every hatch during a timed run. It was, literally, hit-and-miss but we did receive the odd letter from the army expressing their satisfaction so we must have hit something we were aiming at!

In late 1955 I was with 61 Squadron and detached to Cyprus for the Suez Operation. This involved four bombing sorties in Egypt, three of which were very successful. The fourth, a high speed, low-level attack on the Cairo radio station was something of a farce as the combination of speed and height meant that the target was outside the range of the bombsight.

"Estimate by Mark I eyeball," I told my navigator/bomb aimer and he did.

"Bombs gone!" and a string of six 1,000lb bombs landed along the avenue leading to the radio station, the last falling short of the buildings by 300 yards.

"Can't see a thing back there!"

Plumes of sand and smoke from our bombs totally obscured the target from the remainder of the force which emerged more or less unscathed—as did the radio station!

Thor missiles

IN July 1959 I was posted to my first ground tour to be a Launch Control Officer on Thor missiles. After the fun and novelty of crossing the Atlantic in the SS *Statendam* I headed for Davis-Monthan Air Force Base in Arizona.

Here I enjoyed(?) a month of intensive study of ballistic missiles generally and the Thor in particular. It was all *very* complicated but a fascinating and incredible piece of machinery.

Then it was two months at Vandenberg Air Force Base in California studying, being tested over and over again, practice exercises in erecting the missile, loading with fuel and liquid oxygen, and dealing with simulated malfunctions. Finally, I witnessed the actual launch of a Thor—tremendous!

It wasn't all hard graft: I explored the magnificent desert scenery and the local Wild West legends like Tombstone where the Boot Hill graveyard contained such gems as *George Jackson: hanged by mistake*. I stayed with a distant cousin in Los Angeles. He was a movie agent and so I was introduced to several stars but cannot remember a single one!

I returned to England in 1959 and was posted to 254 Squadron at Melton Mowbray, a satellite of North Luffenham, Leicestershire. This was a long tour, with very little action, except for the occasional exercise. I felt ambivalent about this job; the missile was a nuclear deterrent which meant that if it had been used it would have failed in its purpose, but if it wasn't used we had wasted a lot of time and effort learning how to use it!

Boscombe Down

IN November 1963 I was posted to the Aircraft and Armament Experimental Establishment at Boscombe Down, Wiltshire, as a pilot on the Transport and Trials Squadron testing equipment in aircraft. It was a marvellous job enabling me to fly many different types of aircraft and to visit exotic parts of the world.

I completed a course at De Havilland's for competency on the Comet 4c that we flew all over the world on radar and navigation trials, tropical and cold weather trials and polar flights. We 'cold-soaked' the aircraft for twenty-four hours in the open at Thule AFB in Greenland. We'd check the temperature:

"It's minus forty."

"Centigrade or Farenheit?"

"In these temperatures does it make much difference?"

"You know, I'll bet Scott was positively *warm* in the Antarctic compared with here!" I said through chattering teeth. Even so, we had to fly the Comet for an hour before switching on any heating.

There was never a dull moment—like the time, in 1969, when I took off in a Comet 4c from Boscombe Down for a flight to Sweden. It was very cold and foggy with the runway covered in deep slush except for an area cleared by snow ploughs where the slush was about an inch deep. Just as rotation speed was reached the nose-wheel hit deep slush, spewing heavy spray into the engines. There was nothing for it but to abandon the Swedish flight. I returned to Boscombe Down, climbing to jettison fuel before attempting to land.

On my first attempt I overshot. My second attempt was on the button and I landed but there was no question of finding the cleared area. I landed in deep slush.

Geoff Boston

Tons of slush hit the flaps and wrecked them. I did not retract what was left of them so that the mainplane was not damaged. Expressions on the faces of the ground crew as I taxied onto the apron were worth a guinea a box. I thought it prudent to go on leave...

It was customary for officers to request where their final tour should be taken and I naturally asked for Boscombe Down which was granted. It was a splendid finale to my RAF service.

Last round-up

I'll just finish with a couple more funny stories. While engaged in night-flying at South Cerney, Gloucestershire, on Prentices with a would-be instructor, taking it in turns at circuits and bumps, the visibility gradually worsened until we could hardly see the airfield from the down-wind position. No one in the other aircraft said anything on the radio but my colleague and I gave up and radioed,

"We're coming in for final landing on account of the weather."

This was acknowledged and, with considerable difficulty, we landed. Groping our way round the peri-track we suddenly realised our windscreen had misted up. It was as clear as a bell outside!

During a night bombing sortie on Oxmoor range during my Canberra training days we identified a triangle of lights on the range and bombed successfully. Next day we discovered that we had bombed a vicar's garden party! No casualties, fortunately, but insult was added to injury when the vicar was subsequently fined for displaying illegal lights!

I had been very lucky to have had a lifetime of flying and I have now hung up my helmet—or headset as it is now called! I amassed nearly 18,000 flying hours and decided enough was enough, and I haven't flown an aircraft since!

Gerald Carver

DSO, DFC

Pilot

37 and 78 Squadrons

Sergeant Gerald Carver, aged 19, autumn 1941 with 37 Squadron, Sallufa, Suez

P/O Gerald Carver during the summer 1942 at 7c OTU, Limvady, Northern Ireland (Coastal Operational Training Unit) as an instructor after returning from Middle East— newly promoted 'show-off'!

Civilian Gerald Carver, summer 1989

Gerald Carver

Gerald (Gerry) Carver enrolled in the RAF in July 1940 at Cardington, Bedfordshire. He was awarded his pilot's brevet in March 1941. He trained in Britain where his Operational Training Unit instructor concluded he was "inclined to be lazy ... could have done better." His link trainer assessment was "below average". Nevertheless, he was posted to 37 Squadron, Bomber Command, flying Wellingtons after which he spent time as an instructor with Coastal Command before returning to Bomber Command's 78 Squadron flying Halifaxes for a second tour. He flew a total of fifty-eight operations and was awarded the DSO and DFC and was Mentioned in Despatches—not bad for a 'below average', 'lazy' type.

Top secret raid

ON 17 August 1943 Gerry Carver took part in the raid on Peenemunde, an island in the mouth of the River Oder between Germany and Poland, where the German V1 and V2 rockets were being developed. He takes up the story:

It was, arguably, the most important Bomber Command raid of the war. If successful it would delay the launch by the Germans of the V1 and V2 rockets with their potentially devastating effect on the Allies' war effort, and particularly the execution of the second front—the invasion of Europe.

High security surrounded the raid and once the target was known we were confined to base. If it had been delayed due to bad weather we would have had to stay put until it was completed.

The raid was cleverly planned with diversionary Mosquito attacks on Berlin, some 120 miles to the south, to coincide with the time of the main raid. It was also the first use of a Master Bomber (Group Commander John Searby DSO, DFC) whose job was to stand off the target area and direct the bombers by radio to drop their bombs more effectively, having observed the results being achieved.

In the event, enemy opposition proved relatively weak, at least in the initial stages of the raid. The results were successful, as bombs were concentrated in the development and production areas of the site as was proved from subsequent photographic reconnaissance.

The raid was organised in three waves—we were in the middle wave. Some 600 aircraft employing precision radar and standard marking techniques achieved results from about fifty minutes over the target. The losses were forty-one aircraft, mainly from the third wave for, by the time they were at the target, the enemy had been able to concentrate his fighters and harass the departing bombers.

The attack was carried out mainly from a lower than usual level: 8,000 feet. We experienced some light flak from flak ships strategically placed en route. A smoke screen was employed to try to obscure the target but it was not very effective. The total flight time was seven hours, twenty-five minutes.

Altogether, it was a most satisfying trip—I had a feeling of having really achieved something for the war effort and German plans were set back by about nine months.

Wimpeys...

HOWEVER, not everything went so well. Gerry recalls a bad experience when flying Wellingtons, or Wimpeys as they were affectionately known:

Some fifteen Wellingtons were dispersed at an advanced desert airfield in North Africa known as LG09, bombed up and fuelled awaiting take-off time for a night operation. Suddenly, there was an almighty explosion and bits of aircraft flew everywhere.

One of the squadron Wellingtons, about a hundred yards from us, had blown up, killing five of the crew outright. The second pilot with whom I had trained, was seriously injured and in great pain.

I was on the spot and able to direct the blood wagon to the crew through the bedlam of exploding ammunition, scattered fires and incendiary bombs. The injured man was made as comfortable as possible in the first aid tent but died in the early hours of the morning, still in terrible pain. The crew who were killed had been very popular—they were great characters. It was a very sad incident and it really sticks in my mind.

The reason for the explosion has remained a mystery.

Another incident involving Wellingtons was when we were waiting to take off for Crete in October 1941. We were first off and heavily laden with high explosive and incendiary bombs. As usual, I held the aircraft down to build up airspeed before climbing away. There was a bang as we left the ground.

"What the—?" I said involuntarily. Our height was of no more than fifteen feet. There were flames to my left as our port undercarriage leg struck something.

"Looks like a petrol bowser," I heard one of the crew say as we bit the dust rather rapidly and violently.

"Some bloody idiot left it right in the way just at the edge of the airfield," we were told afterwards.

The bowser blew up and the bombs scattered everywhere. Finally, the aircraft came to rest. Those behind us, on seeing the explosion, thought we had been killed and were somewhat to surprised to see us back in the assembly tent for coffee!

"What the hell are you doing here?"

"We thought you'd bought it!"

"Sorry to disappoint you but we're here safe and sound—more or less," I replied. I had a deep cut under my left eye that needed three stitches but no one else was injured.

37 Squadron wrecked Wellington aircraft and remains of a petrol bowser after collision October 1941

Gerald Carver

Yet another story concerning Wellingtons was, ultimately, a very sad one. We were detailed to bomb Derna, a German fighter base in northern Libya. The weather was poor with the cloud base down to 4,000 feet necessitating a lower level attack than normal.

On the bombing run-in we encountered accurate light flak. Our starboard engine was hit and stopped but we completed our bombing run and inflicted aiming point damage without further damage to us. Unfortunately, Wimpeys are not good on one engine and so we couldn't afford to hang around.

We set course for home. Our direct route was initially over the sea, normally some two-and-a-half hours' flying time, but with only one engine it took almost four hours. Having jettisoned all surplus equipment it became clear we were not going to make it back to base.

The WOP/AG was having no success in contacting Sidi Barani, an emergency landing ground, and so I decided our best chance was to ditch in the sea as near to land as possible. Dinghy drill procedures were confirmed by the crew. Conditions were not ideal, for it was pitch black with no moon. The landing was somewhat rough but all crew members got out. The dinghy broke loose from the aircraft of its own accord and drifted away. Nevertheless, four of us reached it and clambered in but, regrettably, the navigator and the WOP/AG had become separated and were carried away with the current. We maintained verbal contact with the missing crew members and used flares and rockets to try to guide them. In the meantime, attached by a rope, I swam round the dinghy to try to

locate and rescue them, but to no avail. Eventually, we lost all contact and it became strangely quiet. A horrible silence fell over the four of us in the dinghy when no more voices came to us from the darkness. We were very despondent.

Aboard the dinghy we assessed our injuries: one broken rib, one dislocated shoulder, various cuts and bruises, but nothing disastrous. Nevertheless, we had under half our normal muscle-power to man the paddles. We set out for the shore some one to two miles distant but a heavy current kept us out at sea—or so it seemed. However, we hit shore at first light after about three hours.

I managed to secret the three crew members in a disused pill-box and set out to get help. I returned ten hours later with an ambulance having trekked for two hours to hitch a lift in an army lorry and spent a further two hours journeying to a field hospital at Mersa Matru without too much difficulty. We all spent three days in hospital before returning to base some 400 miles to the east.

The other crew members needed extended recuperation and convalesence whereas I was lucky enough to be able to spend a week convalescing in Palestine before returning to the squadron and completing my first tour in Malta.

Because of the sad loss of two of my crew, the remaining members, after being passed fully fit for flying once again, would be split and would crew up again with a new skipper. I was lucky to be able to resume and complete my operational tour with the crew with whom I had trained and brought out from the UK in June 1941: two Englishmen, two Scotsmen, an Australian and a New Zealander.

19

'Friendly fire'

IT was on the Berlin raid in August 1943 that Gerry and his crew were a victim of 'friendly fire':

Approaching the target on the bombing run, a bomb from another aircraft above us, also on the bombing run, punched a hole through our port wing, narrowly missing the outboard engine and a petrol tank. It was thought to be a 500lb bomb. We pressed on and managed to get back on track and complete our bombing run without further mishap.

We experienced a number of combats and a few near misses with enemy fighters. Our rear gunner shot down one Me109 which was confirmed and another unconfirmed. Other fighters with which we had a brush were an Me110 and a Ju88.

Three months after the 'bomb through the wing' incident, we were approaching the target area—Ludwigshaven—and had a near miss from a heavy burst of flak. Shrapnel damaged the hydraulics. Fortunately, the bomb aimer, who was preparing to guide me into the target on the final run in, was not hurt.

When the time came to release the bombs, we couldn't. The shrapnel had damaged the bomb release mechanism as well.

"We're going round again," I told the crew. It wasn't a popular move. Once over the target was enough. We went round again and the bomb aimer tried once more. Nothing.

"I'll try and shake them loose. Hold tight," I told the crew as I weaved, dived and corkscrewed and tried every other violent manoeuvre I knew. We continued at various intervals all the way home to try to shake off the bombs but to no avail. The bombs remained firm except for five cases of incendiaries which dropped away. But that was all. There was nothing for it but to return home with the remainder of the bombs. It was an uncomfortable and frustrating trip back. Fortunately, we managed, somehow, to avoid the unwelcome attentions of the enemy. Three and a half hours with 15/20 per cent flap droop, bomb doors open and a nearly full bomb load of live bombs that the slightest jolt on landing could blow us to kingdom come.

On return to base my mind was so focused on those bombs that I made the smoothest landing in my entire flying career!

We got on well as a crew; we were a mixed bunch—Scots, English, Canadian and Australian—and our survival was due to teamwork, vigilance, professional gunners and a good slice of luck.

Chips with everything

ON take-off at the start of a night operation to bomb a munitions factory in France I noticed that the airspeed indicator was not registering. I estimated the airspeed to be about 60mph and decided to abort the take-off in the hope of bringing the heavily laden aircraft to a stop within a short distance. However, despite cutting the engines and applying full flap, we trundled on over the airfield boundary, across a road and ended up in a potato field with the starboard undercarriage collapsed. All the crew got out safely but the somewhat elderly aircraft was a write-off. As we surveyed it, my crew shrugged and said,

"Bit long in the tooth anyway, wasn't she?"

"Seen better days."

"Probably done ourselves a favour—better here than over France."

I had to agree but I was never to live the incident down. The field became known as Gerry's Potato Patch, to which my response was,

"Well, at least we haven't had our chips!"

George Cash

DFC

Navigator/Bomb aimer/Wireless Operator

139 and 571 Squadrons and 1409 Meteorological Flight

*George Cash just commissioned as
Pilot Officer 4 January 1944...*

...and in 1997

George on 20 April 1944 safely back from a 'trip'

George Cash

George Cash enrolled in the RAF in July 1941 at Oxford. He trained as a navigator and served in 139, 1409 Meteorological Flight and 571 Squadrons with 8 Group (Pathfinder Force), Bomber Command, flying Mosquitoes. He was taken prisoner of war in July 1944 and released in May 1945. He was awarded the DFC and is a member of the Caterpillar Club.

Joining the Caterpillar Club...

I had been on ops. for nearly a year and Tuesday, 18 July 1944 began like any other day—but little did I know what lay in store!

That evening, when we went into briefing, I had no undue feelings of trepidation— certainly not like the 'butterflies' that I had when I first flew on ops. Experience and the knowledge of what to expect helped to allay one's fears although, however much experience a man had, I don't think that any airman could truthfully say that he did not feel some apprehension before setting off on a mission.

This time, I saw that A Flight—ours—was to go to Cologne and B Flight to Berlin. Accordingly, I began to get out maps and charts of the Ruhr in readiness when I noticed that our names were not on the A Flight list. When I pointed this out to my pilot, who was always known as 'Doddy' (S/Ldr Terry Dodwell DFC and bar), he nodded and remarked that we were going to Berlin instead.

"There's a sprog crew in B Flight," he said, "so I offered to take their place—they can go on a short trip some time to break them in gently."

In the Services, one was always told never to volunteer for anything. A dangerous job in the line of duty was one thing but you did not stick your neck out needlessly and go looking for trouble! Somehow, deep inside me, I had an uncomfortable feeling that this was 'It'.

We had the usual briefing: target, routes into and away from 'The Big City', deployment of defences along these routes, met. report and so on. During the briefing, the Intelligence Officer warned us of the Germans using experimental jet-propelled night fighters over Berlin. I didn't pay much heed to this for I had heard it all before. (Big head!)

After preparing my flight plan and marking my maps and charts with information that I would need, I packed my things and Doddy and I walked across to the crew room to get our Mae Wests, 'chutes and dinghies. We were unusually silent and I wondered if he sensed what I was thinking.

It was time to go. The crew bus arrived, we clambered on and soon we were dropped off at our dispersal. We climbed into the aircraft, stowed our gear and while I fixed my charts and flight plan, Doddy carried out his pre-flight check. When he came to run up the engines, he found that the port engine had a mag. drop and, consequently, was u/s.

We collected our things, climbed out of the aircraft and sent one of the ground crew to get a van to take us over to the reserve aircraft. By now, the rest of the squadron had taken off and were on their way. We raced round the 'drome to the reserve aircraft, climbed aboard and, after hurried checks all round, took off well behind the rest. All this rush and frenzy had been most unsettling—it was a very bad start. We were more than fifteen minutes behind and could never make up that time which meant that we would be 'Tail-end Charlies' out behind the mainstream. This would make us very vulnerable—an easy target for flak or fighters as we knew from experience—and yet, strangely, I remember that I wasn't particularly perturbed by the prospect.

As we climbed to our operational height—28,000 feet—we began to settle down and by the time we levelled out, we were quite calm and I was too busy with my navigation to worry about anything else. We were approaching the enemy coast and, as normal, we began to siphon fuel from our overload tanks to the outer tanks in the wings to replace fuel that we had used.

We had just crossed the Dutch coast when a stream of tracers from below indicated that enemy fighters were on to us. Doddy immediately took evasive action—always difficult with a 'cookie' on board. We ran the gauntlet of a couple of Ju88s. We shook them off eventually and resumed our course, each of us in our own way breathing a sigh of relief.

I suddenly realised that, in the heat of the moment, we had forgotten to turn off the petrol siphons. The outer tanks had filled and we had been discharging precious fuel into the slipstream. We must have lost a considerable amount and it crossed my mind that we might not have enough to get us home. This must have occurred to Doddy too, as he gave vent to a few choice phrases but, once again, I wasn't particularly bothered.

It seems, in retrospect, that I was sub-consciously preparing for the worst—that we wouldn't be coming back anyway. This had put us further behind and, although the next part of the route was a dog-leg round a heavily defended area near Wittingen, we decided to take a chance and fly straight across. I worked out the new course and just as we were thinking that we had got away with it, all hell broke loose. Shells burst round us too close for comfort.

Doddy put up the nose, opened the throttles and climbed as fast as we could go. It seemed ages before we got away but not before a huge lump of shrapnel had smashed through the back window into the 'Gee' box by my side—another few inches and I wouldn't be telling this tale!

Engine fire

We arrived over Stendal—our last turning point—and, in the distance, saw that the target indicators had already gone down over the railway marshalling yards north-west of Berlin—the target. The raid had begun.

Ahead of us were searchlights and bursting flak. Doddy decided to skirt round them and come in from another direction but, just then, we were coned. We were blinded by the glare. Doddy, once more threw the kite around, diving and banking, turning and climbing, in an effort to get away but to no avail. Then, suddenly the searchlights dipped—we had shaken them off—but we ought to have known better!

We were now in sight of the target indicators and I noted in my log: *0200 hours. Target sighted, preparing to bomb.*

I stowed my equipment and knelt down ready to crawl into the nose to the bomb sight. I had hardly moved when we felt a quick succession of thumps as cannon shells smashed into the fuselage. A tremendous whoof and the port petrol tanks exploded. The port engine burst into blames.

I realised, all too late, why the searchlights had left us. A night fighter had homed on to us and had flown up beneath us to deliver the coup de grâce—we had been a sitting duck.

With the cockpit now well ablaze, Doddy said, "Come on, we've got to get out of here!"

I pulled up the cover of the escape hatch and threw it into the nose. When I got up, I found that I was on my own. Doddy had exited smartly through the top hatch. I couldn't blame him—his seat was on fire!

(In dry runs on the ground, we had practised getting out in a hurry through the conventional exit below the navigator's position. We had to aim at getting out in ten seconds. With all our cumbersome gear, Mae Wests, parachutes and harness and dinghy, we couldn't get out in ten minutes!)

It was dangerous going out of the top (to be done only if the aircraft ditched or crash-landed) since, in flight, there was the great risk of striking the tail fin and rudder or the tailplane. But, there I was, in a blazing aircraft, spiralling out of control with a 4,000lb bomb still on board. The 'G' pressure was like a heavy weight, pressing me down onto my seat. I did what any man in my position would do: I breathed a quick prayer, "God, help me."

Suddenly, despite the heat in the cockpit and my perilous position, a calmness came over me and my mind was clear. A fierce draught fanned the flames so that the whole cockpit was ablaze and full of smoke. There was nothing for it—I had to go: out of the top hatch.

I struggled round on my seat to reach behind me to get my parachute from its stowage. As I turned back, my elbow caught the ruined 'Gee' box by my side knocking my 'chute from my hand. It fell down the escape hatch... but it stuck half-way down where I could reach it and clip it onto my harness.

In those few seconds, I suddenly remembered reading an account in *Tee Em* magazine about how a Mosquito navigator had baled out by climbing out of the top hatch and rolling onto the starboard wing before letting go. I took three deep breaths of oxygen, took off my mask and helmet, threw them down and proceeded to do likewise.

I was carried away by the slipstream, clear of the aircraft and, after counting the requisite "One, two three" I reached up to my parachute pack, which was now above my head, and pulled the release handle. Nothing happened! I reached up with both hands and pulled open the flaps of the pack.

There was a plop as the canopy sprang out and filled with air. There I was floating through the quiet, peaceful sky. Then I looked down and, immediately below me, or so it seemed, there was our Mosquito in a field, blazing away with the 'cookie' still on board. If it had gone up then, I would have gone up with it. I continued drifting a little way away then, suddenly, innumerable fingers were scrabbling at me—I had the fleeting thought of falling into the hands of a lynch mob. But they were twigs—I had come down in a tree! I was dangling there, my night vision completely gone and I couldn't see or feel the ground. I needed to get away as fast as I could. I pressed the release button and I fell ten feet into a bush below the tree. Except for a few scratches, I was unharmed. I was on terra firma, albeit enemy terra firma, but I was down and that was how I qualified for the Caterpillar Club.

My claim to fame

For my claim to fame—if it can be called such—I am one of a very few men who baled out from the top hatch of a Mosquito and lived to tell the tale. Also, I am one, probably of many, who climbed down from a tree which he had not climbed up!

I set off walking in a westerly direction, putting as much distance as I possibly could between myself and the blazing Mozzie. The 'cookie' did go up after about ten minutes, with a great crump and a terrific orange glow—I felt the blast even at that distance.

I was now on my own, my last link with home had gone. I kept going for nearly two days but, on the way through a small village just outside Magdeburg, very late at night, I had the misfortune to walk into a Volksturm patrol who were out looking for the crew of a Flying Fortress that had been shot down earlier in the day. I spent the next three days in the civvie jail in Magdeburg before I was transported to the Interrogation Centre at Oberursel, just outside Frankfurt-am-Main.

A few days later, I was entrained with about 200 others—180 Americans and twenty British—to Barth in Pomerania on the Baltic coast. I marched into Stalag Luft I with this contingent on Tuesday, 1 August, 1944—my twenty-third birthday—just two weeks after I had taken off from Oakington for the last time. I was to spend nearly ten months in Germany before returning home at the end of the war.

The hand of fate

There is a short corollary to this part of my story: an episode that occurred in the POW camp. The weather in February 1945 was atrocious—freezing cold with ice and snow underfoot. To keep us occupied, the senior officers in the barrack block organised a bridge tournament. In one round, my partner and I were drawn to play against a couple in an adjacent room. As was normal, we exchanged pleasantries before commencing our game—we asked each other about the aircraft which we had flown in and with which squadron, etc.

One of our opponents was a F/Lt Thompson who

informed us that he had been with 571 Squadron when he had been shot down. When I told him that I had been on 571 as well and that I didn't remember him, he said that he had been on the squadron for only a couple of days and had been shot down on his first trip. He went on to say that he and his navigator had been due to go to Berlin two nights before but had been taken off the Battle Order and put down as reserve crew.

When I asked him when this was, he said that it had been on the 18 July and that they had been shot down over Hamburg on the 20 July. His navigator had been killed. I put two and two together—they had been the crew that Doddy and I had replaced. When I put this to him, he confirmed that the crew who had taken their place on the Berlin trip had not returned and we both realised that Doddy and I had been that crew.

I wondered then, and I have often wondered since, what would have happened if we hadn't taken their flight that night. Perhaps we may have returned from our respective missions and my pilot and his navigator would not have been killed. But this is only conjecture—we can only assume that their number was up and fate stepped in to do the rest. At that time, I had no idea what had happened to Doddy and it was a considerable time after the war that I was to find out what did happen.

"Komm' Herr Terrorflieger - for you the war is over!!"
Cartoon George drew in his logbook-cum-diary while a POW

Truth can be stranger than fiction

This brings me to the second corollary to my story. A number of years ago, a fellow named Barry Blunt was researching the history of 571 Squadron. In due course, I learned from him what had happened on that disastrous trip.

Apparently, we had been tracked and shot down by a German night fighter ace— Oberleutnant Heinz Strüning—of 3 NJG (Nachtjagdgeschwader—Night Fighter Squadron) flying a Heinkel 219A-5 (Uhu— Owl) which was armed with Schrage Musik (the code word for upward firing guns fitting to the aircraft). To enable them to keep up with faster aircraft, as we were, their engines were fitted with nitrous-oxide boosters which could be used for about ten minutes or so to enhance their speed. Heinz Strüning was awarded the Oak Leaves to his Knight's Cross with Swords and Diamonds on 20 July 1944 for shooting us down!

From an account in the German archives, the body of S/Ldr T.E. Dodwell had been discovered, with his parachute unopened, in a clump of trees near Laudin, thirty-five miles west of Berlin, close to the site where the aircraft had crashed. From the appearance of the body, it had been deduced that he was dead before reaching the ground having been fatally injured by striking part of the aircraft (the tail?) on baling out. Hence the unopened parachute.

Having the fanciful idea of going to Germany to meet Heinz Strüning, I requested further information about him. Apparently, he had been promoted to

Oberleutnant Heinz Strüning who shot down George's Mosquito

Hauptmann a few weeks after our incident and posted to 9 NJG as a Flight Commander. He enjoyed considerable acclaim as a night fighter ace with a squadron of Me110s flying over Holland. On Christmas Eve 1944, a force of our heavies was out and Strüning's squadron took off to try to infiltrate them. Unknown to him the heavies were accompanied by a couple of squadrons of Mosquito night fighters.

Dr Theo Boiten, a member of the Dutch Aircraft Recovery team, reported the following information obtained from German Military Archives.

Investigating the wartime crash site of an Me110, he was told that on the night of 24/25 December 1944 the aircraft in question, Messerschmitt Bf110 G-4, Nr 740162 of 9 NJG, had been flown by Hauptmann Heinz Strüning who had fifty-six night victories including two Mosquitoes with 3 NJG. Strüning's aircraft had been shot down by a Mosquito night fighter and crashed near Bergisch-Gladbach/ Rheinland.

The radar operator and air gunner baled out safely but Strüning hit the tail of the Me110 when he baled out and was killed. His body was found two months later and interred.

These incidents make up a remarkable and ironic coincidence. In the first case, a Mosquito pilot, shot down by a German night fighter— Strüning—was killed on baling out by striking the tail of his aircraft. The German night fighter pilot— Strüning—was shot down by a Mosquito and was killed on baling out by striking the tail of *his* aircraft! Truth can be stranger than fiction!

EXTRACT FROM LONDON GAZETTE
DATED 18 AUGUST 1944

The King has been graciously pleased
to approve the following award in
recognition of gallantry and devotion
to duty in the execution of air
operations:

Distinguished Flying Cross

Pilot Officer George William CASH (169975)   RAFVR
No 1409 Flight

Pilot Officer Cash has completed thirty six
operational flights, involving a variety of tasks;
the majority of these calling for deep penetration
into enemy territory by daylight,

His work in 1409 Flight has been carried out
efficiently and well, the number of successful
sorties indicating the high standard of planning
and preparation attained. At all times his skilful
navigation and his determination to cover the route
ordered have contributed largely to the success of
these missions.

The information brought back on these flights
materially assisted in the selection of targets
for major attacks.

George's citation for the award of Distinguished Flying Cross

Geoff Cole

DFC

Pilot

103 and 214 Squadrons

*Geoff Cole at the outbreak of war.
Cambridge, September 1939*

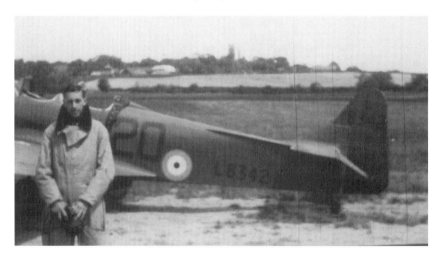

Geoff after completing his first solo flight at Redhill, 6 May 1939

Geoff in 1998

Geoff Cole

Geoffrey Cole joined the RAF Volunteer Reserve in early 1938 at Derby. He trained as a pilot and wanted to join Bomber Command with a view to becoming a civilian airline pilot. He was awarded his pilot's brevet in 1939 and joined 214 Squadron in July 1940, then 103 Squadron in 1943. Amongst other places he was based in Lossiemouth, Stradishall, Elsham Wolds and Blyton. He flew Wellingtons with 3 Group and Lancasters with 1 Group, Bomber Command, and, after completing fifty-four operations he became an instructor on Lancasters and Halifaxes. For a short time he was seconded to the Royal Navy aircraft carrier, Argus. After the war he achieved his ambition of becoming an airline pilot with BOAC, Skyway and Court Line. He amassed a total flying time over 20,000 hours worldwide. Geoff once flew the Wellington R-Robert which ditched in Loch Ness and was raised a few years ago. It is now undergoing restoration at Brooklands Museum.

Frightened by a dragon

I saw my first aircraft in 1926 when I was six years old. I was playing in the woods near my house with a friend when we heard a terrible roaring noise and something swooped above the trees. We were terrified.

My friend identified it as a dragon then we fled in terror into the house. My mother allayed our fears and told us,

"It's an aeroplane, not a dragon. There's nothing to be frightened of. I think it's landed in the field just down the road. Go and have a look."

Still somewhat apprehensive, we ventured forth but my courage grew as my brother and his friend joined us. Just as my mother had predicted there was the aeroplane. We watched from the edge of the field as instructed by the field owner. He went out in his car to talk to the man standing by its side. Eventually, the aeroplane was turned around, 'wound up' and came racing towards us. It took off and soared over our heads. The pilot waved to us and finally disappeared. We watched until it was nothing more than a speck in the distant sky then we raced back home.

"We saw it fly into the sky!" I told my mother excitedly. "It just ran along the ground then went right over us into the sky! But it never moved its wings—how can it fly if it doesn't flap its wings like a bird?"

"I don't know, dear. You'll have to ask your father when he comes in—he knows all about aeroplanes."

When my father came in I told him the story and asked him how it flew.

"It's obvious, my boy. Sky-hooks, that's what keeps it up."

"Sky-hooks?"

"Yes." I puzzled over that for some time. Finally I said,

"Yes, Dad, but what holds up the sky-hooks?" (I was a little boy with an enquiring mind.) He said,

"Bigger sky-hooks." I realised then that if grown-ups didn't know the answer they told you a story!

I finally learnt the truth about how aeroplanes fly from a Christmas present in 1931—*Every Boy's Hobby Annual* had a chapter on how aeroplanes flew and an article about some fifteen year-old apprentices at a place called RAF Halton who had actually built a real aeroplane. I did not realise it at the time but I was hooked on aeroplanes.

Crewing up and seeing how it's done

I was called up for regular service three days before war was declared in September 1939 having already attended various courses and clocked up solo flying hours as a pre-war Volunteer Reserve. I became a fully qualified pilot (twin-engined) in June 1940 at RAF Ternhill, Shropshire. From there I went to Lossiemouth—a new OTU flying Wellingtons with two newly commissioned Pilot Officers and Sergeant Pilot Cattle (pronounced C'tell not Cattle), who became a friend.

It turned out that the aircraft were not dual controlled and we were to be instructors, which we didn't fancy at the time, and so we went to see the newly arrived Wing Commander. We requested not to be instructors and said we wished to go to war.

"All right," came the reply, "Get yourself a crew!"

So we went round the hangar, talked to the chaps working there and acquired a crew. This consisted of LAC Flanagan, LAC Cook, LAC Hide and Sgt Butcher, a direct entry Sergeant

Navigator. We called ourselves No.1 Crew, No.1 Course, Lossiemouth. There was one small snag: I had trouble with my take-offs and Cattle had trouble with his landings!

Our first flight together in a Wellington from Lossiemouth (now known as No.20 OTU) was round the top of Scotland and lasted about four hours. A pilot, Sgt Douglas, who had been on ops, accompanied us and 'knew all about it'. Towards the end of the flight he said,

"I'll show you how things are done on the squadron." We were duly impressed when he got right down on the deck—really low—and for the last thirty miles or so came roaring back at minimum altitude.

Unfortunately, he had been used to flying the latest Wellington, the Mark Ic. This one was a Mark I and had a hydraulic system that had to be off-loaded by means of a power cock. Before putting wheels and flaps down it was necessary to turn on the power. Sgt Douglas forgot all about this and we ended up in a heap in the middle of the field. It must have been the quickest evacuation on record!

Accident when flying with Sgt. Douglas, Lossiemouth, June 1940
Sgt Cattle on top of aircraft retrieving parachutes; Sgt Cole with back to camera next to Sgt Cook; Sgt Douglas walking away from aircraft; Sgts Hide and Flanagan inspecting front turret. Photo taken by Sgt Butcher with aircraft's camera.

Quite 'armless

I'VE said that Cattle was no good at landing and I was no good at taking off and so we swapped over when it was time to land or take-off. Obviously, this couldn't go on and so we put in some practice. One particular day returning from a cross-country flight we discovered there were two squadrons of Blenheims lined up on the far side of the field at Lossiemouth. Cattle was due to do the landing and, as often happened, he touched down well into the field; only this time it was worse than usual. However, he managed to turn the aircraft. We were now going sideways at a rate of knots but heading for a gap between the two squadrons. At that moment, a Blenheim appeared in the gap from behind the other Blenheims.

"This is it. This is my lot," I thought, "I've had it."

The Blenheim's propellers would slice right into us. I could see it coming. Cattle swung the aircraft again at the last minute and, instead of his propellers chopping us, ours chopped his nose off.

After a speedy evacuation from both aircraft it was discovered that the navigator of the Blenheim had been in the nose. We got him out. He was fully conscious but the propeller had chopped his arm off at the shoulder—clean as a whistle! We tried to staunch the bleeding with our shirts while the ambulance came—but it never did. We realised that no one on the airfield had seen the accident happen as they had all gone to the NAAFI for tea. The RAF was still operating under peace-time conditions.

Eventually, our navigator raced the full length of the field to get the ambulance. When it arrived the 'armless' navigator was sitting up smoking a cigarette. He got up casually, strolled into the ambulance, somebody put his arm in behind him—and off he went.

A year later he returned to Lossiemouth on a visit from Canada where he had been instructing navigators. Cattle and I were both back there as instructors having completed our first tour. He told us that the accident was the best thing that has happened to him as out of eighteen crews on 21 and 57 Squadrons (Blenheims) only four survived their fortnight at Lossiemouth.

Up to this time Cattle and I had taken turns to be captain but after this incident Cattle was made permanent second pilot by the CO.

Part of Geoff's crew at Lossiemouth, 1940.
Left to right: *Sgt Hide, unknown, Sgt Butcher, Sgt Cole, Sgt Cattle*

Trigger-happy

WE had been chronically short of equipment—so short that up to now we had had no guns and so, whenever we went out, the gunners just came along for the ride! Eventually, we actually got guns in our turrets and set off on a gunnery exercise. I was taxiing out in preparation for take-off when I felt a vibration from behind. I wondered if there was something wrong with the tail wheel or if it had collapsed. I asked the rear gunner,

"Tail wheel OK?"

There was a slight pause then the rear gunner replied.

"It was me, skipper."

"You?"

"I just fired my guns into the ground."

"You did *what*? I asked incredulously.

"In the 14-18 war gunners had to fire their guns into the ground just before take-off to test them. Standard practice," he said.

"I see." I had a suspicion that I had not heard the end of this.

We continued with the exercise and on return I wasn't in the least surprised to be summoned to see the Station Commander—on the double. I had to give my gunner all the support I could and explained exactly what had happened, praised his outstanding ability and keenness, proved when he said it was standard practice to test the guns by firing into the ground during the last war.

"Maybe it was then but it isn't now. Perhaps, Sgt Cole, you'll be interested to know that the entire camp took to the air raid shelters, including me. In future, when you do things like this will you warn me first?" and I thought I detected a faint smile.

"Yes, sir."

"Dismissed."

Chased by a star

WE had just completed our first raid. This was to Schipol airport, Amsterdam, and we were on our way back. I was now second pilot to Pilot Officer Filluel who had taken over my crew. Tension was high as there had been many rumours about German night fighters with lights on them. We had left the target about ten minutes when the rear gunner reported a light coming up behind.

"You sure?"

"Positive."

Filluel dived and turned trying to lose the light but it remained steadfastly behind us. He ordered the navigator,

"Go take a look through the astrodome."

"Definitely a light, skipper," reported the navigator. I then suggested,

"I'll go and look." Sure enough, there was the light. No matter what we did or where we went, it stayed with us.

"How about giving him a burst with our guns?" I suggested to Filluel, "let him know we've seen him."

"OK."

The rear gunner blasted into the night sky. What a surprise—we had been trying to shoot down Venus—the morning star!

In retrospect it was laughable but at the time, with nerves stretched to breaking point and an atmosphere of fear and tension, the slightest thing could spark imagination and defy reason. Shooting at Venus was just one of many similar incidents created, I suspect, by tension and anxiety.

I believe other crews had also tried to shoot down Venus. It was, of course, the first year night bombers had operated and not many people had observed the early morning planet.

Where was Hitler when we needed him?

TWO years into the war—14 September 1941. It was the day the war could have ended if we could have found Hitler. We were to bomb a railway station at Ehrang in the Harz Mountains where, according to intelligence, Hitler was spending the night in a train. There was a lot of cloud but we let down through the cloud to about a couple of hundred feet and found the railway line and followed it but couldn't find the station.

We decided to drop a flare. We'd never dropped a flare before and the navigator went to do this. He came back,

"It's stuck, skipper."

I went back to help him. It was wedged in the flare chute—not only that but the nose of the flare was already out. The flare's nose had a propeller and when the propeller came unscrewed the thing exploded. I was fiddling about with it when it started to fizz ominously.

With an almighty shove I pushed it out. It fell into a field about 200 feet below us and killed a cow. By the light of the burning flare we found ourselves on the side of a hill, climbed to clear it and back into the clouds but they obscured our target and we never did bomb the station.

Had we achieved our goal, and killed Hitler instead of the hapless cow, maybe the war would have ended much sooner.

A tale of two parachutes

MINE was one of three aircraft that took off thirty minutes before the main force of sixty aircraft detailed to light the target, Dusseldorf, on 17 October 1940. On the way back we ran into a lot of cloud and so I decided to climb above it. We reached 14,000 feet when both engines stopped—iced up. I had had my aircraft fitted with a hand-operated, alcohol-pump that was supposed to de-ice both engines but they still would not start. There was nothing I could do as we steadily dropped. At 6,000 feet I ordered,

"Parachutes on. You know the drill."

The parachutes were separate from the harness and kept in a rack by the entrance door so that as you left you took your parachute and jumped out. At least, that was the theory. The drill was that the navigator would sort out the parachutes and hand them out. I looked round and was amazed to see the navigator on his knees praying. I also noticed my co-pilot had stopped pumping. Although I'm not a religious chap I offered up a prayer myself at the same time saying,

"Pump, you bastard, pump!"

Suddenly the starboard engine started but we were below 4,000 feet.

"We're OK. If she keeps going we can make England on one engine," I tried not to sound too jubilant because our altitude was 2,000 feet and dropping—maybe we couldn't make it after all. On top of that we were attacked by ground defences. We were so low by this time that the searchlight beams looked almost horizontal and reflected on the sea; we realised we were heading over the North Sea at just 500 feet. We pressed on and rose to 1,000 feet. The port engine started and we made it back home.

The next day I was called into the parachute section.

"Where's your parachute, Sgt Cole?"

"In the aircraft."

"It isn't. There's one missing and it's yours."

I told them what had happened. In handing out the parachutes, the navigator had probably accidentally dropped one through the open door. If we had had to abandon the aircraft I would have been parachute-less. My mind went back to seeing the navigator praying—had be been praying for himself or me?

From then on I always wore a pilot-type parachute on which I sat. (Incidentally, of the three aircraft that led the raid, I was the only one to return. The main force of sixty all turned back due to bad weather.)

It was on my second tour on Lancasters with 103 Squadron, on a raid on Bochem in 1943, when we took a lot of flak. Even so, we came back relatively unscathed or so I thought. The next day the parachute section called for me.

"I can't have lost a parachute *again*," I thought. I knew I couldn't because I had actually been sitting on it and it was attached to me. I went to see what the problem was. I was shown a black, sticky mess hanging from the rack.

"Your parachute, F/Lt Cole."

I was handed a piece of shrapnel about four inches long.

"Where did that come from?"

"Your parachute."

On inspection of my aircraft I discovered that this piece of shrapnel had gone through the bomb doors, through a can of incendiary bombs, through the floor of the aircraft, through the bottom of my seat and into my parachute. It had stopped there. Being red hot it had melted the artificial silk into a burnt, glutinous mess. Had I not been wearing this type of parachute I wouldn't be here to tell this story!

Near squeak for Baggy

PILOT Officer (as he was now) Cattle and I were instructing on Wellingtons at Lossiemouth from 1941-2. There was also a New Zealander, F/Sgt Bagnall ('Baggy') and another chap whose name I've forgotten.

On 22 August 1941 we were on night training exercises with pupils—circuits and bumps. I finished my shift and waited for the others. Cattle and the other fellow came in but there was no sign of Bagnall. We waited a while and presumed he must have gone home. The flare path was being cleared and the airfield closing down for the night.

"Wonder what's happened to Baggy? He's not signed in," said Cattle. "Let's check with the flight office." The flight sergeant confirmed that the aircraft was still out. We called the Observer Corps.

"Nothing flying at all, sir. No aircraft airborne in Scotland at this time," came the reply.

"He must have crashed."

We notified the CO and he raised the camp and a search party to search the cliff tops.

Cattle and I did a square search of the sea just off the coast. A Whitley from RAF Kinloss did the same thing and the lighthouse keeper also put on his light as a guide. In those days we didn't carry radio—just speaking tubes—so there was no contact with the ground once you were airborne. We started our search, combing the sea with our landing lights on at a height of 200 feet or so.

Suddenly, we noticed air-to-air gunfire to port. An enemy intruder had joined us. I switched off the navigation lights immediately. The lighthouse did the same, so did the Whitley from Kinloss and the airfield. In the total darkness the three aircraft—two British and one German—flew round not knowing where the others were. I waited for the crash that I was sure would come...

Finally, as dawn broke we landed safely back at the base but no one had seen a sign of F/Sgt Bagnall.

"Poor old, Baggy, what a way to go—lost on circuits and bumps."

Cattle and I retired to bed having been up all

night thinking we had lost a good friend.

In circuits and bumps the pupil, in effect, flies a square, four-legged circuit round the airfield and comes into land then takes off again, turns, goes round in 'legs', lands again and so on. It's easy to forget which 'leg' you're on and thus continue in a straight line.

This happened to a pupil the morning after Baggy disappeared. The instructor let him carry on and waited for the pupil to realise his mistake but the pupil didn't. Eventually, after five miles or so down wind near the Spey estuary the instructor suggested it might be an idea to turn back to the airfield. The pupil, no doubt embarrassed at his lapse in concentration, did so. At that moment the instructor glanced out of the window and noticed a dinghy floating in the water with two people in it.

It was Baggy and his pupil! (How lucky can you get?)

The rescue people went out and the two were brought in and taken to hospital. We went to see him,

"What happened, Baggy?" was our first question.

"First take-off on the circuits and bumps the full flaps came on, the aircraft struck a hangar, damaged the propeller, knocked off the airspeed indicator, the engine caught fire and the next thing I remember was being in the sea. The aircraft sank but the dinghy floated to the surface. We scrambled in and sat there the rest of the night. We watched you searching and we waved like mad but you never saw us."

Three weeks later he returned to circuits and bumps. (Sadly, F/Sgt Bagnall was later reporting missing in action while flying Stirlings on his second tour of operations.)

Sixth sense?

I was Squadron Leader in 1662 HCU Blyton near Gainsborough, Lincolnshire, in October 1943. I was just twenty-three years old. One particular occasion I was Officer-in-Charge of night flying and was about to go off duty as all the aircraft were back except one. He should be back any time, I told myself, but there was no news. I waited and waited then the telephone rang.

"RAF doctor here. There's been a mid-air collision between two aircraft about ten miles away. I think one of them is yours."

"We're expecting one back. What happened?"

"No survivors from one, I'm afraid. Not sure about the other. Would you mind going to the crash site where there were no survivors? My corporal will go with you and he'll bring the body bags." The other RAF doctor was away on leave and it was an RAF requirement that there had to be an officer present at clearing up after such an accident.

The wreckage was still burning when I arrived at the scene. The corporal and I began our gruesome task and put bits and pieces in body bags. I saw a flying helmet on the ground not far away and picked it up. There was a head still in it and I looked into the face of a young lad I had been speaking to only four hours before.

We finished our grim task as dawn broke and returned to the airfield. Before going to bed I went over to the mess and ordered a late lunch for two o'clock. When I returned at two the mess was empty. As I was hanging up my coat the mess telephone rang. No one came to answer it and it continued to ring. It rang and rang. Suddenly I got the odd sensation that it was for me. What's more, I sensed it was the mother of the boy whose helmet and head I had found.

I forced myself to pick up the receiver. A gentle, woman's voice said,

"Is that RAF Blyton?"

"Yes," I said.

"Who am I speaking to?" I had a strange feeling she knew without asking. I stalled for time.

"I'm afraid I can't say but can I help you?" She told me her name—it came as no surprise—and continued,

"My son's a bomb aimer in Squadron Leader Cole's flight. He's my only son—he's everything to me," her voice trembled slightly, "I'm a widow, you see." There was a pause. "I know this sounds silly but I woke suddenly at four o'clock this morning and I had a horrible feeling that something had happened to him— that he had been killed. I couldn't sleep after that and all morning I've been thinking about

him. I just had to ring up and find out. I do hope you don't mind. I've been so worried," she paused, "has there been an accident?"

I couldn't tell her that I had been looking into the face of her beheaded son only a few hours ago. What does one say at a time like this?

"I believe there has," was a much as I could say, "I'll put you through to the adjutant. He'll be able to help you." Thankfully I transferred the call.

All the time I sensed she knew who she was speaking to—even though we had never spoken before. Four o'clock had been the exact time that the accident had happened.

Was it a mirage?

I was on duty at RAF Lindholme and there were just three aircraft flying that night. It was winter with a slight mist over the hollows that would soon clear. The first aircraft took off and crashed shortly after take-off about two miles from the end of the runway. I sent the emergency vehicles—fire engines and ambulance—and notified the civilian people who sent their emergency staff and equipment.

I put the other two aircraft on hold while all this was being sorted out. Very soon the telephone rang. It was the Air Commodore. I told him what had happened and that, until the emergency vehicles and staff were back on the airfield, I was holding the remaining aircraft which struck me as the most sensible and safe thing to do.

"Don't you know there's a war on? Get them airborne immediately!" came the angry reply.

"But, sir—" I began.

"Get them airborne," insisted the air commodore. I was very reluctant to do this for what if they crashed too? It was unlikely but...

The next aircraft went off and it too crashed about five miles further on. Of course, there was nothing I could do about it. There were

no emergency services—nothing. I told the duty clerk to tell the air commodore but I had to send off the third aircraft and this one also crashed about three miles beyond the second crash. I now had three burning aircraft— eighteen young men needlessly killed.

There was a sequel to this. About three years later I was a captain with BOAC and was flying out of Bordeaux one evening. Forest fires had been burning and smoke and mist was forming in the low-lying areas and drifting across the airfield. I told the crew to hurry up and take-off as quickly as possible before the fog came down.

We took off and at about 200 feet, the First Officer grabbed the controls. I looked up and was horrified to see that we were flying upside down! Above me was a perfect picture of the ground with moving vehicles, streetlights, house lights—everything.

I snarled at him to check the instruments. Slowly he let go, checked the standby instruments and then mine. He relaxed slightly and sat back. The instruments were correct but we were apparently flying upside down. At 600 feet we flew clear. It was the strangest sensation I have ever experienced.

My mind went back to the three aircraft that had crashed at RAF Lindholme. The meteorological conditions were almost the same. There was smoke and mist and I have often wondered how many aircraft crashes have been due to this phenomenon with the pilot ignoring his instruments and believing his visual sighting. To suddenly see the ground above you is unnerving, to say the least, and to someone with relatively little experience of night flying, could prove fatal.

Geoff's experience of the perils of civilian flying: Cyprus in the late 1950s

The remains of Hermes GACD blown up by a bomb in passengers' baggage at Nicosia, Cyprus. The bomb went off as the crew were about to do their ground checks. The flight engineer was blown off the wing and, miraculously, suffered only a broken wrist. Three months before, Geoff had unwittingly carried a bomb from Nicosia to Bahrain which, fortunately, had failed to go off and was discovered on landing.

Gordon Collinson

Pilot

202 (RAF), 760 and 761 (Fleet Air Arm) Squadrons

Gordon Collinson 1944

Above: Gordon flying a Harvard Mk. IV
1943 at 34 Service Flying Training
School, Medicine Hat, Alberta, Canada

1989 retirement treat to celebrate fifty years' service
at ICL: a Tiger Moth flight from Little Gransden,
Cambridgeshire.

Gordon Collinson

Gordon Collinson joined the RAF Volunteer Reserve in 1941 at Oxford. He was awarded his pilot's brevet in 1943 after training in Britain and Canada flying Tiger Moths and Harvards. He later attended a conversion course to fly twin-engined aircraft before being posted to Killadeas in Northern Ireland to fly Catalina flying boats in 1944. He was with RAF Coastal Command's 202 Squadron from 1944-5 then in the Fleet Air Arm from 1945-6 with 760 and 761 Squadrons flying Seafire IIIs. He flew twenty-five operations. He was demobbed in 1946 and throughout the 1950s was CO of No. 248 (Letchworth) Squadron Air Training Corps.

No second chance

IT was mid afternoon on 8 April 1945. I was flying as second pilot with Captain John Baldry and crew in a Catalina IV, JX204, belonging to 202 Squadron based at Castle Archdale, Lough Erne, Northern Ireland. Although the end of the war was looming hostilities weren't over and it was our job to be on the look-out for German submarines that might still be lurking in the North Atlantic.

Suddenly, a crew member in one of the blister turrets said excitedly,

"Snorkel and periscope to the rear of the aircraft!"

We turned starboard through 360 degrees to attack. The navigator, lying in the nose of the aircraft, prepared to drop depth charges. Standing above, him the front gunner with his feet on either side of the prone navigator, readied himself for the attack. He adjusted each foot on the port and starboard steps until he was steady.

We reduced height to fifty feet—perfect. Absolutely spot on.

"Bombs gone," said the navigator as he pressed the button to release the depth charges—except they stayed put. "What the hell—?" Nothing happened.

"Again! Again!" Still nothing.

"Hang on," called the navigator. "It's your bloody leg!" he addressed the front gunner.

"What's the matter with my leg?"

"You've bloody well knocked the cover of the intervalometer back." (This device controlled the spacing between depth charges.)

The gunner looked down to see that his boot, in pushing the cover back, had allowed a projecting screw to trip a vital switch in the mechanism causing it to fail and hence the depth charges did not drop.

"Oh, bloody hell!" uttered the wretched gunner.

"I can fix it." The navigator quickly put things right but it was too late.

"Any sign of our German friend?" asked the skipper without much hope. The U-boat had disappeared without trace.

For the skipper it was a dreadful moment! He was on his third flying boat tour and it was the first time his crew had ever sighted a U-boat.

"I could weep," was all he could say.

It was a serious offence to sight a submarine and not drop depth charges. There was a court of inquiry. The crew was exonerated and somebody in the armament section got a rocket for a botched modification—it wasn't much consolation.

43

Gordon Collinson

How not to take-off in a Catalina

THERE was another incident also in 1945 and again I was second pilot with F/Lt John Baldry of 202 Squadron at Castle Archdale.

To assist in manoeuvring on water a Catalina has two drogues (sea anchors)—one to port and one to starboard. They are streamed from bollards aft of the blister turrets. Each drogue is linked to the aircraft by a wire hawser when in use. After landing, the aircraft approaches a mooring buoy which has a floating strop to be picked up by a crew member, in the nose, by means of a boathook. The captain approaches the buoy as slowly as he can, using the drogues to keep the aircraft into the wind, to make the strop pick-up and attachment to the bollard as easy as possible—sometimes in difficult conditions. The drogues were often left streamed after mooring up and one of the first things a crew should do when boarding an aircraft for another flight is to ensure that the drogues are inboard.

On this particular trip, two drogues were taken in and the aircraft made ready for flight. It was lightly loaded, being a short training flight, and should have got airborne very quickly. It did not.

"What's going on?" said the skipper. The Catalina felt heavy and awkward.

"I don't know. No reason why she shouldn't take off."

"Give her a long run." We did but were still on the water. We aborted take-off.

"Try again." But the second attempt was just the same.

"What the hell's the matter with her? Everything's OK. Maximum power—let's go!"

At the third attempt we managed to haul the aircraft into the air. It felt like flying a brick and as though we were being dragged back all the time.

"Hey! Know what?" came a shout from the blister turret, "We're streaming a drogue from the starboard bollard."

"We can't be! We took two in."

"Well, we are. Look!"

And indeed we were. There was the culprit—but the drogue was only doing its job—trying to anchor us! Somehow the crew hauled the drogue in. Why there had been a third drogue in the water we never did find out.

When we returned we found ourselves the object of puzzled admiration.

"Never seen anything like it!" said one chap from Flying Control.

"How the hell did you take off at all?"

"Amazing!"

"Thought you were off on a fighter affiliation trip!" quipped someone else referring to the drogues used for 'target practice' by nippy little fighters. 'Nippy' was not a word you could use to describe a Catalina!

"Hardly! Not exactly what the Catalina was designed to do!"

Catalina flight August 1992. Gordon with Capt. Paul Warren Wilson, ex-Harrier pilot responsible for 'rescuing' this Catalina in South Africa in the 1960s.

John Cooper

DSC and Bar

Pilot

760, 761, 809, 881, 882 Squadrons
Fleet Air Arm

(Died 1998)

No photographs available

John Cooper

John Cooper joined the Royal Navy in February 1940 at Cambridge and was awarded his 'Wings' later that year. He served with the Fleet Air Arm in Atlantic and Arctic convoys and became an instructor on Hurricanes and Spitfires. He was awarded the DSC and Bar. John wrote his reminiscences in a privately prouduced book and it is from this that these extracts are taken.

Log book entry February-May 1940

HMS St Vincent, Gosport, and training in naval discipline, custom and assessment prior to acceptance for Flying Training.

This opening title in my flying log book should not really be there because HMS *St Vincent* was a naval shore establishment, a barracks at Gosport. The Navy has always been in the habit of calling shore stations after ships. It was, in fact, a series of buildings, rumoured to date from Napoleonic days, built around an enormous parade ground in which stood a tall mast for seamanship training. The whole was enclosed by forbidding walls with gates that were locked at night.

Before the war *St Vincent* had been used for receiving, screening and knocking into shape boys or would-be ordinary seamen seeking a career in the Royal Navy. Its wartime role was to be similar but the intake suddenly became volunteer pilots and observers who were potential officer material. Should they pass through the disciplinary and academic ground training at *St Vincent* and be sent on to flying training with the RAF, they could possibly qualify as full-blown pilots and officers within six months.

If they failed to get their Wings at the end of these periods of training they stayed put on the lower deck and went back to square one—a dreadful fate to contemplate. They could then well find themselves bouncing up and down on a destroyer escorting arctic convoys as ordinary seamen forever and a day.

We *St Vincent* trainees were called Naval Airmen which, in rank, was really the equivalent of ordinary seamen, and we were paid something like three shillings a day. As far as I can recall the only minimum requirement for being accepted for training at *St Vincent*, other than passing an interview, was a secondary education. My pilots' course, therefore, consisted of about fifty or sixty young men who came from all sorts of social backgrounds and now included, for the first time, a number of university graduates.

I myself had been to Cambridge University and had gained an Honours degree in economics and law. I had then worked in our family woollen business in the West End of London for a year before returning to the university with a few like-minded friends to be interviewed and accepted as a trainee Fleet Air Arm pilot. Needless to say, acceptance included having to pass a rigorous physical test, certainly as far as eyesight was concerned. Quite a number of people failed.

As you can imagine this new situation at HMS *St Vincent* came as a bit of a social shock both to the instructed and to the instructors, many of whom were Chief Petty Officers or Petty Officers. Large dollops of good humour and goodwill were necessary on both sides to make life tolerable.

The discipline was extremely strict with unlimited square bashing and we were wakened each morning to that well-known call, "Wakey-wakey, rise and shine. Lash up and stow!" as we rolled out of our hammocks and folded them away.

The parade ground was a bit draughty in February, especially for raw recruits in seaman's fore and aft rig—one got very cold around the neck! We also cast anxious eyes at the enormously high ship's main mast with its rigging which we prayed we would never be asked to climb as our predecessors had been

obliged to do—a prayer that, thank heaven, was granted.

Needless to say, some of us fell into the usual training traps and I was one of them. When our stentorian Petty Officer instructor called for "anyone who could chauffeur a Daimler" to step forward, I did so, and was instantly ordered to go and clean out the Petty Officers' heads [toilets]. He kindly accompanied me to advise on the best method to be used. More than thirty-four years later I am still doing the same job at my little country church which is not on the mains! "Stick your bloody arm down!" the Chief had ordered and that is what I still do.

Shore leave stories

IN accepting intakes of Fleet Air Arm aircrew volunteers with public school and/or university backgrounds, the navy circles in the Portsmouth area had to get used to ordinary seamen with Oxbridge accents breaking long standing conventions.

One unforgettable evening a fellow trainee of mine, a very good friend from my Cambridge days, Sandy Jackson, together with two other chaps, went out on the town on shore leave in the evening to wine and dine. Sandy was a wealthy young man who had taken a First Class Honours degree at the university, had driven around in a Ferrari and had impressed all of us fellow students by having a delightful mistress. Leaving all these luxuries behind him Sandy had now become a Naval Airman Second Class earning three shillings a day and he was doing it all with the greatest good humour.

One particular evening he led us from Gosport via the Portsmouth ferry to a famous hotel on the seafront at Southsea and into its extremely luxurious lounge bar. A dreadful silence fell because there was a number of very senior naval officers propping up the bar with yards of 'scrambled egg' up their arms. They

were struck dumb at our appearance because, of course, Other Ranks were certainly very much de trop in that particular hotel.

We whispered to Sandy that we should retreat as convention clearly indicated but, undeterred, he advanced to the bar and asked the white-coated and white-gloved barman for four large dry martinis. The poor man told Sandy that the bar was for officers and that he certainly could not serve members of the lower deck.

Sandy replied that both he and the senior officers present would undoubtedly agree that he and his friends could and should be served when he explained the position.

"What position is that?" asked the barman.

"I own this hotel" said Sandy.

There was a general roar of laughter by everyone in the room followed by a discussion on the novel social situation now developing at the local pubs and clubs. It transpired that Sandy did not own the hotel outright but was a leading shareholder in the financial group that did.

How well I recall travelling from Pompey to London on a weekend leave with Sandy. When the train started from Portsmouth station he took a suitcase along to the loo and changed into a Savile Row pin-stripe suit with a silk tie and even sported a button hole. When he returned to our carriage an old lady told him that he could not sit down as that seat was already taken by a sailor!

Sandy survived the war. He had a very good brain indeed and passed all the tests at *St Vincent* and at RAF courses on engine maintenance, navigation and so on at the very top of the form but, when it came to flying, he had little judgement and was a danger both to himself and to anyone near him, frequently getting lost or 'wandering' when flying in formation.

He once took off in a Fairey Battle from Netheravon on Salisbury Plain on a solo navigation test to fly to Peterborough and finished up on the Welsh coast—that took some doing! Sadly, he eventually relinquished his attempts to earn his Wings and found himself aboard a destroyer in the Atlantic as the seaman detailed to take cocoa up to the bridge.

Happily, his failure to become a pilot resulted in his survival. Casualties in that course were to be extremely high and it was sad to lose so many very good friends in the years to come.

Most of our shore leaves in the evening were spent in Portsmouth, travelling to and from Gosport on the harbour ferries. I remember coming back late one night from Portsmouth after the ferry crossing to Gosport had been long delayed by air aids and warnings. I was escorting an attractive young girl, extremely well dressed, to her home at about midnight. All public transport had stopped and she lived in a very imposing house at Alverstoke where many senior officers had houses.

When we got to her house I accepted her invitation to come in and have a cup of cocoa—liquid refreshment that was a bit out of character for me! Down the stairs, at one o'clock in the morning, came her father in his dressing gown. He turned out to be an Admiral and was very interested to meet one of the new *St Vincent* intakes. He was concerned that my evening shore leave had long expired and was amused when I told him that getting into HMS *St Vincent* at night presented no difficulties to someone used to climbing into colleges at Cambridge!

49

Ken Dixon

Observer

816, 854 and 857 Squadrons

Fleet Air Arm

*Ken Dixon during his wartime service
with the Fleet Air Arm*

Ken today

Ken Dixon

Ken Dixon volunteered for the Fleet Air Arm in 1940 but was not called up until October 1941. After a lengthy period of training at various naval establishments in the UK and a final period of flying training in Trinidad he was commissioned as an Observer with the rank of Sub Lieutenant (A) Royal Naval Volunteer Reserve in 1943. He served on the Russian convoys and in the Far East before leaving the Fleet Air Arm in 1946.

On the Russian convoys

MY first appointment was to HMS *Chaser*, an American-built escort carrier which I joined at Gourock in Scotland. My first task was to act as assistant to the Air Staff Officer. Early in 1944 we took on board a composite squadron (816) with eleven Swordfish and eleven Wildcat aircraft. I flew regularly with that squadron.

In February 1944 the ship joined the close escort for a Russian convoy (JW57) bound for Murmansk. After stopping for a few days at Scapa Flow we joined the convoy which also had the cruiser *Black Prince* and seventeen destroyers as close escort. Not long after joining we were shadowed by Ju88s that the Wildcats engaged but were afflicted by gun stoppages due to the cold weather.

We could tell by HF/DF (high frequency direction finder) where the U-boats were operating—fourteen were stationed in two lines across our path. The Swordfish, our anti-submarine aircraft, were slow but very manoeuvrable and were armed with eight rocket projectiles. The weather soon turned foul and one dark, stormy night the destroyer *Mahratta* was torpedoed and sank despite heroic efforts by the crew of HMS *Impulsive*. Only seventeen of her crew of two hundred were saved. The snow and the storm swallowed up the rest.

In those dreadful conditions the Swordfish suffered from landing on a dangerously pitching and rolling carrier and before long only six were serviceable; whilst, on the ship barrier machinery, arrestor wire sheaves and guns seized up. But the remaining Swordfish continued to hunt the U-boats and kept them away from the convoy so that it reached the Kola Inlet to Murmansk without further loss.

At Kola Inlet much work was done repairing defects; the fighter pilots visited a Russian fighter base, enjoyed alcoholic hospitality and had to be carried back on board! We also had a visit by the choir of the Russian Arctic Fleet and appreciated their splendid singing. My strongest and most moving impression was seeing forty-three merchant ships of our convoy steaming steadily up the Inlet keeping perfect station on their way to Murmansk.

We left Kola Inlet on 2 March with thirty-one ships of the homeward-bound convoy RA57. We sailed for two days undetected; indeed, the blizzards and raging seas scattered the convoy over a wide area. After the storm abated and the ships had resumed formation, the Swordfish had some success. Two U-boats, U472 and U355, were hit by rockets and sank. One ship in the convoy was hit by a torpedo but, as it had a cargo of wood, it did not sink for days! At this time the U-boats were circling the convoys and escorts firing torpedoes that were difficult to avoid.

Later I received a Russian medal which was awarded to all the sailors who went to Russia—

Ken Dixon

the Arctic Medal, if I remember rightly.

The ship's stay when we were back in Scapa was not without incident.

Swordfish as used in 816 Squadron in 1944 when Ken Dixon regularly flew with the squadron

shock, as I was very inexperienced and he was the CO! But wiser counsel prevailed and a Lt Squires was given the position. On their first

We were moored near the passage between two islands. The wind got up and funnelled through the gap at a tremendous speed—enough to snap the mooring cable. As the ship was having its boilers cleaned there was no power from the engines and we drifted gently ashore, breaking off a rudder in the process. The ship was towed to Rosyth for repair and after a while I joined a naval air station at Fearn in north-east Scotland to crew up on the Fleet Air Arm's latest torpedo-dive bomber, the Barracuda. It was plagued with problems that took some time to sort out. (The Barracuda was difficult to get into and even more difficult to leave in a hurry. At first it used to shed its wings in a dive due to faulty rivets! It was also underpowered and could not be used in hot climates where the air was thinner.)

We were then sent to Ceylon where we retrained on American-built Avenger aircraft— an efficient and well-tested torpedo-glide bomber. Early in 1945 I joined 854 Squadron on HMS *Illustrious*. The squadron took part in two attacks on the very important oil refineries at Palembang in Sumatra. It was the largest operation by the Fleet Air Arm with some 140 naval aircraft taking part. Forty-one were lost but the refineries suffered heavy damage.

The Commanding Officer of 854 Squadron was killed at Palembang. He was replaced by Lt Cdr Nottingham, RNVR, who was the CO of 816 Squadron on HMS *Chaser*. He knew me and said I would be his observer. This was a

operation the plane was shot down: Nottingham escaped but Squires was killed—a lucky escape for me!

We then sailed on to Sydney and became part of the British Pacific Fleet. I joined 857 Squadron on HMS *Indomitable* and for two months was engaged on bombing attacks on the Sakashima Gunto, a chain of islands south of Japan. These islands all had coral airstrips that the Japanese used to 'stage' aircraft back to Japan and to Okinawa where the Americans had just invaded. It was something of a pointless exercise as our 500lb bombs hitting those coral airstrips made only small holes that the Japs soon filled in. We also bombed an airfield in Formosa; it was mountainous and inhospitable and we were greeted by a particularly heavy anti-aircraft barrage when we hit the airfields—but we survived.

The Japanese surrender found us in Sydney and we were immediately rushed to Hong Kong to take it over from the Japs. This was a satisfying task: rounding up the Japs, helping restore the railway to working order and generally tidying up some of the damage.

We had hardly dropped anchor on Hong Kong when boats of Chinese laundrymen came alongside offering their services.

Later we returned to Sydney and soon departed for home leaving a large number of troops due for demob and some civilians who had been imprisoned by the Japs. I had reached the rank of Lieutenant (A) RNVR.

Derek Eden

Air Gunner

38 Squadron

Derek Eden at Gunnery School in Kabrit, Egypt, just before his nineteenth birthday...

...and Derek just a few years after his nineteenth birthday!

Derek Eden

Derek Eden joined the RAF in 1941 at Cardington, Bedfordshire. He knew he "hadn't the maths" to be a pilot or navigator or bomb aimer. After square-bashing at Great Yarmouth he went to gunnery school in Kabrit, Egypt, and qualified as an air gunner with 38 Squadron based in the Middle East, bombing targets in North Africa and Italy. He was awarded the 1939-45 Star, the Africa Star and Clasp, Italy Star and Victory Medal. He was a 'Special' after the war in the police force and earned the Long Service Police Medal with two Bars. He joined the Aircrew Association thirteen years ago and found it was like being back on the squadron! Recently, Derek has taken to recapturing his RAF days in poetry.

Dear Dad

Those silver wings upon my chest
I am so proud, like all the rest,
At last I'm ready for the fray
Now, tomorrow, or any day.

Those older crews who have got some in,
The ones in the mess, who make all the din,
Oh, how I envy everyone,
They've done some things that I've not done.

Each night they've been to hell and back—
Gerry, Johnny, Fred, Ron and Mac.
I know the ops. are tough to do;
I'm told it makes a man of you.

In the mess, I look at empty chairs.
A short time ago that crew had no cares
But I know it will be OK for me
For mine is the best crew in the flight, you see.

Don't worry, Dad, for I will be back,
Look after Mum, don't let her crack,
Love to Billy and my girl, June,
'Bye for now—I'll write again soon.

Your loving son Sgt Pilot Bill Brown

Air Gunner Off Duty

He strolled through the field of grass so green
among the flowers, he felt serene,
all around the flowers bloomed;
the busy bees close by him zoomed.

He stroked the daffs, he picked a rose,
inspected buttercups, rows and rows.
The old oak tree seemed to smile and say:
"Welcome here, on this peaceful day."

He sat in the sun, watched clouds roll by,
stretched out his arms, let out a sigh,
"If I could stay here, let the war go by!

"But perhaps in heaven, it's like this all the time,
with beautiful girls, serving the wine,
angels and harps, and old friends too."
Of course, if he was there, he'd be with his crew.

Then back to briefing to hear the worst—
with what dodgy target would they be cursed?
But he thought: "If we get the chop and heaven's
like this,
with all those girls it'll be perfect bliss!"

Derek Eden

The Pilot

He gripped the control column and stared ahead
Beyond the searchlights, the fires were vivid red;
Above the crashing and the bangs, he heard his bomb aimer call,
"Sorry, skip, it's round again—can't see the target at all."

He banked H-Harry round again, to get back in the stream.
Once more he heard the voice: "Left, left, steady" as if in a dream.
The searchlights tried to cone them but he flew on straight and true,
The flak burst all around them, but on and on he flew.

At last the welcome call, "OK, skip, bombs away!"
Bomb doors closed, throttles forward. It's time to leave the fray.
His thoughts turned to nicer things: that ginger WAAF called Kay...
The gunner's shout of "Corkscrew port!" soon brushed that thought away.

The cannon shells laced the tail and soared just overhead,
But the 109 came unstuck from our mid upper, Fred.
So once again he turned for home, the job at last was done,
Another op. in the bag—that makes twenty-one.

The Flight Engineer

He sits by the pilot, the flight engineer,
Known in the crew as the 'ginger beer',
He studies the dials, checks the gauges,
Hydraulic system—this goes on for ages.

Under-carriage warning horn and light—
Is that balance cock screwed in tight?
Suction gauge, de-icer pump,
Bleeding things give me the hump.

Flap controls, feathering switch,
Pressure gauges, intercom switch,
Bomb release, landing lamps,
Booster coil, push up the amps.

Cowling gill, close all hatches—
We're starting up, check the watches.
How can I think of the WAAFs and the beer
With all these checks, I can't, I fear.

Derek Eden

The Cook

Being a cook isn't much fun,
Just another job that has to be done.
I'm told it's important, they rely upon me,
Dishing the food up, pouring the tea.

Still we all have our tasks on the squadron to do,
It's as important, I'm told, as being aircrew.
Well, someone has to feed them—I really care
'Cos I've seen them come back from that trip in the air.

I've seen weary fitters, armourers too,
Out in the flights from early morn through.
Theirs is a cold and horrible job,
My mate's a fitter—I feel sorry for Bob.

But, like me, they soldier on,
We'll be here long after the aircrew have gone.
I'm standing here dreaming—time does fly;
Now what's the menu today? Ah, cottage pie!

The Wireless Op.

The wireless op., with his box of tricks,
The one the nav. turns to for a fix.
Some wireless ops. are WOP/AGs
And with their guns they aim not to please.

A very important part of the crew—
Without a good radioman, what would we do?
We all get used to his dit-dit-dah—
He even practises when we're at the bar!

We stood on the tube platform as the girls passed by—
I gazed at them longingly, one gave me the eye.
I turned to our W/OP, said: "Did you see that?"
He was turning the words on a poster to dit-dah-dit-dat.

The trouble with W/OPs, their minds are one track,
It's all Morse code and fixes, even when dodging the flak.
But we all love him, he's the best in the flight,
A good bloke to be with you, in the thick of the fight.

Derek Eden

The Navigator

The tired nav. bent over his maps
It's OK, don't worry, chaps.
Now I took a fix, just about there
All was OK, why are we here?

The lads all trust me—they say I'm the best—
On every op. I've stood the test.
I've taken them to Hamburg, Berlin and Essen,
Bremen, the Ruhr—that was a session.

I've guided them through fog and flak
Whatever conditions, we always get back.
Oh, I see what is wrong, a slight deviation
This won't take me long—oh, elation!

Nav. to skipper—just steer oh-two-three
And at five-forty-five we'll sit down to tea.
Skip to nav.—I got it! Steer oh-two-three.
We're on the town tonight, your drink's on me!

Fitter 2E (Engines)

It's not much fun as a flight mech. or fitter.
The weather's a problem, on the airfield it's bitter.
We grovel around in the oil and the sludge
Struggling with bolts that just will not budge.

Then along come 'Chiefy' with his eagle eye,
 "Look at the state of that engine!" he'd cry,
 "I want that running and gleaming as well!"
I knew if it wasn't, he'd give me hell.

Still, I can't complain of the job that I do
When I think what the aircrew go through
So I make sure that my engines are sweet
But sometimes I'm so weary, I'm out on my feet.

The tension of waiting for my aircraft to get back—
A jolly good crew, my favourite's old Mac,
What with his grin and infectious laughter,
He slips me a choc bar, says, "I know what you're after!"

When P-Popsie takes off,
I feel very sad; I also feel proud, and then I am glad,
P-Popsie in the circuit—she sure looks great
Although I know tonight she will keep me up late.

The Intelligence Officer

I'm the intelligence officer, known by the lads as the IO—
The one that stands out in the front, and tells the poor sods where to go.
I gaze down upon the young upturned faces
I tell them of Berlin, Essen and other dodgy places.

I try to sugar the pill, and say:
"You're lucky, this one's a milk run today!"
I can tell by their looks that they've heard it before
But what can I say? We're fighting a war.

As I look around, some faces are missing;
I tap on the map and say, "Now, lads, listen,
If you go north at this point here
You'll miss most of the flak, but not fighters, I fear.

"So gunners, be alert, keep your eyes open wide
Those fighters are cunning, from them you can't hide
But I know you will all give of your best
I've sent you all over and you passed every test.

"Believe me when I say, I'd rather be you
Than standing up here, knowing what you will go through;
So do your job and hurry up back
Into debriefing, then hit the sack."

The SWO
(Station Warrant Officer)

A man of power, we all love to hate,
Always immaculate, and never late;
He struts round the flights, cane under arm,
He is a figure, the erks, view with alarm.

He has no time for aircrew: "Jumped up sods—
They just chucked stripes at the stupid clods
Because they do a bit of flying. They make a fuss,
A disgrace in the mess where they drink and cuss.

If I had my way, they'd be AC2's
And in between flying, they'd clean out the loos;
They'd sleep on camp beds, in old wooden shacks
With old leaky roofs and walls full of cracks.

I'd give 'em chocolate and bacon and egg!
For a couple of slices of bread they would beg,
And when they came to ask for a pass
All they would get would be a kick up the arse."

On Ops.

"Skip to rear gunner!" I hear the call,
he wants to know if I'm on the ball.
A bevy of bandits, coming fast,
I try to get one as they zoom past.

To my surprise my hands are steady.
I turn the turret, I am ready.
A cannon shell flies past my head—
a little lower and I'd be dead.

I fire a burst and watch the glow
of tracers falling far below;
the fighter banks, and turns again,
the sweat stands on my brow like rain.

He fires a burst and turns away
but he misses, and we're OK.
I feel the sweat run down my back—
is the b——d coming back?

I picture again my Mum's sweet face,
 I feel again that last embrace.
"Take no chances, son," she said,
"always take care, use your head."

I wondered if the fighter's Mum
had said the same words to her son.
And here we fight, high in the sky—
we both wanted so much to fly.

If I come through this and have a son
let him have girls and wine and fun.
Please not for him, this awful life
but a well paid job, and lovely wife.

The WAAF Driver

When I first got the job, to drive the crews
I could hardly wait to spread the good news.
What a lovely job, driving those cheerful young men—
I fell in love with them all, especially Ken.

But I found it does no good to lose you heart;
They have no future, death keeps you apart.
So now I love them in a sisterly way
And when they take off, I kneel down and pray.

Please, God, protect them, they are but boys,
Not long ago they were playing with toys;
They are so young, they were eager to fly,
Oh, please bring them back, don't let them die.

It's hard to stay aloof, and smile when they say they love me;
I love them but there is no future with them for me.
I want a boy, safe on the ground with me to stay,
Not from all of these ops. your boyfriend did not return today.

The Bomb Aimer

He lays there flat upon his face
But of the target there is no trace.
He peered again through the haze and smoke
But the target was covered, as if by a cloak.

He knew he would have to utter, that dreaded refrain:
 "Sorry, skip, can't see it, we'll have to go round again."
He could sense the sweat, the fear in the crew,
But if he can't see the target what can he do?

"Well, here we go, is that a gap in the haze?
Yes, OK, skip—left, left, steady, open bomb bays.
Hold it, skip, hold it!" He presses the switch
The bombs go away smoothly with never a hitch.

"Close bomb bay doors, skip, bombs all away.
Let's go home, lads, that's all for the day.
This is op. number thirty so now we are done;
Tonight we'll be legless so back for the fun!"

Derek Eden

In the Turret

I sat there, gazing down,
and watched the horror unfold.
The vivid red, the white and black—
enough to make the blood run cold.

I turn the turret left and right
and gaze upon that fearful sight.
The flak leaps at me, slow at first
then speeding up, and then a burst
of vivid flame before my eyes,
but does not hurt me, to my surprise.

How many nights of hell like this
must I endure?
I hold my breath, clench my fist,
I scan the heavens and search for foe,
all hell is breaking loose below.

I hold back my tears,
I fight the fears;
my mates back there, rely on me,
I am their guardian in the sky, you see.

We turn to go, another op. gone,
another five before we're done.
Oh, Lord above, watch over us,
take us home without a fuss.

We touch down, we arrive,
and say: "Thank God, we're still alive."

Don Foster

DFM

Wireless Operator/Air Gunner/Pilot

49, 240 and 408 Squadrons

Don Foster early 1939 in the
hangar at Scampton with
Handley Page Hampden
aircraft

Don in June 1942 at
Magdelene College,
Cambridge, on a pilots'
initial training course

The 'forgotten aircraft' - Handley Page Hampdens - Britain's latest front-line light
bomber in which Don had done 49 operations by 1943.
240 (RCAF) Squadron with Timmerman in the lead, Clayton and Don Foster (WOP/
AG) in No.4 aircraft practising formation flying before daylight ops. in September
1942 from Syerston, Nottinghamshire. Soon after this photo was taken Don was
awarded the DFM after being attacked by Me109s and Focke-Wulf fighters.
(See A new squadron p.69)

Don Foster

Don Foster was born in Cleethorpes and moved to Hull when he was thirteen. He joined the RAF in December 1937 at West Drayton. He initially trained as a wireless operator/air gunner but left Bomber Command for Training Command when he went on a pilots' course in 1942. After obtaining his 'Wings' in Canada he returned to the UK. Following an advanced flying course he was posted to Coastal Command and flew Catalinas including one from Oban to India in South East Asia Command (twenty operations). He served with 49 and 408 (RCAF) Squadrons in Bomber Command (forty-nine operations). He was awarded the DFM although the first he knew of it was when his mother wrote to him and sent a cutting about it from the Hull Daily Mail! *Not to be outdone, the Cleethorpes local paper also claimed him as 'theirs' and ran a story about him!*

A great skipper...

MY first 'interesting' op. was on 23 April 1940—a security patrol round the island of Sylt looking for any activity from magnetic mine-laying flying boats—with Canadian F/Lt Timmerman as my skipper. We found two flak ships and dive-bombed them from 6,000 feet down to their decks. Their anti-aircraft fire was intense to say the least. When Timmerman pulled out at zero feet and climbed away I was staring eyeball-to-eyeball with the enemy gunners! They didn't hit us but we admired the wonderful display of coloured strings of tracer bullets.

After that we stooged around a bit and—lo, and behold, there was another flak ship.

"Same drill again, fellas," said Timmerman. "Hold tight!" We dive-bombed them.

"Got him! Got him!" came a triumphant yell.

"Sunk?"

"Yes, skipper." (At the time we thought we had him but now I doubt it.)

But the main thing about that op. happened on the way back. I got a radio message: "Fog at Scampton—land at Upper Heyford." There was 10/10ths cloud beneath us and I could not raise any RAF stations. Our navigator didn't have any idea where we were. All was blackness. Dare we descend? Time ticked by. I was suffering from cold and a lack of oxygen, not to mention tiredness. (Pilots and navigators actually had *a sleep* prior to take-off—not AC2 WOP/AGs—we were down at the flights toting Vickers' gas operated guns into our cockpits and tuning the radios.)

Anyway, I could not raise any of the stations that should have been listening out for us and could give us a QDM—codename for a course to steer to reach them. It was then about five in the morning and we hadn't a clue where we were. I had already been in contact with MF/DF Heston and received a fix from them. I wanted a QDM from *another* two MF/DF stations that would take radio bearings on our aircraft's transmission, plot each bearing on a chart at Heston and where these lines crossed was where we were. Heston would then give us a three-letter three-figure code which told us where we were.

I switched coils to Medium Frequency again and called them up. A reply, loud and clear. I requested a QDM. Silence. Then,

"FO9B... 6 IMI." 'IMI' meant 'interrogative'—he was challenging me as, for all he knew, I might have been an intruding enemy aircraft. I scrabbled through the code papers and gave the correct three-figure reply. There was a long wait.

"Come on, *hurry up!*" I shouted at the set.

"4 IMI," it said impersonally. *Another* challenge. Once again I sent the appropriate three-figure reply thinking I must have sent the wrong one the first time. Another long wait. *A third* challenge. I sent back a reply.

"FO9B—press your key and transmit..."

At last! He gave me a QDM and we swung round heading for home. Timmerman pretty well guessed his way round the circuit and landed in thick fog, taxied off the flight path and promptly ran out of petrol.

As we climbed off the Hampden, Timmerman uttered those welcome words,

"Well done, Foz, you saved our bacon this time!"

...and a not-so-great skipper

IN mid 1940 I flew with a P/O Hunchback (that wasn't his real name). He was the exact opposite of Timmerman and everything an aircraft captain should *not* be: remote and uncommunicative. He never spoke a word to me after I had many times brought him home after a long, complicated and exhausting trip with fixes and bearings—not a word. He scrambled down after taxiing to the dispersal, jumped into the transport and drove off leaving me to slog back to HQ on foot for de-briefing. To top it all, when I arrived he proceeded to buy his navigator a beer and one for himself but none for me! (All other skippers bought all their crew drinks—but not him.)

By the end of August that year I was getting fed up. I'd done over thirty night ops. and after the first Berlin trip (just over nine hours), I flew with a P/O Lewis for eight hours two nights later.

The next night I was down for the Hamburg trip with Hunchback. My heart sank. Three trips in four nights seemed to me a bit thick—especially as we had several spare W/OPs who were 'rested'—and flying with Hunchback was the last straw.

I told Hunchback I did not wish to go with him and he was to get someone else.

"You've had two nights in bed and I've had none in the last twenty-four hours. And another thing: why didn't you see that someone else flew with P/O Lewis?"

"We're flying tonight, Foster, and that's that."

I was fuming and marched off to see the O/C of A Flight about it but to no avail. Obviously, Hunchback wanted a practised hand on the wireless telephony key.

Peaches in the Mess

IN May 1940 we WOP/AGs were all made sergeants with an accompanying rise in pay—not much, mind you, but it was entry into the sergeants' mess that was the best thing. Scampton, being a modern peace-time station, had good food and accommodation, comfort and all the trimmings.

Its fame spread and anyone landing there before midday was assumed to have done so merely in order to get a good lunch! There was even a civilian butler who presided over meals and laid out a sideboard groaning with roast meats, joints, vegetables and all the refreshments our hearty appetites could wish for when returning from a hard night out—in Lincoln, for instance!

Half the squadron used to visit the Theatre Royal in Lincoln on Monday nights. One memorable occasion was when a famous fan-dancer called Peaches Weston was head of the bill, she was invited back to the officers' mess by a bevy of young pilots headed by F/O Learoyd (later to be awarded the VC) and to everyone's surprise she came. This was regarded as a victory over our rival, 83 Squadron, also based at Scampton.

A new squadron

IN August 1941 I was posted to the newly formed 408 (RCAF) Squadron at Syerston. To my delight F/Lt Timmerman (now Wing Commander and a DFC) was my CO and F/Lt Pitt Clayton DFC was my flight commander. Thus began the most enjoyable part of my flying career.

As we were a new squadron, the first RCAF squadron in 5 Group, the powers-that-be had earmarked us for some daylight flights, in formation, over France, with escorts of Hurricanes and Spitfires. This was after the Battle of Britain, and Fighter Command was spoiling for a fight. The weather was glorious and our aircraft were painted duck-egg blue as camouflage against the summer sky. We had lots of formation flying in 'boxes' of six. Practice, practice, practice. We had it off to a T. It was an exciting change from perpetual night operations.

Eventually, we set off across the Channel for real: take-off time: 1535 and flying to 12,000 feet in a close box of six. WOP/AGs had the cupolas up and two pans of one hundred .303s already on the guns. It was quiet at first and Clayton's voice came through,

"Can you see the fighters yet?"

"No."

"Keep a lookout then."

"OK."

I had barely uttered the words when the sky was filled with Spitfires and Hurricanes weaving back and forth behind us, rank upon rank, tier upon tier, squadron upon squadron, higher and higher above us until they disappeared from sight at 30,000 feet hoping to tempt the FW200s and Me109s into battle.

Wham! The first ack-ack fire broke around us. The fighters disappeared. As we were in close formation we could not weave but had to concentrate and 'take it'. The firing stopped. This meant that German fighters were around somewhere. And they were! Someone's tail-fin flew past us followed by three or four Messerschmitts passing head-on with cannons blazing. As they flashed by I shot my guns but I was too late—they had gone.

And so it continued: heavy anti-aircraft fire

followed by fighter attacks. We were to bomb Marquise power station. Timmerman was in the leading Hampden and Clayton and I in No.4. We flew straight and level. We weren't far away from the target. We held our breaths. We were all to bomb on the leading bomb aimer's instruction. We waited for the signal... and we waited. Finally it came:

"We've passed it! It's too late! Missed it!"

And so we had. There was no chance of a second pass over the target for the Spitfires' endurance didn't allow it and so we flew on in a curve to port, still with bombs in place. Red faced we returned to base a little worse for wear. We had fifteen holes as battle damage. Talk about an anti-climax...

Some days later we returned and, this time, we well and truly plastered the target. At one point though, I mistook a FW200 for a Spitfire on fire before realising it was a FW's cannon fire smoke!

408 was a smashing squadron. With chaps like Timmerman and Clayton it could hardly be anything else.

"I'll pick a nice easy one, Foz," Clayton would say. (How different it was from my time with Hunchback!)

I was sorry when we returned to night operations—daylights were more fun. (With hindsight, I must have been an idiot to take this view as I wouldn't still be here if we had not changed!)

The RAF still retained a smidgen of 'bull' but 408 had virtually none. It was all first name terms and there was no standing on ceremony. If I wanted a day off I just said to Clayton,

"OK to have a day off tomorrow, Pitt?" He'd look up the schedule and say,

"Yes, OK—see you Friday" and off I'd go to Nottingham to the Flying Horse pub or the Victoria Ballroom.

Mind you, all this easy-come-easy-go attitude had its drawbacks. One afternoon Pitt rang me in the sergeants' mess.

"Foz, terribly sorry to bother you but you couldn't do me a favour, could you?"

"What is it?"

"Hate to ask you but I'm in a bit of a spot."

"What's the matter?"

"Would you mind flying a trip with another pilot?"

"Where's his W/OP?"

"No one seems to know. Buzzed off somewhere, I expect."

"OK."

"Thanks, Foz. I'll buy you a drink when you get back."

I got all togged up and went off with the pilot and his crew. As we taxyed to the beginning of the take-off path and lined up, I could see over the tail to the main road to Nottingham. A car rolled up and stopped. A small blue-clad figure shot out of it, climbed the fence and hurtled towards us. It was the missing W/OP! He dodged under the wing, opened the door, climbed in, relieved me of my helmet, log book, flying suit, boots and parachute and took over.

"Thanks, mate," he said settling himself in.

"Don't mention it," I replied somewhat taken aback. I climbed out and watched them take off.

Charlie Fry

Wireless Operator/Air Gunner

50, 76 and 102 Squadrons

Charlie Fry in 1943...

... and in 1997

Charlie Fry

Charlie Fry was born into a large family in 1918 in the Lancashire mining town of Haydock. He started work at the age of fourteen in a local colliery. It didn't take him long to discover that this was not for him and he went to Liverpool three times to volunteer for the Royal Navy. Twice he was unsuccessful but on the third occasion the enlisting officer told him that he would not be accepted because coal mining was a reserved occupation. The only way he could get away from the colliery was to volunteer for flying duties in the RAF. Charlie did just that and on 26 November 1940 he reported to Padgate, Warrington, for a medical and other tests.

In February 1941 he went to Blackpool for Morse training, and in September passed the Morse Code exam at eighteen words a minute. He was then sent to Fairwood Common in Swansea to gain experience and took part in Direction Finding courses for lost RAF fighter aircraft returning from sweeps over the Channel.

Charlie was then posted to No.7 Air Gunnery School for a gunnery course that he passed. He was then a qualified wireless operator/air gunner sergeant in 50 Squadron and later in 76 Squadron when he was commissioned.

Remembrances of pilots past

AFTER training it was on to 1661 Heavy Conversion Unit at Upper Heyford in Oxfordshire to crew up. I was pretty old for aircrew—twenty six—but our skipper seemed to me to be particularly young. He was small and slight, only nineteen—twenty at the most, I thought. He was a nice lad, a gentle sort who wouldn't say boo to a goose. I often wondered how he'd managed to become a pilot because it sometimes needed a fair amount of strength to handle a Lancaster and this lad couldn't have weighed more than nine stone wringing wet!

On 2 January 1944 we were posted to 50 Squadron at Skellingthorpe, Lincolnshire, flying Lancs. Less than two weeks later we were bombing Brunswick and soon after that Berlin—three times.

In February we were on the Leipzig raid—our fifth op.—and, after dropping the bombs, our aircraft was attacked by a Ju88. Cannon shells ripped through the port flap and fuselage and both tyres were punctured. My skipper chose to make an emergency landing at Manston and had great difficulty keeping a straight course for, on touch-down, the aircraft slid all over the place—a bit alarming, to say the least. However, our skipper handled it well and we finally came to a halt.

On the night of 20-21 February we were detailed to bomb Stuttgart. Half way there our skipper said he felt unwell and was returning to base. However, four days later we set off for Schweinfurt but again returned early due to the pilot's sickness. The next day our skipper was posted to 53 Base but he was back with us in time for the raid on 20-21 April—the marshalling yards at La Chapelle near Paris.

The next night it was Brunswick and two days later, Munich—both completed and making a total of ten ops.—well on the way to 'a tour'. It seemed as though we were 'back on course' again with our regular pilot.

Schweinfurt was the target on the night of 26-27 April. Everything seemed to be going fine but then our skipper was ill again and we returned early. A few days later we heard he had been posted to 53 Base and we never heard another word about him after that. It was all a bit of a mystery and somewhat disconcerting.

In early July (1944) I was posted to 102 Squadron, Pocklington, and did various trips as a spare WOP/AG on Halifaxes. After that I was sent to Holme-on-Spalding Moor—76 Squadron on Halifaxes again—where I crewed up with F/O Bert Throstle. I was granted a commission in 76 Squadron.

I always remember another pilot. He was a bit of a character and insisted that we sang *South of the border, down Mexico way*. It was his favourite song and it became something of a mascot or good luck charm—if we didn't sing it something awful would happen! We always sang it and, I'm glad to say, it worked.

I was discharged on 3 August 1946.

Douglas Fry

Air Gunner

15 Squadron

Dougl Fry, aged 18, taken at No.2 Air Gunnery School, Dalcross, Scotland, at the beginning of 1943. He had just emerged from a Defiant aircraft after completing a firing exercise.

Doug in 1995

Douglas Fry

Douglas Fry was born in London on 3 May 1924. He started work in the City of London in May 1939 in a marine insurance office. As a boy Doug had a great love of aeroplanes and had joined the Air Defence Cadet Corps. It followed, therefore, that he would eventually join the RAF as aircrew and duly did so in 1942 aged eighteen.

He trained as an air gunner in Dalcross, Scotland. In 1943 he was a sergeant air gunner with 15 Squadron, 3 Group, Bomber Command, operating from Mildenhall in Suffolk and flying Stirling aircraft. His crew of seven comprised P/O George Judd (pilot), Sgt Bill Wells (wireless operator), Sgt Sid Long (bomb aimer), Sgt Dennis Brown (navigator), Sgt Dick Richards (flight engineer), Canadian P/O Ken Banks (rear gunner) and Doug himself as mid upper gunner. Four were killed when their aircraft was shot down on a raid on Remschied in July 1943. Doug was wounded and became a prisoner of war.

Raid on Remschied

ON the night of 30/31 July 1943 we were briefed to operate against Remschied as part of a force of some 250 aircraft. My aircraft was EF427 A-Apple. The outward flight was uneventful but on arrival at the target and on our bombing run we were caught in a master beam searchlight and quickly coned by several other lights. Heavy flak immediately got our range and we were hit by the first salvo. However, we did not take evasive action but dropped our bombs on the selected markers and whilst we were still flying straight and level in order to obtain our photo, I realised that the port side of the interior of the fuselage was on fire.

Since there was no chance of a fighter attack whilst we were still under flak fire, I left my turret in order, if possible, to deal with the fire. As I stepped down a shell burst just behind us and I was hit in the stomach by a chunk of shrapnel. Almost immediately we received a direct hit on the front of the aircraft that then went into a very steep dive. I was pinned to the top of the fuselage by the force of gravity and resigned myself to the inevitable end. Then the aircraft pulled out of the dive and I believe that

my pilot, although he must have been badly wounded, had regained control.

I then found that my parachute had broken loose from its rack and had disappeared. I found it some way along the fuselage and having clipped it on, baled out of the rear escape hatch that had already been opened by the flight engineer who baled out first. Whilst I was putting on my parachute I saw the rear gunner leave his position and bale out. My parachute opened almost as soon as I had left the aircraft which was flying away with flames streaming from her—and four of my crew still on board. I think I baled out at about 5,000 feet. It was a clear night and I was just able to see the ground coming up to meet me. It was then that I realised that I was drifting towards a wall. I just managed to avoid hitting it by lifting my feet at the last moment.

On landing

I landed in what turned out to be the garden of a house in the village of Manheim. By this time I was feeling quite unwell because of my wounds. I had just released my parachute harness and taken off my life jacket when I passed out, leaving the parachute hanging over the wall and into the street. I had at first tried to find a way out of the garden with a view to escaping, but I could not find a gate and, in any event, my wounds were now affecting me badly and I drifted into unconsciousness.

The sound of the 'all clear' roused me. I heard someone shouting, "Helloo". A soldier, presumably on leave, emerged from a door at the back of the garden and helped me to my feet. He led me out of the garden and into the house where several people, including three or four children, had just come from an air raid shelter. A little motherly type of lady shook her fist at me but then helped me to a chair in what seemed to be the kitchen; they loosened my clothing to reveal the wound in my stomach. The lady gave me a cup of water and made signs for me not to drink but just to rinse out my mouth. Everybody seemed most concerned and when a huge man in a black uniform wielding a large pistol came in and, I believe, wanted to shoot me on the spot, they argued with him and sent him on his way!

Then two young men—I think they were air raid wardens—came in with a stretcher on which they gently put me and carried me a short distance to a doctor's house.

F/O Ken Banks, Doug's Canadian rear gunner - also wounded and taken prisoner

They placed me on the pavement outside the doctor's house. He came out to put a pad on my wound and give me an injection. He then placed me onto the back seat of his car and we drove off into the night.

(Before I was taken from the house on the stretcher I had wanted to give the children my two bars of chocolate—part of my flying rations—but, unfortunately, they had fallen from the top of my flying boot where I used to keep them for easy access. I learned later that our aircraft had crashed in a field at Bennen Winkel where it had completely burnt out together with the four crew members who had been unable to escape. Sadly, like so many others, they have no known graves.)

Whilst in the doctor's car I kept losing consciousness and falling off the seat and so I have no recollection of where we were going or of the arrival of daylight. The next thing that comes to mind is pulling up outside a house in another village or town. It was a sunny morning and, I think, very early because the road was deserted except for a man in a black uniform who I saw in the distance.

Reunited

There were steps going up to the front door from the pavement and I remember a woman, wearing glasses, whose fair hair was swept back into a bun. I found myself in what I suppose was the hallway of the house. It was empty except for a stretcher leaning against the wall. I was put onto it but again drifted into oblivion. Before I did so the lady bent over me. She offered me a cigarette. I shook my head; I didn't smoke anyway.

With the jolting of the stretcher I regained semi-consciousness. I was being taken out of the house and down the steps. I saw an ambulance into which I was put on the bottom shelf. It was then that I heard a familiar voice coming from the top shelf—it was our Canadian rear gunner, Ken Banks, who had also been wounded.

Although delighted to know he was there I again drifted off. During all this time I had not felt any pain—that would come later and with a vengeance. The next time I opened my eyes was when we were going through Düsseldorf —at least I think it was Düsseldorf. It was dusk but through an open window in the ambulance I could see the tops of bombed-out buildings.

After that I was not aware of anything until I felt people undressing me. I was in a brightly lit room and lying on some sort of table. Nearby lay Ken Banks.

Someone in a white coat bent over me and by way of sign language asked me if I had false teeth. I shook my head and then a pad came down over nose and mouth and I blacked out. I regained consciousness some three or four days later. (It may have been more but nobody ever told me exactly.) Someone was cutting an enormous dressing from around my body. It was darkly stained all over and I caught the odour of dried blood.

A Polish doctor, also a prisoner, operated on me but did not locate the piece of flak which is, in fact, still in me! I had a few uncomfortable and painful days, the bed was not exactly comfortable because it was merely a paper sack filled with sawdust and woodchips. The place where I received this treatment was the reserve hospital at Stalag 6J at Gerrsheim, a short distance from Düsseldorf. (I had no treatment at all from German doctors or staff but only from the Polish doctor and French orderlies.)

A prisoner of war

After a few weeks I was fit enough to travel and so Ken Banks, my rear gunner, and I, together with a one-footed Canadian were told to prepare for the journey to Frankfurt and my clothes were handed back to me. Two armed guards took the three of us from the camp by public transport bus into Düsseldorf where we caught a train to Cologne. We changed trains at Cologne and were soon under way.

It was a beautiful journey, notwithstanding the hard wooden seats and the fact that we were POWs and had nothing to eat or drink all day, because the line runs along the Rhine for nearly the whole way and the scenery was magnificent.

We changed trains again at Koblenz and arrived at Frankfurt in the evening just as it was getting dark. We were put into a large room over the station and it was already full of shot-down British airmen, some of whom were injured and heavily bandaged. After a restless night came the dawn when we were herded downstairs and into the street where we boarded a streetcar.

Some German fellow travellers shouted abuse at us. Eventually, we arrived at a place in the suburbs of Frankfurt where we were off-loaded. We were then split into two groups: those who were injured or recovering from wounds like myself and those who would be going straight to Dulag Luft for interrogation. My group was then taken off to Hohmark Sanatorium, a splendid place in its own grounds. We were ushered upstairs to a long corridor at the end of which was a bathroom.

We were actually going to have a bath— wonderful! I had not indulged in this luxury for about six weeks. My turn came and in eager anticipation I turned on the hot water tap. The hot water ran until there was about a quarter of an inch in the bottom of the bath then it turned cold and so I ended up with a cold bath! It was still very enjoyable though. I was given a long nightshirt and told to get into bed. It was a nice room with four big comfortable beds and a washbasin.

So it was that four of us shared the room. We waited to see what would happen next. We found out that there was a British staff, presumably chaps who had given their parole, and who seemed to get on very well with the German staff—rather a curious set up, I thought. Soon a German doctor turned up to look at our various injuries, although by this time I had healed up quite nicely and needed only a small dressing. This was changed as it had become soggy when I had the bath. The food was not plentiful but it wasn't bad. Red Cross parcels were available although they were not issued to us individually.

After a couple of days I was summoned to the end of the corridor where a Luftwaffe officer was sitting at a small table by a window. I felt a bit of an idiot prancing along in my long nightshirt but I sat down and waited for the inevitable questioning. The officer merely asked me to fill in the so-called Red Cross form. We knew all about these forms and so I simply filled in my name, rank and number and assumed a blank, disinterested look. The interrogation officer tried to persuade me to complete all the other details such as squadron number and other pertinent information but when I refused he gathered up his papers and left. I returned to my room well satisfied.

Next day I was moved to a room of my own and Adolf, one of the German orderlies, brought me a book to read, *Three men in a boat* by Jerome K. Jerome—marvellous. It was not long before another Luftwaffe interrogation officer arrived, this time for the real interrogation. He told me he had been educated at Oxford and knew and liked England—this was the softening-up process. He then showed me the large file containing details and information on 15 Squadron. There was even a picture of the Squadron crest on the inside cover of the file. The top page listed all my crew and against four of the names were marked small crosses. He told me they were dead and I told him that I already suspected they had been killed. He then went on to inform me when I had joined the RAF and where I had trained, etc. This news was, presumably, to lead me to believe that they knew everything and that there was no point in keeping anything from them as they merely wanted confirmation of certain facts.

I was asked many questions about the operation against Remscheid, all of which I could have answered, but I played dumb and pleaded ignorance and tried to appear uninterested. The officer, no doubt, suspected my game but he merely collected his file and papers, said goodbye and left.

I was soon given back my clothes and allowed to wander about the allocated floors with the rest of the chaps.

After about two weeks several of us were taken to Dulag Luft to await transfer to a permanent camp. At Dulag Luft we were photographed with our POW numbers round our necks and fingerprinted. I wrote a card home from Dulag Luft—I still have it together with several other cards and letters I sent to my mother. I was actually posted as missing for three months. We were herded into cattle trucks for a five-day journey up to Stalag Luft VI at Heydekrug in East Prussia. I now had a POW number: it was 6479.

Life as a POW

Some 200 of us marched from the railway siding to our new 'home' and arrived at Stalag Luft VI. We went first into the Vorlager (outer compound) where we had to strip off to be searched before going through into 'K' Lager. This was a new compound consisting of two huge blocks that were divided into twelve barrack rooms—six rooms to a block. There were enough of us to occupy the first three rooms and I went into 'K2' and nabbed a lower bunk at the far end away from the door which opened directly into the room, thus hoping to avoid any draughts, especially as winter was approaching. There were, as I recall, about thirty plus two-tier bunks in each room. At each end there was a stove, a brick-built construction some six feet by four feet and about four feet high with a cement top and a huge hot-plate. It didn't work very well, mainly, I suppose, because it was not possible to maintain in a continuous and well-stoked fire, as we had only a meagre ration of poor quality coal bricks.

We new Kriegies (prisoners of war) were kitted out from the store according to our needs and I received a pair of boots, a greatcoat and some underwear, all RAF issue and provided through the Red Cross. Soon after our arrival a Heydekrug, about 5 October 1943, a new intake of 800 men were transferred from Stalag Luft I at Barth on the Baltic coast. Amongst them was my flight engineer, Dick Richards. He expressed some surprise at seeing me alive and well, then apologised for not helping me escape from our aircraft when he passed me on his way to the rear escape hatch. Seeing me lying there with flames streaming past, he naturally thought I was past help.

With the arrival of the 'seasoned' POWs things soon settled down to what one might term a 'normal' and routine POW life. The great day was when the mail arrived but there were only a couple of letters for my room and I was not one of the lucky ones. However, a few days later more mail arrived and it was my turn to get a letter: it was from my mother.

Time plodded on and Christmas came and went. I eventually received a personal parcel from home. This contained lots of 'goodies' like soap, boot polish, toothbrush and dentrifice, socks, a sweater and handkerchiefs as well as chocolate and chewing gum—marvellous! However, a pair of pyjamas was listed but they had been stolen. The Germans used to check the contents of our parcels and so they had already been opened when we got them.

Eventually, the bitterly cold East Prussian winter turned to spring and then into summer. It became warm so that we could spend more of the days outside. One morning, in June 1944, two Scots laddies and I were messing about with a volleyball. There was nobody about and it was raining on and off with a blustery wind and low, scudding clouds. Suddenly we heard a shout from 'A' Lager and everyone came running out from all over the camp. Someone had heard an announcement over the German loudspeaker that was installed between the compounds that there had been a landing in France. It was 6 June 1944—D-Day!

Soon it became obvious that this was 'it' and all our hearts and prayers went out to the forces taking part—particularly to the armies who had to go ashore. How splendid they were! As usual, the German version of these momentous events was distorted and made it appear like another Dieppe, but we had our own 'canary' (secret radio) and so we got a true picture of the situation.

After the first twenty-four hours when our people were pressing on, we became totally confident of the outcome and speculated as to how long it would be before we were liberated. We reckoned we would be home for Christmas—we Kriegies were always optimistic!

On the march

However, we then got news of the V1 and then the V2 rockets being launched against southern England and we knew that it wasn't over yet—there was still a vicious sting in the tail of this particular beast.

By this time the Russian armies were advancing towards the Baltic countries which meant that East Prussia was threatened and, indeed, in the distance we could see columns of refugees silhouetted against the skyline as they fled westwards. It then came our turn to evacuate and whilst 'A' Lager and part of 'K' Lager went by rail to another camp, I, with the rest of 'K' Lager, some 800 or more men, went by cattle truck to the port of Memel. There we boarded a ship, *Insterburg*. A few sick men were allowed to stay on deck but the rest of us were battened down in the filthy hold where one dim light bulb dangled and toilet facilities consisted of a bucket lowered down on the end of a rope. Once or twice drinking water was also lowered in a bucket—probably the same one.

As I was one of the last down into the hold there was no room left on the floor and so I had to find myself a spot on a girder about a foot wide, three feet long and four feet off the deck. Thus, I spent three days and nights, the length of the voyage on the Baltic Sea, squatting on my little shelf. We duly arrived at the port of Swinemünde on the Baltic coast and disembarked straight into cattle trucks that were waiting on the quayside. Whilst there, the sirens went and we heard the Americans flying overhead, unseen because it was overcast. The Germans immediatley threw up a smokescreen and the cruiser *Prinz Eugen* that was berthed alongside opened fire with her ack-ack guns. We saw a U-boat slide past making for the Baltic. Our boots were now taken from us and the doors slammed shut. We were off again. Eventually, we arrived at our destination, the railway sidings at Kiefheide where we were given back our boots and, after yet another count, marched off.

Soon we saw an incredible sight: kit strewn the full length of the route of our march to the camp—about two miles or so. German guards with machine guns skulked in the woods on each side of the road; we also spotted some with movie cameras. When we arrived at the camp, Stalag Luft IV at Grossetychow, we saw that all the chaps from the first column were still milling about or lying down outside the camp. Hauptmann (Captain) Pickardt, resplendent in a well-pressed, light coloured uniform, was waving a pistol about and screaming his silly head off.

We soon learned that the men in the first column had been manacled in twos and forced to run up the road at bayonet point, the Luftwaffe guards having been reinforced by a bunch of young thugs from the Kriegsmarine (German navy). These specimens of the master race were very free with their bayonets and stabbed several chaps or frequently hit them with their rifle butts. The German guard dogs bit other men and all the time the Germans were screaming abuse. We were kept hanging around outside the camp nearly all day without any food or drink. We particularly needed a drink as it was a very hot summer day: 20 July 1944. Eventually, after protest, a bucket of water was passed around and we slaked our thirst.

When we were eventually let into the camp all our kit was taken from us. Our compound was not finished and so we were directed to small huts like big dog kennels that had been erected in the compound for American prisoners. There we ensconced ourselves: ten men to each hut; it was somewhat crowded. We could not stand fully upright and we slept on the bare boards.

There was an air of foreboding over the camp and a sense of impending disaster. The doom-laden atmosphere was not helped by the scarcity of food. During a violent thunderstorm lightning struck one of the 'dog kennels'—it was like a bomb exploding. As it was not yet raining everyone had been sitting outside because of the oppressive heat and seven chaps were struck by the blast. One, a pilot called Roy Stevens, who had been a POW for quite some time, was killed although he did not die until some hours later in spite of non-stop artificial respiration by one of our chaps. I do not know why the Germans refused to take him to hospital.

Two days later a Luftwaffe electrician, harnessed to a pole, was working on the perimeter lights. Suddenly he stiffened then dangled from his safety harness. It transpired that one of his mates had accidentally switched on the current and electrocuted him. I couldn't help but wonder if fate had had a hand in this rough justice.

Still on the move

We eventually moved into the new compound. The stoves had not yet been installed and there were no lights either. We then had our kit returned to us although it had obviously been well picked over by the Germans. I lost some items including my brand new, navy blue, roll-necked sweater that my mother had sent.

The barrack rooms had eight two-tiered bunks so that there were sixteen men to a room. This soon increased to twenty when four American airmen joined us as there wasn't room for them in the American part of the camp, even here they had to make do without bunks.

Food was very scarce and even the Red Cross parcels had reduced to a trickle; we got one parcel between two which wasn't much when you took into account the sparse rations issued by the Germans.

The Third Reich was falling apart and, in spite of Allied successes everywhere, our future was becoming increasingly uncertain. Rumours abounded that we were to be moved, presumably westward because of the advance of the Russians. The winter set in with heavy falls of snow and Christmas came and went.

So it happened that very early one morning, 6 February 1945 to be exact, we were awakened by the cries of, "Raus! Raus!" (hurry) and told to parade outside. There was already about two feet of snow on the ground and a blizzard was blowing when we lined up outside at about six o'clock that morning. In view of the rumours about moving we had endeavoured to prepare ourselves. I had altered a small sort of kitbag, that my mother had sent me, so that it was now like a knapsack for carrying on my back. I had also sewn my two thin German blankets together to form a sleeping bag that I felt would be more practical.

We were kept hanging about for two hours or more in the freezing cold and did not move off until about half-past eight by which time it was daylight. We were handed two Red Cross parcels each—the entire stocks, so it was said. However, we were not allowed to stop to pack the stuff into our knapsacks and so, as we walked away from the camp, we opened the food parcels and stuffed as much as we could into our knapsacks and pockets. Foolishly, most of us discarded tins of margarine and other sundry items thinking that, in the present situation, they were the least of our requirements, especially as we were led to believe we would be marching only a few miles to another camp.

It was snowing and the going was heavy. The roads were inches deep in snow and ice so that it was difficult to keep one's feet. It was, of course, dark by about half-past three and, I suppose, the object was to get somewhere for the night before dark. However, the guard in charge of our particular column and who had a map, turned out to be a useless navigator and we got lost. There we were, traipsing around in pitch darkness, in alternating rain and snow, looking for the farm where we were supposed to sleep that night.

We did eventually find it and discovered that the other column had arrived long since and had bedded down. I found myself stepping over bodies that I could not see, trying to find a space in the hayloft into which we had climbed. I finally slumped down in my soaking wet clothes and although frozen stiff and hungry went straight to sleep. When I awoke at daybreak, I found I had been sleeping on the very edge of a gaping hole with about a ten-foot drop into the barn below.

Each day was as bad as the last as the weather was atrocious and food was in short supply. One day we were marching past some tiny cottages where two or three little old ladies, dressed in black, peasant-type garb, came out of their front doors and put buckets of water by their gates so that we could grab a drink as we went past. The guards had other ideas and promptly kicked the buckets over—and these were 'ordinary' Luftwaffe chaps. I couldn't help but think how courageous those old ladies were.

Soon all our Red Cross food was exhausted and so one day, when we rested up for a day at a farm, Vic Clark, our camp leader, scouted about and found a stock of parcels, enough, I think, for one between two men. Vic had to give his parole in order to do his searching on an old bicycle that he had managed to scrounge. (When the various forced marches began, the Red Cross made it their task to ascertain, as far as possible, the routes that the Germans had mapped out and had placed parcels at strategic places.)

More forced marching

The march continued next day in foul weather although the issue of the food parcels had lifted our spirits. One day when we had halted for the first five-minute rest period of the day, I tried to undo my pack to get something to eat—I thought I might still have a piece of bread or something—but my hands were so cold that I could not unfasten it. I gave up, leaned back to rest my weary body and promptly fell asleep. If I had not been awakened, or for some reason had been left lying there, I would have frozen to death in my sleep. It is quite true that, in such circumstances, one very soon succumbs to tiredness in spite of cold and hunger.

On or about the 15 February, after completing some 120 miles since we left camp, we arrived at a place called Pritter, two-and-a-half miles from the port of Swinemünde, after a record march of twenty-eight miles that day. Here we had to sleep in the open as there was not a farm or barn in sight. It was bitterly cold and raining and by morning most of us were covered in frost. However, there was some consolation in that we were issued with Red Cross parcels, one between two, as we moved off the next morning. We marched to Swinemünde where we boarded a ferry to cross to a place called Usedom from where we continued over the bridge to Anklam. After several more days of marching we eventually had another rest day, probably for the benefit of the guards, more than for us.

The weather was still wet and raw and we were, as usual, hungry. We had not received a bread ration nor anything else and our last issue of Red Cross food had long been eaten. As usual, we milled about in the mud, trying to keep warm and trying not to think of food, although always hoping something would turn up.

At one farm I spotted a brick-built lean-to, wandered over to it and looked inside. There was a heap of swedes or cow-turnips as some chaps called them. I grabbed one and put it under my coat but it was seen by one of the guards who immediately started ranting at me and ordered me to put my 'loot' back. I lost my temper and started arguing with him. He threatened me with his rifle. I said a few unprintable words to him and then turned my back on him. He then swung at me with his rifle but a couple of chaps yelled, "Look out, Doug!" and I instinctively ducked but took a glancing blow across my back.

Then I really lost my temper and I think would have struck the German if he had not cocked his gun and levelled it at me. This made me think that discretion was the better part of valour and I backed off. Hearing the commotion the Feldwebel (sergeant), a club-footed bloke who rode around on a bicycle, called me over to him and said that they were the 'masters' (his very words) and that I must do as I was told. I told him that very soon now we would be the masters, and then watch out. He shrugged his shoulders and moved on.

I returned to my pals, rueing the fact that I had lost my cow-turnips. After many more weeks of marching and sleeping, sometimes in barns and sometimes in the open, we crossed the River Elbe at Domitz. One morning we passed through a town full of wounded Germans. Many buildings seemed to have been turned into hospitals and there were lots of German soldiers, some sporting bandages, looking out of the windows as we went past.

Bombed

We soon left the town and, after about a mile or so, were crossing open ground making for a path through some woods, when a large formation of B17s, together with a big escort of Mustangs approached and passed overhead. Immediately, their lead bomb aimers dropped their loads in which there were bombs trailing smoke, a signal for the others in the formations to drop their bombs. The ground shook as the bombs hit the town we had just passed through which was a rail junction. There was no opposition from the Germans but, seeing the smoke bombs go down, the German Commander in charge started shouting, "New weapon! New weapon!" thinking that the smoke were trailing from shot-down aircraft. As there was neither German fighters nor flak, he, poor chap thought a new secret weapon was responsible for what he mistook for crashing aircraft. He was, of course, sadly disappointed.

We eventually came to a town called Ebstorf

where our Luftwaffe guards, who had been with us from the camp, handed us over to army guards. We were then herded into filthy cattle trucks and were again on our way to yet another uncertain destination. The next day, 29 March, we arrived at a place called Fallingbostel where there was an old established POW camp, Stalag 357. We were put into huge marquees where we were to sleep on the ground.

When we arrived at Fallingbostel we received a Red Cross parcel, one between two men, but the only food we got from the Germans each day was a bowl of what purported to be soup—greasy water with one or two turnips floating in it. After eleven days in this awful place we were ordered to march again, this time eastwards, as the British army was advancing rapidly towards us and the Germans would not let us stay in one place to be liberated. They were treating us as hostages.

By this time the weather was quite mild and sunny. Since we felt it would not be long now we set off in high spirits. We set quite a good pace, although we were again going away from our potential liberators, but before long we were called to halt because the German guards, some of whom were quite old, could not keep up with us and it was obvious their morale was beginning crack.

We arrived at a village early in the afternoon; by now the days were drawing out and we had time to look around and bag our places in a barn. The barn faced onto the village square with a flower-bed in the middle surrounded by a low wall. Several villagers were milling around and staring at us curiously. Sitting on the wall was a young, fair-haired woman who was heavily pregnant. I was still wearing my 'flying sweater' and the woman looked at it enviously. My chum, Danny Heath, and I had no food and so I thought I would try a bit of bargaining.

I asked the woman if she could get me a loaf of bread in exchange for my sweater. She agreed immediately and made signs that she would unravel the wool and make clothes for her baby. Thus I parted with my dear old sweater which had served me well through the bitter cold weather. In return I obtained a huge, freshly baked, three kilo loaf—far better than the official issue of black, sawdust-like bread—when we had any at all. Danny and I could now eat. (If that baby survived it will now be fifty-three years old!)

On 17 April we crossed the Elbe once more on a large raft lashed to the side of a motor launch. As we tramped across a field away from the river two RAF Spitfires appeared and whilst one kept top-cover at about 1,000 feet, the other did several tight turns over us at about 200 feet waggling its wings in recognition and encouragement. What a morale booster! We stood cheering and waving like mad. The Germans dived to the ground in terror. On the 21 April we arrived at Cammin where we were to stay the night in barns close by a river.

At about one o'clock in the morning I was awakened by the sound of aircraft and then a loud explosion close by. At first I thought the plane had crashed but I heard it flying away, then it came round again. Through an opening high in the wall opposite me I saw the flash of guns and streams of tracer coming straight at us. I turned my face to the floor and all hell broke loose.

Cannon shells exploded setting the thatched roof on fire. Blazing thatch dropped into the barn setting light to the straw on the floor. I felt a blow across my back and knew I had been hit. (It turned out to be just a small cut from a tiny shell splinter.) The two chaps on either side of me were killed: one, an American, and one, Reg Brown, who had been a POW for some years. Several men were badly wounded and a Canadian died later of his stomach wound.

Everybody made an orderly exit from the barn which was, by now, well alight. On my way out I lost a boot and my sleeping bag. When I got outside I saw my chum, Joe Boyle, who had been badly wounded in the neck and leg, sitting on the muddy ground, leaning against a wall. I was about to go over to him when I realised that I could not paddle about in the mud with only one boot. I returned to the burning barn and, lo and behold, there was a boot lying a few feet inside the door! It was not actually my boot but it was the right size and foot and so I was quite satisfied.

By the time I emerged from the barn again and put my boots on, the casualties had been taken to a house on the other side of the river, and their wounds dressed. I knew I was not badly hurt but could feel the blood trickling down my back. As my body and clothes were dirty, I thought I ought to have my 'scratch' cleaned up.

We were all taken by horse-drawn cart to a small POW camp to get cleaned up and receive some treatment. This camp was just outside a town called Schwerin. Here we were treated in the sick bay that was staffed by the POWs themselves, amongst them at least one French doctor.

Freedom

On the morning of the 2 May 1945, the day before my twenty-first birthday, and after we had been at this camp about ten days, an early-rising Kriegie came into the hut. He told us that the guard boxes were empty and that there were some broken rifles lying on the ground outside the wire. The Germans had fled and we were free. We could not really believe our good fortune until about an hour later when we were looking out of the camp towards the road. A jeep went past with a Browning machine gun mounted on the back and crewed by a couple of cheerful Americans. We yelled and waved at each other, but they continued on their way, going east.

By this time thousands of German civilians and columns of servicemen were converging on Schwerin and the camp and the huge field at the back was full of refugees from the Russian front. Deserting German servicemen, some wounded and bandaged, were coming through the nearby woods and some even had

Drawing Doug made in his wartime 'log book'. These 'log books' were given to British prisoners of war by the YMCA for leisure use.

their families with them. It was chaos. The Russian prisoners in the camp immediately armed themselves and, I think, took their revenge there and then on many Germans. Hearing sporadic gunfire throughout the night I began to feel that perhaps the dangers were not yet over.

It was not long before the Americans brought us a huge supply of their excellent 'K' rations. We 'liberated' a pig, slaughtered it and cut it up. There was half a hundredweight of butter and sacks of potatoes, all from local farms. We had not seen so much food since we had left England. Our stomachs, of course, could not take so much food and we soon found that our eyes were bigger than our bellies.

Owing to congestion on the roads leading into and out of Schwerin as the Germans came in to surrender with all their equipment, it was not possible to transport us out of the camp, although priority was given to the sick and badly wounded chaps like Joe Boyle.

Thus it was about four days before we were taken to the British sector at Lüneburg where we were billeted in the German barracks. Good food with white bread was the order of the day as well as copious supplies of hot water for showers. We were supposed to fly home in Dakotas from the Lüneburg airfield but when the departure time arrived we were informed that many severely wounded army chaps had to be got home in a hurry for treatment and so would we mind waiting a little longer? We could not object and felt that the wounded men should have priority. After all, another day or so was nothing to us, whereas it meant everything to the wounded. In the event, everything turned out fine because arrangements were made to fly us back from Lübeck instead.

Going home

Off we went in British army trucks, once more crossing the Elbe but this time over a pontoon bridge. On 10 May 1945 we met the crew of a Lancaster bomber in which we were to fly home and as the mid-upper gunner had nipped home for a quick forty-eight hour leave, the skipper allowed me to ride home in my old position—the mid-upper turret. I noticed the crew were not wearing life jackets or parachute harness. When I mentioned this, the rear gunner said that, as we ex-POWs did not have this equipment, the crew would also fly without it. What a splendid gesture!

We had a good flight back over Hamburg—one of my old targets—and landed at an airfield in the Midlands. As we got out of the Lanc, there were WAAFs waiting to take our arms and carry what little kit we had. They truly welcomed us home and even as I recount these events my heart goes out to these lovely ladies who led us to a hangar decked out with bunting. There were tables laid with tea, cakes and sandwiches. A small RAF dance band was playing and the WAAFs invited us to dance. The whole welcome was quite overwhelming.

At the other end of the hangar, transport was waiting and we were soon on our way again. This time it was a short journey to the No.106 Prisoner Receiving Centre at RAF Cosford. Again there was a marvellous welcome: brightly lit billets and beds made up with clean sheets, with 'hospital blue' suits laid out pending the issue of new uniforms. We had been given a telegram form to send to our families to say we were on our way home. We were kitted out, medically examined and given double-ration cards and, of course, some pay. We were not allowed to walk anywhere and were even driven to the mess where we had good old fish and chips. (I think we were too overwhelmed and excited to eat much and, when we later went into the mess bar, we just could not drink the pints we had ordered—it was disappointing after so long looking forward to good food and a pint of beer!)

Next day we caught the special train to London. It was obvious that the people in the houses lining the railway knew that the special trains were full of returning POWs because

87

there were 'Welcome Home' signs painted on the houses and on banners in the gardens. What a splendid homecoming!

After arriving in London I took a taxi home to Islington. I had survived several operations against Germany; I had survived being shot down and near fatally wounded; I had survived prison camps; I had survived weeks of marching in atrocious weather; I had survived hunger and thirst. Now, here I was looking out of the taxi window at the old familiar streets near my home. I told the cabby to stop outside my house. There was bunting and a banner across the front of the house with the words 'Welcome Home!' There was a also a

huge key hanging on the door in celebration of my twenty-first birthday which had been on the 3 May, the day after I was liberated by our American friends. My mother was waiting anxiously at the top of the steps in anticipation of my arrival.

Thus another member of 15 Squadron made it back to base, albeit somewhat late.

By way of a postscript: I have a copy of a videotape from the Ministry of Information film entitled *The Biter Bit* some of which was shot a few hours before we met our demise over Remscheid and which includes a few seconds of me.

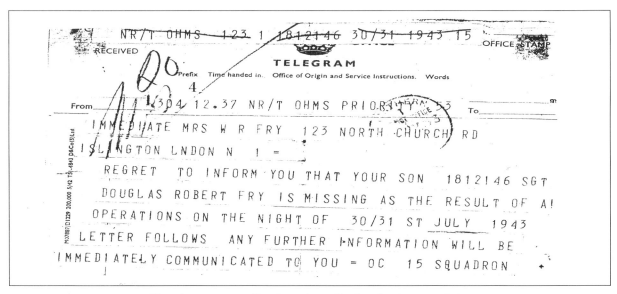

The telegram sent to Doug's mother telling her that he was missing

Happy ending - the telegram Doug sent to his mother saying he would be home soon

Letter sent by the Foreign Office to the German authorities regarding the treatment of prisoners as experienced by Doug Fry.

0103/6123(P12)   W.C. Ref. No. 747 of 16/1/
45   F.O. Ref. No. 2/110
<u>Memorandum</u>

    With reference to the Federal Political Department's note No B. 52.Gbr. (1) 5 - NL/Bi (No.57753) of 16th November, 1944 transmitting reports on the treatment of British prisoners of war on the journey from Stalag Luft VI to Stalag Luft IV and a copy of the German Foreign Office Memorandum R.4177 T of the 4th October, 1944 in explanation of one part of the complaint, it is requested that the Swiss Legation at Berlin may be informed as follows:-

His Majesty's Government is shocked at the conditions reported to have obtained on board ship when prisoners were crowded in the holds where the heat was excessive and the ventilation was inadequate. Very little water was made available to the prisoners. Although many of them were sea sick, only one man at a time was allowed to go to the latrines and all requests for better treatment were refused.

    On arrival at the port of disembarkation most of the kit belonging to prisoners of war had to be left in the ship.

    The conditions on the rest of the journey to the camp are equally perturbing. Prisoners were crowded into goods wagons, handcuffed in pairs and on arrival at Kiefheide were closely surrounded by guards with fixed bayonets. They were marched to the camp at a fast pace, and on the march were struck with bayonets and rifle butts and even bitten by dogs. Under this treatment many were obliged to abandon their remaining kit. At the camp all personal property was taken away during the search, and badges of rank were stripped from the prisoners, who were again struck by the guards. Similar treatment was given to two further parties of prisoners of war arriving from Dulag Luft Wetzlar, and this to such as extent that on one occasion the German Conducting Officer himself registered a protest.

contd.

The excuse advanced by the German authorities that special measures had to be taken owing to the obstreperous and provocative manner of the prisoners is hardly acceptable. Prisoners who were thus handcuffed, accompanied by a heavy armed guard, and forced at the point of bayonet to keep up a fast pace, could not be in a condition to cause serious trouble to their custodians. The fact that some prisoners had to be treated on their arrival for injuries confirms the view of His Majesty's Government that the complaint of the Man of Confidence was fully justified.

This treatment is in clear breach of the Geneva Convention and in particular Articles 2 and 26.

It is accordingly requested that the Swiss legation at Berlin will represent the views set out above to the German authorities and to express the extreme dissatisfaction felt by his Majesty's Government in this matter and will press that a full enquiry be held into these incidents and that a list should be supplied of those who suffered injuries as a result of their ill-treatment, setting out particulars of the injuries sustained.

FOREIGN OFFICE, S.W.1.
27th January, 1945.

Distribution by P.W.2.

F.M.	High Commissioners:-	M.I.9
D.F. (D)	Australia	Cas (PW)
D.A.G. (A)	Canada	F.4 (PW)
D.G.A.M.S.	New Zealand	A.M.D.5
Colonial Office	South Africa	L.M.2 (A)
India Office		
Admiralty		
Air Ministry		

Letter sent after the war from the former German commander, Helmut Wahle, to Vic Clark, British POW camp leader mentioned in Doug Fry's account. The letter is copied verbatim. Vic Clark died before the letter was delivered.

```
Helmut R. Whale  [signed Wahle]
Hamburg
Germany                    Bad-Neustadt, November 26th 46.


Dear Mr. Clark !

        According to circumstances I would like to contact
you again. It is now considerable time we have seen us last
and obviously my letters in the last year never reached you.
It is now by some important reason I write to you again :
the case Pickardt!

        I have met my friend Baron von Guttenberg(formerly) in
the mail-censoring department) again and today I am with him
for some days. We have discussed the case Pickardt and we
find it our duty to bring this case before the authorities
providing you or T/Sgt.Paules have not yet done it on your
part. We have trapped Pickardt and found he made for the
Russian Zone. This is the situation. Furthermore I remember
our last meeting in the camp before we were transfered to
the  Russian frontier. You and T/Sgt. Paules told us to
contact you as soon as possible after the war for any
support of help if necessary. In view of the fact that we
have decided to follow the advise ouf our friends and
relatives abroad we want to emigrate when an opportunity is
given. A statement of yours would certainly give us
preference in obtaining the permission for leaving the
country. Would you therefore be kind enough to give us a
statement as soon as possible, which shows the situation in
the camp and our activities. I am certain you will remember
if you read as follows :
    "Baron von Guttenberg and Mr.Helmut Whale have been
    interpreters from 1941-1945 in Pow-camps of the German
    "Luftwaffe", holding Airforce personell of the Allied
    forces.
    During that time they have been very helpful in every
    respect in eleviating the strain of Pow-life, thus
    gaining our confidence. In summer 1944 I have been
    British camp-leader at Stalag-Luft-4 Grosstychow,
```

Pomerania. By the brutal mistreating on the part of the guards under their Cpt-Pickardt by about 3o Pow's were bayonetted. Preparations and trainings were in progress for organized shootings into the camp. When the a/m interpreters were transfered to this camp, I - the British camp-leader - and T/Sgt.Paules have asked them both to help us in our more than desperate situation knowing that these two were the only ones who would have some understanding in our situation and who would be prepared to take the considerable risk of taking up activities against the a/m Cpt. who was strongly backed up by the Nazi-party. Therefore we have asked these interpreters to do their best to prevent this captain in carrying on in his activities pointing out that they would certainly save the life or at least the health of hundreds of Pow's and to do away with the enormous strain on the whole camp of approx. 1oooo immates. We have offered them any possible help if necessary after the war, which was refused by them in claiming that they would do everything possible, but would hate any idea of "payment". Both interpreters were completely successful in their efforts. I can only state, that we the camp-leaders feel grateful that these interpreters had the courage in resisting a powerful party-officer in that camp."

This was the situation, dear Mr. Clark, as you will well remember, and if you would acknowledge these facts both of us would really feel more than grateful, because it possibly helps us to built up a new life somewhere abroad. Will you please therefore send your letter containing this statement in double to :

> Baron Wolf von Guttenberg
> Herschfelderstrasse 13
> Bad-Neustadt/Saale (13a)
> Germany/American Zone

I would like to hear from you bout your well being and would appreciate if this correspondence could be continued giving all of us a new start for understanding each other.

> Kind regards from me and Baron von Guttenberg

> yours

> [Helmut R. Wahle]

John Goldsmith

Pilot

1635 Heavy Conversion Unit
Flying Training Command

John Goldsmith at the start of his RAF career

"What a pilot!"

John in 1997

John Goldsmith

John Goldsmith joined the RAF Volunteer Reserve in October 1942 after attending the Aircrew Selection Board at Lord's Cricket Ground, St. John's Wood, London. He was only seventeen when sworn in and had to wait until he was eighteen before he could begin training as a pilot in South Africa flying Tiger Moths and Harvards. He was awarded his 'Wings' in September 1944 before being posted to 1635 HCU North Luffenham, Leicestershire. He flew mostly Lancasters with Bomber Command and after attending many courses on different aspects of flying bombers became something of a one-man crew in himself!

All flying and no fighting!

I don't think I have any real stories to tell but I have in mind the peculiarities of my career in the RAF Volunteer Reserve. It seems to me that I spent the whole time on courses whilst the intention was to fly and fight!

I commenced doing my ITW (Initial Training Wing) course which was prolonged somewhat by my contracting yellow jaundice. I went on to do twelve hours' flying and was subsequently selected for pilot training in South Africa. Having completed the course, instead of going on to OTU (Operational Training Unit) on Hurricanes I had to wait for an interview by two officers from Group Headquarters who told me that I had been selected for a staff navigators' course. (This was the price I paid for doing too well in navigation in the pilots' course: top in practice and second in theory!)

Eventually, I returned to the UK and after waiting for further selection it was to learn that I had been selected for a flight engineers' course and to fly as second pilot on Lancasters. I had just completed the course when VE Day came along and I could either go on Meteors or be made redundant. Because I was in a reserved occupation when I joined the RAFVR and my job was waiting for me, I had no alternative other than to be made redundant.

I thoroughly enjoyed my flying career but it was all courses and in some ways a complete waste of time but it did allow me to occasionally fly privately which I thoroughly enjoyed.

There were some dicey moments such as when, in training, the previous pilot had sensed a fault in the instruments whilst flying at night but did not report it. On taking off I felt the aircraft had not the correct flying attitude and only by sliding the hood back and flying by looking at the horizon in the dark was I able to complete a circuit and land safely. It was, to say the least, nerve-wracking!

Dennis Griffiths

Air Gunner

7 and 195 Squadrons

Dennis Griffiths, 7 Squadron, Oakington, Cambridgeshire, in his Lancaster's rear gun turrent before take-off to Heligoland, April 1945.

Dennis's Lancaster crew

Back row left to right: *Dennis (rear gunner); Reg (mid upper gunner); Smithy (pilot); Tex (navigator).*
Front row: left ro right: *Tiny (bomb aimer); Geordie (wireless operator); Pete (flight engineer). Pete is holding raffle prize P/O Prune doll made by Group Captain's wife. Sadly, P/O Prune (along with maps) blew out through the astro hatch which came off somewhere over the Fatherland!*
(See poem *Yesterday's youth* p.79)

Dennis Griffiths

Dennis Griffiths was accepted for aircrew at RAF Cardington, Bedfordshire, in 1942. He enrolled in August 1943 at the RAF Aircrew Reception Centre, St. John's Wood, London, and attended No.1 Air Gunners School, Pembrey, South Wales, before being posted to Operational Training Unit at Westcott, Buckinghamshire. Then it was on to Heavy Conversion Unit at Woolfox Lodge, Rutland, and after that, 195 Squadron, Wratting Common, Suffolk, 3 Group, Bomber Command. He was finally posted to 7 Squadron, Oakington, Cambridgeshire, 8 Group, Pathfinder Force.

In the beginning...

MY earliest flights were as an air cadet in 1941. Cadets were given the opportunity to fly as 'Air Experience'. First was in a Handley Page Halifax of Coastal Command at Holmesley, Hampshire, then the following year in the De Havilland Dragon Rapide at RAF Hornchurch, Essex.

In 1947 I had to attend a course at RAF Kirkham, mid-way between Preston and Blackpool. A soccer match between the two towns was scheduled with Tom Finney playing for Preston and Stanley Matthews for Blackpool and I went to see it at Preston.

When it was over the crowds flocked to buses and trains and so I decided to hitch a lift to Kirkham. Whilst I was standing by the roadside thumbing a lift a coach pulled up, the door flew open and two portly women grabbed me and pulled me inside. The coach was full of similarly large ladies.

"If you want a lift, lad, you'll have to dance for it!" they shouted at me.

They prodded me good humouredly, if determinedly, and, with shaking knees at this impromptu performance, I danced from Preston to Kirkham! It turned out they were Blackpool landladies returning from a beano!

... and in the end

AFTER my wartime service with the RAF, I elected to accept an offer to stay in the RAF for a further three years. I was an aircraft recognition instructor, concentrating mainly on Russian aircraft. I remained with 7 Squadron until November 1949, still on flying duties and spent a lot of time on courses and overseas visits including a week on B-29 Super Fortresses with USAAF 92 Bombardment Group at RAF Skulthorpe, Norfolk, as well as flying in Avro Ansons and Lancasters, and Vickers Wellingtons.

After leaving the RAF in November 1949 I served on paid Class E Reserve for four years. Eighteen months after expiry of this situation, the RAF Records Department informed me that I had never been discharged from the reserve!

They requested that I sign for a further two years retrospective which I did. I was then sent back-pay for eighteen months and further monthly payments for six months!

Dennis Griffiths

A real brick

SOME time back I was reminded by one of my former crew members of the fact that I always took a house brick with me on operations. In a recent issue of the *Daily Mail* was an article headlined 'British bricks in Japan'. Apparently, our bricks are something of a curiosity over there and they have a number on display in a museum. I mused over this and decided to write to the editor who chose to print my contribution:

British bricks are in demand in Japan and Germany has a few, too. When German flak came up, fifty years ago, I used to lob one out of my rear gunner's turret. Those still alive from our Lancaster crew remind me of this futile gesture whenever we meet. (Daily Mail, Thursday, 14 May, 1998)

The bricks I carried came from the dock area of the East End of London—there were plenty lying around after the Blitz. I used to think, "You knocked them down—you can have them!" Sometimes I'd write on them 'A present from London'.

Some bods used to throw out quart beer bottles. It was said that they sounded like 2,000lb bombs. Heaven knows who or how they that came to that conclusion!

The Seven Deadly Sins of A.G.s No.4: Inability to identify aircraft (From Tee Emm, published by HMSO, Crown copyright)

Yesterday's youth

Eighteen years plus, off to dispersal in the crew bus.
Check over the aircraft, now await dusk.
Off down the runway, clawing the night air
Carrying a cargo of destructive fare.
Up to 10,000, on with your mask, re-check your guns, stow away your flask.
Crossing their coast we are greeted with fire by the unwilling host.

Over the target, plenty of flak.
Bombs all away? Then let us get back.
Throttles wide open, we turn away
Avoiding the searchlights and their constant play.
All eyes scan the dark sky, look out for fighters, it's their turn to try.
The screech of hot tyres on the tarmac—once again we've made it back.

Off to debriefing via the crew bus, let's get it over without too much fuss.
Now to the locker room, get shot of your gear, then off to the mess as dawn draws
   near, for bacon and eggs and next stop, bed.
Back to the mess, lunchtime that day, we drink to those who went astray.
No 'op' tonight, so up to town. Please let us have seven glasses of brown
   for Smithy, Tex, Pete, Reg, Tiny and Geordie,
We burst into song both decent and bawdy.

Later that night you think of tomorrow, where next will we plant
Our seeds of sorrow?
You of today, you have time to play,
Just make sure you keep it that way.

(See photo of crew on p.98)

John Guy

Pilot

Flying Training Command

John Guy in 1943

John in 1997

John Guy

John Guy joined the RAF at Oxford. He trained in Canada and Wiltshire. He was awarded his pilot's 'Wings' in September 1943 but then, owing to a loss of centrral records, had to go through the system twice! After that he went to the Staff Pilot Training Unit at Cark in Cumbria where he took courses in navigation and bomb aiming. He was then posted to 7(O) Advanced Flying Unit, Bishop's Court, Northern Ireland and served in Training Command.

Missing in (in) action 1943-4

THE message 'Missing in action' would strike fear into the hearts of an airman's loved ones but, in my case, no anxiety was felt by family and friends because, during the 'missing' ten months, I sent regular letters from a hotel in Harrogate.

"Harrogate?" you ask? "Which Stalag was that?"

Since some explanation is required, perhaps I should begin at the beginning, in fact, at 31 PD, Moncton, New Brunswick, Canada.

Proudly exhibiting newly won wings, airmen were normally batched together in thousands for return to UK. I shall never really know how 149 other pilots and I were picked out except that our surnames began with 'GU' or 'HA'. As a batch of merely 150 we travelled unescorted to the port of Halifax in Nova Scotia where, on the dock, in the shadow of the *New Mauritania*, we were met by an RCAF Warrant Officer (Second Class) service policeman. He explained that he knew nothing about troopships (nor, indeed, as a prairie man, about ships of any description). His orders were to meet 150 pilots on the dock and to instruct them in the duties of security aboard preparatory to the arrival, four days later, of 6,000 US infantrymen whom we were to assist as we and they sailed to some unknown destination in England.

Four days—and no one really knew what our precise duties should be. The WO2 divided us into three watches and marched off the first fifty whilst the other hundred drew fifty hammocks from ship's stores and, uninstructed, attempted to sling them in a very crowded mess deck. The pattern was beginning to emerge. One third on duty, one third in hammocks shaking dust and debris upon the remaining third as they endeavoured to eat or rest at the mess tables below.

As the WO2 marched the first batch around the maze of ship's corridors, he came to what he thought would be good sentry posts. At these he would peel off a man and instruct him to remain alert for two hours until relieved. Having so positioned sixteen men, he marched the remainder back to the mess deck. Retracing steps took about one hour because the *New Mauritania* was a very large ship and, having never been finally fitted as a civilian liner, there were no directional signs.

Eventually, stumbling upon the mess deck, the WO2 wisely decided that he had better set out immediately to relieve the original sentries. Unfortunately, he could not find them, partly because he could not remember where he had stationed them but mainly because, being airmen with lots of initiative, they had seen no point in guarding nothing and had therefore slipped up on deck. Some had discovered the route to the gangplanks and were exploring possibilities of wine, women and song in the port of Halifax.

Four days of chaos then ensued before trainloads of soldiers began to arrive—6,000 GIs and all obviously rookies. The vast majority had only three medals up and so we reckoned that they could not have been in the army for more than three or four months. This proved to be correct: one General Service gong (for having enlisted during wartime), one General Efficiency Medal (for having fired a rifle on the practice range) and one very new looking gong: the Atlantic Medal, given for reasons which are obvious, although some of us unrewarded RAF bods thought they might have waited to cross the gangplanks before sewing the ribbon onto their tunics.

We sailed for England. An American troopship is a 'dry' ship, or at least it should be! Whilst GIs crowded every corridor playing 'craps', British Merchant Navy men mysteriously appeared around corners carrying unlabelled bottles of all shapes and sizes which contained an off-white brew. Bottles and large bundles of dollars were exchanged. Soon the drunken cries of "Crap" became louder mixed with those of "cheat" and "swindler". Fisticuffs and the sound of breaking bottles ensued. We, the preservers of the peace, were issued with rifles and six live rounds. The 'war' had started somewhat earlier than expected.

It had been announced that one of the ship's four main boilers was u/s and that our sea trip would consequently be extended by one or two days. We suspected that one boiler might have been out of action because an astute British crew had converted it into an illicit still.

Eventually, we came to Liverpool where the American troops were ordered to prepare for landing the next day. Each GI accordingly occupied his time busily sewing on a fourth ribbon: the European Theatre of Operations Medal. I had not previously thought that Liverpool was such a dangerous place.

For the GI disembarkation, the quay was lined with top brass: Lord Lieutenants in plumes, local dignitaries weighed down with chains and two bands, one American army and the other a Liverpool civilian band. It was indeed a splendid welcome.

One hundred and fifty UK airmen had to stay aboard a further night before disembarking on the same quay to be greeted only by a line of inquisitive customs officers.

What has all this to do with 'Missing (in) action'? Well, it would seem that when the records of 6,000 GIs were off-loaded from the *New Mauritania*, those of 150 RAF men went with them and were never to be found again. Servicemen without any central records are deemed 'not to exist'. Thus, for ten months, we hung around Harrogate before the powers-that-be decided that, to prove we really existed, we had better start all over again: another Elementary Flying Training School and Service Flying Training School in England. After that, it would seem that we were all considered to be over-trained and ripe only for Training Command. Had it been otherwise, one might wonder how many of the 150 sprog pilots would have survived in Bomber Command in 1943-4.

(K)night's interception

HAVING been grounded for some time in Harrogate, three of us decided that it would be appropriate to make a night sortie over the moors to a well-known target the Black Swan (aka the Mucky Duck).

We set course in bright moonlight, our engines throbbing at the intake of pure Yorkshire air and our undercarts rhythmically rattling the runway below. For three miles we saw no sign of friend or foe and were somewhat surprised, on arrival at the target, to swing open the hangar doors to find the interior packed with convivial company.

Some hours and pints later, we donned heavy flying kit and hit the cold night air for the return to base. Halfway home the moon disappeared behind 10/10ths cloud and we found ourselves proceeding in pitch blackness keeping on course only by that innate sense of direction which pilots have...

About one mile from base our progress was impeded. We had collided with inanimate objects on the flight path and our undercarts buckled. One of our party lit a flare and, by this limited light, coupled with judicious groping, we were able to determine that the bodies of two civilian girls—very young and very drunk blocked our runway. We assumed that they must have been heading for Harrogate. Accordingly, we hauled them inboard and, by slinging two between three, managed to make slow progress. After some time, we reached the outskirts of the town and there shook our cargo into some degree of coherence. In what little light escaped through the blackout, we perceived that they were even younger than at first thought, perhaps only fifteen or sixteen.

Following their unsteady instructions, we found a street of small houses built in terraces of ten with narrow passages between each terrace. One girl indicated a front door which, like all the others, abutted directly onto the street. We were about to knock on the door when it occurred to us that, when we jettisoned our cargo, we might face some flak from a maternal 'Queen Bee'. Whilst not wanting to exhibit cowardice in the face of the enemy, we felt that discretion, being the better part of valour, might enable us to survive to fight another day.

Thus we proceeded past the indicated target, counting, "One, two, three, four". Sharp turn to starboard. Keep a steady course for fifty feet. Another hard to starboard and start counting again but, this time, back gates instead of front doors. "One, two, three, four." Open the latch quietly. Creep up the yard with engines throttled well back. Test the back door. Thank God, it opens! Jettison cargo in a heap in the scullery and then full throttle away from the flak zone.

Often, during the passage of fifty-five years, I have wondered what happened when the occupants of the house found two very drunken teenagers in the scullery. Did we in fact jettison them in the right house?

If my two male companions of that night should read this, maybe they will be pleased, at long last, to have received a mention in despatches for their gallant action.

Strewth!

DURING the Second World War Badminton House and park in Gloucestershire was a 'prohibited flying zone'. It was also forbidden to approach the park by road. Airmen were not told why but rumour had it that it was a testing area for a new ground-to-air death ray.

Two airmen had set out from a nearby RAF station for the local pub and had lost their way. Not an unusual occurrence in an English countryside where, for security reasons, most road signs had been removed. Unusual, however, in that they were members of the RAAF and Aussies, particularly from the outback, were reputed to be able to sniff out a watering hole from a hundred miles away. They were, in fact, inadvertently walking *away* from the nearest pub and were on a lane approaching Badminton when they saw a strange vehicle coming towards them. It was maroon in colour, had an impressive front grill and a body, which appeared to be higher than its length.

The vehicle had passed them and was fifty feet along the road when it stopped and an ancient, uniformed chauffeur alighted and walked back to them. He asked them where they were heading and then told them that the nearest pub was a couple of miles in the opposite direction.

"However" he continued, "Her Majesty would be pleased to offer a lift in her car."

When the car door was opened, it could be seen that in the high-roofed body was a stately chair, most regal in appearance, upon which sat an elderly straight-backed lady. Her dress of satin reached from a high-laced collar to her ankles. On her head was a toque and she grasped in her right hand a long, thin, black cane with a silver top. She smilingly beckoned the Aussies into the carriage where they sat on two low stools and were duly delivered in style to the local hostelry.

Clearly, there was no secret weapon at Badminton. It was merely thought that the then Queen Mother should have some peace and quiet in her wartime haven.

Imagine what was reported in the two Aussies' letters from Gloucestershire to Wagga Wagga or some such place: "Dear Mum, dear Dad. Strewth, you'll never guess who gave us a lift in her car…"

It was at that point the censor's scissors would have cut out all reference to names and places which was just as well, as we would not have wished the widowed consort of King George V to be a target of the Luftwaffe.

Joe Hall

Navigator

172, 280 and 281 Squadrons

Joe Hall then...

... and now

Joe Hall

Joe Hall joined the RAF in 1941 at Oxford. Awarded his navigator's brevet in April 1944 after training in South Africa, he was posted first to 172 and later to 280 and 281 Squadrons, Coastal Command. After his training he flew Wellingtons and Warwicks.

JOE tells the story of when he was based at Limavady in Northern Ireland. His station was shared with 518 Squadron which flew Halifaxes used for meteorological purposes.

One airman was having an affair with a WAAF and decided it would be a good idea to do a bit of courting in a Halifax, it having the required privacy if not the comfort. He took her down to the flights one evening and they duly settled into the Halifax. After a while the lady said somewhat reluctantly,

"I'll have to go. Nature calls."

"How do you mean?"

"I need to spend a penny," she said somewhat embarrassed. (It wasn't done then to talk about such things to a man.)

"Oh, is that all!" replied her escort relieved that the evening's fun would not have to end just yet, "there's an Elsan. Use that."

"Where?"

"Down at the back."

"What's it like?"

"Sort of bucket-shaped thing."

The WAAF went in search of the Elsan, returned a minute or two later and the couple continued where they had left off.

It was not until sometime later when the DR (distant reading) compass was behaving oddly and had somehow become wet that the truth emerged. It too was a "bucket-shaped thing ... down at the back..."

111

Bob Hannan

Wireless Operator/Air Gunner

282 Squadron

Royal Australian Air Force

Bob Hannan when air gunner of a Warwick in 1944...

...and in 1992

Defender of the skies: Australian air gunner in tropical kit 1943

Bob Hannan

Bob Hannan joined the Royal Australian Air Force in December 1942. After some pilot training he remustered to wireless operator/air gunner. He was trained in Australia and England. He flew in Warwicks with 282 Squadron from St. Eval, Cornwall, on anti-U-boat and air-sea rescue duties from December 1944 until the war ended.

The ghost on the runway

IT was a hot August afternoon in 1944 at Yatesbury, Wiltshire. We were radio training in a small aircraft called a Proctor. The plane had space only for the pilot and we two trainees with our equipment. The cabin had sliding windows of perspex, a form of clear strong plastic, through which we could see the green patchwork of the hedged fields not far below us and life felt good.

The other trainee, Graebner, was well known to me. In aircrew training we quickly learnt the habits of others. We were about to form into operational crews where our lives would depend on the skills and strengths of our comrades. In this case, Graebner had a serious weakness—he was prone to air sickness but was keeping it hidden from the Flight Commander as he hoped to overcome it.

I was wearing my blue battledress direct from the cleaners as I had a date with my English WAAF friend, Audrey Hill, immediately training was over. I am sure you are now ahead of me in this story...

As the summer air turbulence increased so did Graebner's nausea. For such contingencies, the aircraft was provided with jam tins, the RAF not wishing to indulge sick aircrew by providing anything smarter or, in this instance, bigger. Graebner soon filled the container and I slid back my section of the window panel to freshen the air. I was not to reckon on Graebner seated in front of me. Still feeling unwell, he whipped back his window section and emptied the vile contents of the tin. The slipstream did the rest. With my window panel open, I copped it and my clean attire was a thing of the past.

I was an angry figure trudging back to the living quarters cussing the world and Graebner in particular. Moreover, I was anxious to make a good impression on my new WAAF date, she having already told me her father had warned her about Australian habits. So I was not in the mood for caution and, instead of taking the safe but longer road around the edge of the airfield to my quarters that were directly opposite, I committed the sin of walking across the operating runway.

I was midway across the runway, head bowed, still seething, when I was enveloped in a deafening roar with a Proctor's propeller almost in my face,

Then it happened. Something shoved me in the back and I was hurled sprawling on to the runway. The propeller missed me but the leading edge of the wing gave me a glancing blow to the head. I lay there, shocked and dishevelled in my putrid clothing for a few moments then scrambled to my feet to stammer my thanks to my saviour. There was no one there—only a Proctor climbing away with a pilot cursing my stupidity.

Even today, more than fifty years later, it chills me just to think of it. I could not recreate that shove—it came from behind but there had been nothing and no one there.

Some years after the war, a friend with a spiritual bent, suggested it could have been the spirit of my father who was killed when I was a boy acting as my guardian angel. I have no feasible explanation. Who knows?

And my date with Audrey? Yes, it worked out well that day and we had tea in a café garden as the gentle English sun went down.

As a personal aside to this story, I have been back to lovely England many times since the war. When I go there I catch up with the Audrey of my story and we take afternoon tea and play a little bridge.

WAAF wireless operator Audrey Hill in 1944...

...and as Audrey Langford today

John Hart

Wireless Operator

156 and 170 Squadrons

John Hart's Caterpillar Club certificate

Left to right: *John Hart (wireless operator); Alf French (navigator) - see story opposite - and two other crew members, Gil Hampson (pilot) and Jeff Reynolds (bomb aimer) taken at a 1998 reunion.*

John Hart

John Hart joined the RAF in May 1943. He trained as a wireless operator at Yatesbury, Wiltshire, and flew Lancasters with 170 and 156 Squadrons, Bomber Command. He is a member of the Caterpillar Club.

The language barrier

IN late March 1945 with only a few weeks to go before the end of the war, John "arrived by parachute in Germany in daylight". He was beaten up by a mob but says (laconically) that he "managed to walk away" albeit with the mob following until he was taken prisoner of war. It was then that he sustained damage to his previously "superb set of teeth" through a German thug "clobbering my teeth with a pistol barrel".

While in captivity John and his navigator, whose name was French, were interrogated by a collaborating Frenchman.

John takes up the story:

"Name?" the German commandant demanded, ordering the Frenchman to interrogate the English navigator.

"What is your name?" said the interpreter with a strong French accent.

"French," said French.

"Non! Your name, monsieur?"

"French," said French.

"Non! Non! Your name? What are you called?" persisted the Frenchman.

"French," said French.

The Frenchman turned to the commandant in despair.

"He says he's French."

"He isn't. He's English," retorted the commandant.

"I know he's English but he's says he's French."

"Rubbish! Ask him again, idiot."

"Your name, monsieur?"

"French," said French.

"It's no good, sir. His name is French."

"It isn't—he's English," roared the commandant. And so it went on.

My navigator and I exchanged sidelong glances. I don't know how we managed to keep straight faces.

It was, and still is, a source of great amusement that the Frenchman had enormous difficulty in explaining to the German commandant why French was English!

Peter Kenworthy

Navigator

102 and 216 Squadrons

(Died 1998)

No photographs available

Peter Kenworthy

Peter Kenworthy joined the RAF Volunteer Reserve in August 1941. He trained as a navigator in Canada and was posted to 102 Squadron, Bomber Command, and later to 216 Squadron, Transport Command. In both squadrons he flew Halifaxes.

Hair-raising in more ways than one

PETER told the hair-raising story of an incident on one particular bombing raid ("I can't remember when or where") when both the gunners and the flight engineer became very agitated about an aircraft above:

I looked up straight into the bomb bay of the aircraft and watched nine 1,000lb. bombs come tumbling out of it. They passed between our starboard wing and our starboard tail plane and inches (or so it seemed) from the fuselage.

I could read the markings on the aircraft and so knew who was flying it. Safely back home I said to the captain of that aircraft,

"You dropped your bombs a bit close to us, Joe."

"Yes, I know" he said, "I was cursing you because I thought I would have to go round again when my bomb aimer said, 'It's OK, skipper, I can drop the bombs and miss them.'"

Fortunately, he had been right although it would have been nice to have shared his confidence at the time.

Another time (early July 1944) we bombed V1 supply bases in France. Whilst making our bombing run on one of these targets I was struck on the head by flak. It bounced off! A day or two later on a similar raid we were diverted to land at Snaith in the East Riding of Yorkshire because of bad weather over our home bases. Whilst on the ground at Snaith I met a chap from another squadron whom I knew.

"Hullo," he said, "we thought you were dead. We heard that flak had gone through your head and splattered your brains all over the aircraft!"

That someone with a head so thick that even flak couldn't penetrate it gave rise to many a ribald comment and, for a while, gave me a certain notoriety.

Geoff King

DFC

Bomb Aimer/Radar Navigator

57 and 97 Squadrons

Geoff King 97 Squadron Pathfinder Force 1944/5

Geoff (left) in early 1990s with former crew members.
Centre and right: Vincent Day (wireless operator) and George Lang (pilot)

Geoff King

Geoff King enrolled in the RAF in April 1940 at Cambridge, firstly serving on ground staff as a flight mechanic (E) until remustering and being posted onto his initial aircrew training in January 1942. He was awarded his observer and bomb aimer brevet in January 1943. After OTU at North Luffenham, Leicestershire, it as off to Lincolnshire to Heavy Conversion Unit at Swinderby then a posting to 57 Squadron at East Kirkby, and after his first tour, to 97 Pathfinder Squadron at Coningsby both with 5 Group, Bomber Command. He completed fifty operations and was awarded the DFC. Geoff has written his memoirs in a self-published book entitled A country boy at war *and it is from this book that these extracts are taken.*

Flying the flag?

WHEN I was at RAF Manby discipline was rigid. Both the Station CO, a Group Captain nicknamed Ivan the Terrible, and the Station Warrant Officer followed the book to the letter. Every week there was a station parade on the square and woe betide anyone with a hair out of place.

At one of these the flag was due to be raised. As soon as the lanyard was touched a pair of WAAF knickers suddenly unfurled at the top of the flagstaff and began to flutter in the breeze; the lanyard, which had been cut, then fell to the ground.

A titter ran round the parade, but it was quickly silenced when the CO asked for the person who had rigged up the knickers and cut the lanyard to step forward. Not a murmur was heard. We were then told that the whole station would be confined to camp for seven days. There would be a colour parade on every one of the seven days and, after normal working duties, all personnel (including all the WAAFs) would parade and march around the full camp perimeter. This would continue until the culprit came forward. I am not sure what happened but very soon afterwards we had a new Station Commander.

Formation flying and disaster

THE first of our daylight formation-flying exercises was quite successful although the Lancaster was not the best aircraft for close formation work. On our second exercise, though, a horrific accident occurred.

We were about an hour into our manoeuvres, flying in our formation of three, with a pilot named Van Raalte in the outer port position. Another skipper, Perkins, was in the centre, and we at the outer starboard. Our flight leaders were in three other aircraft, above and just ahead of us.

We had just completed a small manoeuvre to port when Van Raalte's aircraft was caught in the slipstream of one of the leading aircraft above. He suddenly swept across above us, missing our aircraft by a few feet then plunged over us again and straight into the side of Perkins' aircraft. Both immediately started to disintegrate and dived into the fields north of Sleaford.

The squadron was immediately ordered back to base and this was the end of our formation flying exercises. We were all badly shaken up at seeing so many of our friends killed in this manner. The only survivor from the two crews, a wireless operator, later told Vincent that he had no idea how he had managed to get out.

He never flew on ops again.

First trip to Berlin

IN early November 1943 we took delivery of what was to become 'our' aircraft, C-Charlie (JB486). She was fitted with H2S navigational radar equipment and so my operational in-flight position now moved from the nose to the small (and very uncomfortable) bench seat beside Curly, the navigator. My equipment was fixed to the right-hand side of his navigator's table. The H2S proved invaluable on long trips: not only did it provide constant fixes that I could pass to Curly, but it also let us map-read our way (literally) along the route thus enabling us to remain on track within the bomber stream and avoid the more heavily defended areas. It was in C-Charlie that we first went to Berlin.

It was 18 November and, although we didn't know it at the time, it was to be the first of ten trips we were to make to this city. At briefing there was a feeling of deep apprehension when our CO, Group Captain Taaft, announced,

"Well, gentlemen, your target tonight is Whitebait—code name for 'The Big City'." For a few moments you could have heard a pin drop. Then, as our individual briefings commenced, the volume of noise increased— and so did our nervousness. Having by now survived two months of operations, we had moved up from the fourth bombing wave to the first or second; on this trip we were in the second.

We had our usual uneventful trip until the approach to the target. This was from the north-west. It took an eternity, for we hardly seemed to be moving. Ahead of us lay what appeared to be an impenetrable screen of anti-aircraft fire from ground level to well over 20,000 feet, bursting in sequence every so many seconds at all levels. I thought,

"My God! How can we get through this lot?" As we neared our aiming point I concentrated on our bombing run and not on the hell that was going on outside the aircraft.

"Bomb doors open. Left, left—steady, steady." As the illuminated cross on my Mk 14 bomb sight criss-crossed the green target markers, I pressed my bomb release. At that moment, you could feel the bomb load leave the bomb bay, and immediately the aircraft wanted to rise. "Bomb doors closed."

Below, one could see some of our own Lancasters and Halifaxes silhouetted against the inferno. I often wondered how many of these aircraft were hit by bombs from above. (In theory, most of them should not have been there, because each bomber wave had its own height and time of attack—essential with the number of aircraft taking part.) There were also enemy fighters flying with us. If the anti-aircraft fire eased, you knew that fighters were there in numbers but usually they ignored their own defences and pressed home their attacks on some unfortunate aircraft.

It was just like a boiling cauldron below and fires were visible a hundred miles away from the target. I usually remained in the nose until we were clear of the target, keeping an extra eye open for fighters and other aircraft. On this trip 440 aircraft took part, with a loss of nine. It was to be one of the lowest losses on this target.

At about this time the German night fighters were becoming more visible and more efficient. (What we didn't then realise was that some of them could home in on our H2S and precautionary warning systems). Some were equipped with fixed upward-firing cannons (schräge Musik): devastating weapons that could cut a Lancaster apart (they could also be a bit hazardous for the fighter pilot, if he got too close to an exploding aircraft). Fortunately, we didn't at that time realise the full potential of this type of fighter but it may explain a few of the little mysteries, such as damage and losses that we attributed to other causes or to bad luck.

Tribute to two lucky C-Charlie(s)

ON 4 November 1943 we collected JB486 C-Charlie—lucky Charlie—that had just been delivered to the squadron. She was to become 'our' aircraft. C-Charlie (JB486) became a true and trusted friend for on my tour with 57 Squadron she bore us to the end.

C-Charlie

On return to East Kirby and within a few days a new C-Charlie arrived (LM517). Untarnished and bright and ready that night to take us into battle again. On return from each trip our pride in C-Charlie just grew as back in dispersal we handed her back to our proud hard-working ground crew.

In those final weeks, with our faith and her luck, we completed our tour, and Charlie's luck held true, and before we moved on we bade her farewell to carry on safely with another young rookie aircrew.

And to this day my memories live. Still I feel that across East Kirkby's field old Charlie's flying still, and when it's time for me to go, with her Merlins at full power, she'll make one final low approach and roar her last farewell, then tilt her wings and into the distance slowly fade away.

Through thick and thin she carried on despite the ills sustained, out into those troubled nights and safely home again. But on one deeply fated night returning from the fray, old Charlie looked a stricken sight with starboard wheel hung low; as on our weary way back to our base we were diverted to another drome to bring her in to land. With hearts in our mouths we made our approach, with our backs to the main spar pressed hard, as her wheels touched the ground the noises grew loud as old Charlie went into a spin. After several ground loops we came to a halt, all shaken but still in one piece and, as we climbed from the rear, we saw with despair that old Charlie's days were done. Next morning we took a sad final look, as we bade her our last farewell.

Postscript

JB486 C-Charlie returned to operations after repair but sadly went missing during July 1944. LM517 C-Charlie continued flying ops. until the end of the war. Our crew moved to 97 Pathfinder Squadron completing our second tour mostly in O-Orange, S-Sugar and M-Mother but C-Charlie was my first love and has always remained dominant in my memory together with M-Mother.

How did we survive?

MANY times I have been asked how did we survive? I think these are some of the reasons:

George Lang, our skipper's cool, efficient overall control in all circumstances throughout the time we flew together.

Curly (Roy) Davis, our navigator, was 100 per cent competent and always kept us on course.

Jock (Robert) Burns, our flight engineer, was a man whose ability more than lived up to his reputation.

Vincent Day, our wireless operator, kept us in close contact with base at all times and fed us any relevant information.

Flash (Frank) Green, our mid-upper and part-time rear gunner, was always on top of his job and helped to save our bacon early on in our operational experiences. (Both mid-upper and rear gunners experienced the discomfort of cold in addition to all the other horrors.)

Tommy Thomas and Dickie Poulson, rear gunners, were always efficient and always warned us of any likely danger. Flying in the coldest, most vulnerable position in the aircraft, they watched all the horrors unfold. (Flying with Pathfinder Force, with Flare Force and/or with the primary marker aircraft, you were at your most vulnerable whilst over the target. It was then that it was essential for your gunners to be on top of their job.)

Finally, myself as bomb aimer. I was fully confident in the competence of my friends who formed our crew.

In addition, we were flying Lancasters, one of the finest bomber aircraft produced during the war; even today I find the sound of those four Merlin engines deeply moving.

In conclusion: these are just one or two incidents and thoughts of my six years' wartime service in the RAF. Our operational flying experiences were not unique and were faced by many other crews flying at that time; some were just a little more fortunate than others.

Many people are inclined to forget that immediately after the evacuation of our troops at Dunkirk in May 1940, and until the Americans entered the war in December 1941, it was the RAF alone that took the war into the heart of Germany.

As the years have passed I have been saddened and disillusioned by some of the views expressed by a few of our so-called 'expert' academics, demeaning the efforts for which so many of our fellow aircrew gave their lives. I have wondered whether, if these men had lived and fought throughout those years, their views and opinions would be so dogmatic today.

Would Hitler have remained on the other side of the Channel without the wonderful effort and sacrifice of our Battle of Britain fighter pilots and the subsequent early Bomber Command offensive carried out by crews who sadly lacked the aircraft and advanced navigational aids that we were to have later?

Had they failed I am sure that the fate of British people would not have been any different from those poor souls who suffered and died in the concentration camps in such awful circumstances.

Something else that made many of us in Bomber Command very sad was the shabby way in which Sir Arthur 'Bomber' Harris ended his dedicated service, and we were disgusted at the government's decision not to mint a Bomber Command campaign medal. If wrong or weak decisions were made by those in government or command at the time, we at the sharp end—from the lowest to the highest rank—followed and carried out our duties with dedication, many with great distinction.

"How can you live with your conscience?"

IN recent years I have many times been asked that question. I must admit it has been a difficult question to answer. At the outbreak of war I was seventeen; now, in old age and knowing, with the benefit of hindsight, of the horrors experienced in those cities we bombed, my conscience is sometimes heavy with sadness.

On the other hand, however, after the air raids on many of our beautiful cities, and as the horrible facts emerged of the crimes committed against humanity in Germany and the countries that the Germans had overrun, I, like many others, felt fully justified. I well remember the words of our Prime Minister Winston Churchill addressing the US Senate on a visit to America, "He who sows the wind will reap the whirlwind."

As the war progressed I saw the full horror of those words materialise. It has been impossible to obliterate the memories of this period of my life and in moments of deep contemplation I can still recall little incidents—sometimes funny, sometimes sad—that occurred either in the mess or on the squadron. These bring back memories of the faces and the voices of my many friends who were lost. Throughout the time we flew together as a crew and through all the experiences we shared I strongly felt that someone was looking after us when we took to the air. Not one of us suffered a serious injury at any time.

As the time passes I feel sad at the ever-increasing problems we see in our world today. The political greed that contributed to World War II and its terrible consequences seem to have been completely overlooked and forgotten. It is as if no lessons have been learned at all: even our dear old country can no longer be recognised for what it was. I wonder what it will be like in another fifty years' time?

I have two beautiful daughters, both happily married, six grandchildren and, at present, six great-grandchildren. I hope and pray, for the sake of our children and future generations, that our efforts and the principles for which we fought then will not have been in vain.

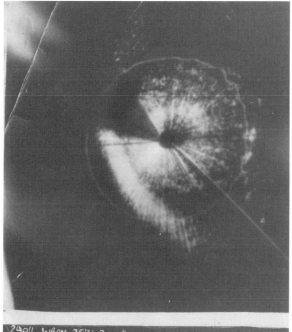

Photo taken from Geoff's aircraft's H2S screen on run up to target (Stuttgart) 25/26 May 1944

Flying with the clouds

We climb up through the mysteries of your mighty stairway to reach the brilliance of the sun that lights the valleys there between your glistening peaks, where sunlit beauty reaches all around.

We fly these paths of brightness, reaching high into the sky, but tonight a different story you will tell, as no longer can we see just where those lofty crags begin or where they end, as into the darkness of the night we fly, surrounded by your swirling mists.

Bound for a distant target we make our hidden way, wondering what mysteries lie within those threatening shrouds as suddenly we feel the anger of your turbulent winds, or is it just another Lanc., so near but hidden by your gloom, but this we'll never know.

Then, like a lightning strike, the ice thrown from our whirling props, smacks with a vicious crack against our frozen craft, as climbing still we hold steady on our course.

As we press on within your freezing mass we wonder when we'll break free of these your mighty peaks. Suddenly, above, we see the twinkling stars and breathe a sigh of great relief, as here and there a spark of light tells us that we are not alone and, there ahead, our target, where already hungry tongues of flame are spreading, reflected now upon your towering mass. Just ahead a flaming Lanc. falls into this mess as fighters strike from the cover of your crimson coloured shrouds.

We say a prayer as we proceed above this place and with target markers in my sights I press my bomb release, then feel our load begin to leave the belly of our craft; a gentle turn to starboard as we set course for home and head back into the curtain of your freezing mists.

As dawn begins to break, the rising sun behind us in the east lights up the beauty of our coastline as we approach once more those green fields of this our dearest land. Where, once again, your towering peaks with all those hidden valleys now begin to form, and herald in the start of yet another day, whilst we descend and land below the beauty of your ever-changing skies.

Ron Liversage

MBE

Air Gunner

38, 101, 148 and 625 Squadrons

Ron Liversage as a rear gunner in 1944

Ron with type of aircraft he worked on as an engine fitter before the war

Ron at a recent Air Crew Association event.
Photo: Dick Harding

Ron Liversage

Ron Liversage joined the RAF in early 1938 and was trained as an aero-engine fitter—part of ground crew. During the war Ron remustered to aircrew in the trade of air gunner. He was stationed in Malta during the siege, then to the Western Desert. He returned to England to 1 Group, 625 Squadron (Lancasters) at Kelstern, Lincolnshire, to complete a tour of thirty ops. over Europe. The aircraft he usually flew in was a Lancaster codenamed CF Easy 2. After the war Ron continued flying as a gunner on Lincoln aircraft with 101 Squadron at Binbrook until jets were introduced. (They had no turret for a gunner so Ron was out of work!)

He joined the RAF Provost Branch and carried out such duties as with the Special Investigation Branch, Counter Intelligence and VIP security. In 1964 he was awarded the MBE (Military) and retired from the RAF in 1971 a very happy man!

He was an early member of the Air Gunners Association, which began just eight years after the end of the war. It was from this that the Air Crew Association was formed to cater for pilots, navigators, bomb aimers, wireless operators and flight engineers.

Operation Manna

OPERATION Manna was the dropping of food to the civilian population of Holland who, by the last weeks of the war, was starving. We heard that about 3,000 a week were dying of starvation. I was involved in late April 1945 when our squadron did eight drops a day. I went four times with about sixty or seventy other aircraft and each time dropped food on the racecourse at The Hague. The dropping zone was marked with a big cross so we'd know exactly where to drop. Apart from the 'X-marks-the-spot' there was one field where the words 'Thank you, boys' had been made in tulips. Really got to you seeing that, you know.

It was great to be dropping food instead of bombs—sacks and sacks of it: Spam, dried egg, flour, yeast, milk powder, cheese, chocolate, dehydrated meat—everything. Of course, some of the sacks burst when they hit the ground but there was no shortage of folks eager to scoop up the contents. I suppose you could say it was an 'organised mob' that ran onto the racecourse when we flew over. The Germans were supposed to hold them back in an orderly fashion while the food was stacked and guarded but they didn't bother much.

On the first one or two drops aircraft had been shot at by the German ack-ack gunners—apparently word hadn't got through that they weren't supposed to shoot or they were just being bloody-minded. Anyway, we loaded up with ammunition—just in case. It was there but we made sure they couldn't see it from below so it looked as though we were unarmed as we were supposed to be.

Well, everything was all right and no one shot at us but it was a nervous moment because we were flying at only 300 feet or so. At that height things wouldn't be damaged too much when dropped but that made us sitting ducks for any trigger-happy ack-ack crew.

As we flew over the rooftops it seemed as though every house in the country was flying the Dutch flag—and there were some Union Jacks as well. I expect they'd had them hidden away just waiting for this day. It was very emotional. We liked to think we were a tough bunch of lads not given to emotion but seeing all this really got to everybody.

On the way back we could let off steam a bit by flying low over the North Sea. We no longer had to watch for intruders sneaking back to shoot us down when we were nearly home and so we got a real kick out of that low flying and seeing the sea flash by so close below us. Thrilling it was! Really exciting!

Going back

1999 will be the twenty-fifth anniversary of the first time I went back to Holland after the war. I've been every year since then. It was about five years ago that I met a Dutch air force Group Captain (or the equivalent) a Kolonel A.P. De Jong and got talking to him about Operation Manna. I told him I came every year.

The next year Kolonel De Jong was waiting for me.

"We've a surprise for you!" he said mysteriously. We were driven to the racecourse at The Hague. "See!" He pointed to the sky and there was the Lancaster from the Battle of Britain Memorial Flight! It was fantastic!

My Dutch host had arranged for the Dutch radio and television people to be there and we were treated right royally. A lady came up to me and said she remembered being there when we dropped the food.

"I remember your droppings," she said. (I hadn't the heart to suggest she rephrase that!)

"There's somebody special to see you," said my host and brought forward a middle-aged chap.

"I was here when you were dropping food for us. I've never met anyone who dropped us food before. I always wanted to so that I could thank you," the man grasped my hand and shook it warmly. "I was about fourteen at the time and I wrote down the squadron letters and numbers of all the aircraft—see." He took a piece of paper from his pocket and there was a long list of numbers.

"That's mine!" I said pointing to CF Easy 2.

"Thank you, sir, thank you so much. You don't know how much it meant," and his voice faded away.

Well, after all that we needed a drink—or two—or three. In fact, the celebrations went on from half-past ten in the morning until half-past eleven at night! Some party that!

The Dutch celebrate Freedom Day every year and I love to be there. There was one occasion, an impromptu party I think, and I had been dancing. I like dancing and, though I say it myself, I'm not too bad at it. We were actually waiting to be interviewed for Dutch radio and I saw an old lady also waiting. She was going to talk about what it was like to be in Holland during the Occupation. Apparently, she was ninety-four but she looked about sixty. I was keen to talk to her and got someone to introduce me to her. It seemed she'd had her eye on me.

"I believe you were here in the Occupation," I began.

"Never mind that! I've been watching you. I want you to dance with me. Get them to play a Glen Miller tune!"

I was taken aback to say the least but gallantly stepped onto the floor with the old lady and we quickstepped our way round. She was a really good dancer! Then we fox-trotted and waltzed until eventually we ran out of steam and had to have a breather. She was amazing.

"I want you to meet my son," she said. "He's been keen to meet someone who was on Operation Manna for a long time." She called him over and introduced us.

"I was sixteen at the time," he told me shaking my hands as though he'd never let them go. I could see the tears were flooding into his eyes (I felt the same) and he smiled, "I wasn't much younger than you chaps flying in those Lancasters. I drove a horse and cart to

pick up the food." By this time the tears were pouring down his face—and mine too!

Every time I go to Holland something different happens. In 1998 my pal, Derek Eden (see p.55), and I went as usual and, almost as usual, we were interviewed on the radio. We were in a little town called Putten and the mayor came and talked to us. When he discovered who we were—that we were former RAF chaps who'd taken part in Operation Manna—he sent somebody back to his house that was quite a few miles away to get his chain of office so that he would be properly dressed to have his photo taken with us!

Schoolchildren's remembrance

IT was about twelve years ago that we (Air Gunners Association) 'adopted' the Christelijke Basisschool de Violier, a primary school in Vaassen, and at that time planted a tree as a commemorative gesture remembering Operation Manna. The local blacksmith had made a plaque, to put near the tree, saying what it was all about.

Thirty of us went (for the twelfth time) in 1998 and met the children who were pretty clued up on the war—more so than our kids, I'm afraid. They asked lots of questions and were thrilled to bits to meet us.

They wanted to know what kind of aircraft we flew, how we felt during a raid, whether we ever had to bale out, whether we lost any friends or relatives during the war, whether we were frightened during a raid, whether we had been prisoners of war and so on. (Long after I returned home I received a surprise letter and a little present sent by the children—they hadn't forgotten our visit.)

This year they presented us with badges with our names on them. These badges were thin slices of wood that had been cut from a branch of the original tree we had planted all those years ago. That was really novel. However, the

original tree, an oak, did not survive but another one has been planted. This time a lime tree—or linden tree—symbolic of remembrance and friendship.

The children of this school look after a memorial in the woods. The site is at Gortel, five miles from Vaassen, where, in 1941, a Stirling (T-Tommy) crashed killing the crew. Every year there's a short service of remembrance and wreaths laid on the memorial. The children know all about it and take part. They aren't allowed to forget.

The whole afternoon is devoted to remembering and the welcome they gave us was, as always, fantastic.

After viewing the Air Gunners' tree, which was followed by tea and 'conversation', we boarded coaches to go to Gortel and the 'T-Tommy' memorial service. The Dutch and British national anthems were played then children planted poppy crosses. Wreaths were laid on behalf of the Royal British Legion and the Air Gunners' Association, as well as flowers. Then came the dedication and Last Post followed by a two-minute silence.

The children even composed a song for us the last verse of which is:

In this song we tried to explain to you
How much we all do love you.
You all risked your lives for our freedom,
We'll never forget all your names, your names.

I suppose if someone had told me at the time—in early 1945—that I'd return to Holland time and again, and make some wonderful friends there who always remember what we did, I wouldn't have believed them. But when I go there now, I know it was all worthwhile. I knew then I was taking part in a momentous event—Operation Manna—but I'd no idea how much it would come to mean to me as the years have passed.

Crew of Lancaster CF Easy 2 at 625 Squadron, Kelstern, Lincolnshire, 1944.
On the left is a WAAF driver, two seated are engine and airframe fitters. Ron is third from right

Mick Maidment

Pilot

8 and 9 Ferry Units

Mick Maidment, Karachi, Pakistan July 1944

Nose of a P-40E Kittyhawk Mk.I and some of Mick's colleagues on a course at Abu Sueir, Egypt

Mick 1994

Mick Maidment

Mick Maidment joined the RAF Volunteer Reserve in June 1941 at Weston-super-Mare. He trained as a pilot in Southern Rhodesia and qualified in December 1943. His OTU in Egypt was the most traumatic period. The six-week course started with about thirty-four pilots in the Spitfire flights and ended with only one injury: a broken arm. The two Kittyhawk flights started with twenty-one pilots and ended with fourteen. Of those seven killed, one had been a room-mate of Mick and of the remaining fourteen, thirteen had serious accidents. Only one escaped injury: Mick. He later served with Transport Command in 8 and 9 Ferry Units in Karachi and Allahabad respectively. He flew, amongst other aircraft, Kittyhawks, Hurricanes, Spitfires and Thunderbolts.

All you need is lust

WE are at 73 OTU, Abu Sueir, Egypt, a peace-time station near the Sweetwater Canal, not too distant from Ismalia. Three Spitfire flights and two P-40 Kittyhawk flights, one in the charge of Canadian F/Lt 'Newt' Newton DFC, and the other, Australian F/Lt Russell, DFC of the RAAF, both of them veterans of the North African campaign. The Aussie is our hero in the tale.

It is soon after midday on a Friday in early March. Russell has a weekend leave which, like a number before him, he intends spending in Alexandria. There, for the past six months or so, has been a detachment of Royal Navy WRNS and our hero has become quite besotted with one of them—and rightly so judging by the photograph now in his hand.

A blonde apparition, beautiful of countenance and in figure and it is a long 'friendship' of some nine or ten weeks. Yet Russell looks troubled.

"What's the problem, Russ? I've lent you the Harvard. I don't expect to hear from you until Sunday evening before the light goes," says Newt.

"Well, we're getting pretty close, and I might get into a situation where... well... I don't know whether she f—s or not," said Russell

with such seriousness that, in spite of the Australian vernacular, a few smiles were raised.

However, fielding expressions of good luck and the odd ribald comment, Russell with cap to head, 'chute over shoulder, bag in hand, climbed into the Harvard and soon lifted off in the direction of Alex and the unknown.

Now, 'tis Monday. The exercise is battle formations: six Kittyhawks at a time, instructor leading. Time for two exercises during the morning. The notice behind the flight office door says that F/Lt Russell is to lead B Flight for the second exercise with take-off around 1130 hours. But that instructor and a Harvard are still missing.

Newt cusses and blinds, throws his battered cap around the office then decides that, although not his flight, he'll lead the formation—which he does. It went well. All land safely. It's nearly 1300 hours. The dust-devils are beginning to swirl across the airfield. Flying has ended. The barbed-wire barriers are being pushed into place. A hush falls over the airfield.

From the north-west a lone yellow Harvard dives over the centre of the dusty airfield—climbs, twists, loops, turns, rolls in sheer exuberance—it damned near turned itself inside out until, heading for the hangars and near ground level, the engine was cut. It landed across the hard standing, turned in through the small gap in the barbed wire almost precisely into the line of P-40s and stopped. About a hundred pilots watched the whole affair with hardly a murmur. Even Newt was quiet.

The canopy slid back. Russell stepped on to the wing, raised a thumb into the air and shouted grinning,

"She does, she does, she does!"

Applause, whistles and catcalls filled the still air. Newt hugged him—and forgave him, such was the great news.

In those days of 1944, such a commitment between two people usually meant that it was total, one to the other. So, in keeping with the morality of those days it must be added that, after about eight months, a Middle East newspaper reached us and in it was a photograph of Russell and his WRN bride leaving an Alexandria church following their nuptials.

One of our aircraft is ... but a Tiger Moth?!

GUINEA Fowl was the name of 26 EFTS because the only signs of life there were those birds in the Rhodesian 'bundu' about a dozen miles south-east from Gwelo in the Midlands. At that time, for night flying, it had a satellite strip, six or seven miles away—just a flat, straight level of ground. When required, the support ground crew left early to light the landing flares by 2000 hours when the first of the sessions started. There were four Tiger Moths, each with an instructor and a trainee pilot, for a two-hour stint of circuits and bumps, dual or solo.

The Witching Hour has passed and the final session concluding at 0200 hours is about to end. A/C Bishop is doing his final solo take-off and rises into the darkness. As all is now quiet, some five or ten minutes having passed, the Officer-in-Charge decides that we can all return to the main airfield. However, one obvious requirement is to count the aircraft and see them away.

"One, two, three... One, two, three? One, two, three... Hell, where's the other one? Who's missing?"

"It must be Bishop, sir."

When all had returned to Guinea Fowl, little could be done in the blackness of the tropical night. Even waking the station CO wasn't very rewarding although a transcript of the

conversation might be both illuminating and colourful.

At first light, before the normal start of flying, all were informed to look out in the area for a crashed Tiger Moth and its missing pilot. It must have been after mid morning that an excited instructor reported the find. Detail suggested that Bishop had lost his engine soon after take-off, glided down the contour of the slope in the darkness until he hit the foliage of gum trees—the windbreak around a farmhouse where the yellow Tiger Moth now rested, some nine or ten miles away.

Three cars with an assortment of personnel tore across the barren field, through the flimsy barbed-wire fence heading for the night-strip and thence the farm. All looked up at the aircraft, little damaged but there was no sign of its pilot. One of the senior officers banged twice on the front door of the farm. It was opened by an elderly, grey-haired lady.

"Do you know that you've got one of our aircraft in your trees, ma'am?"

"Oh, is that where it is? I thought it must be somewhere near," she replied.

"But, where's the pilot? What's happened to him?" asked the officer.

"Sshh! Not so loud. He's asleep in the bedroom. He's had such a trying time, poor fellow."

Bishop, it turned out, had been able to fall to the ground unharmed after getting out of the cockpit. He roused the sole occupant, the lady, who had consoled, fed, watered and, in the small hours of the morning, offered him a bed for the rest of the night. Naturally, Bishop accepted.

The last known location of the said Bishop was at a bungalow not far from Oxford, having retired as a Wing Commander.

Alan Merriman

CB, CBE, AFC and Bar, FRAeS
Air Vice Marshal

Pilot

1 and 263 Squadrons

Happy landing for Alan Merriman? (see story opposite) as depicted by Belgian magazine Radar *5 February 1956*

Alan Merriman

Alan Merriman joined the RAF for his National Service in 1947 as an AC2 Trainee Radar Mechanic. He qualified for pilot training in 1948 under a Cranwell cadetship and three years later was an instructor on Meteor jet fighters. In the mid-1950s he completed an operational tour on Hunter jet fighters as a Flight Lieutenant. After graduating from the Empire Test Pilots' School, Farnborough, in 1958, he tested new transonic and supersonic fighter aircraft such as the Lightning.

A few years later as Wing Commander, he became CO of Fighter Test Squadron developing the Harrier, the world's first vertical take-off fighter. He went on to be appointed Station Commander of RAF Wittering, Cambridgeshire—the 'Home of the Harrier'. In 1977 he became Director of Aircraft Requirements and eventually retired as an Air Vice Marshal. He was awarded the Companion of the Order of the Bath, Commander of the Order of the British Empire Air Force Cross and Bar and Queen's Commendation for Valuable Services in the Air. He is a Fellow of the Royal Aeronautical Society. During his career he flew over 100 different types of aircraft including American, French and Swedish Mach 2 fighters. He was one of the very few RAF pilots to have flown a rocket-powered fighter. Invariably, test pilots have some exciting incidents but his most memorable experience occurred while flying a Hunter on a fighter squadron...

Happy landing?

IT was a beautifully clear and crisp January morning in 1956. There wasn't a cloud in the sky and visibility was unlimited. A full throttle climb out of RAF Wattisham, Suffolk, in the Sapphire-powered Hunter 5 was an exhilarating and satisfying experience. It was sheer bliss for me. To think that the Royal Air Force was prepared to pay me for doing what I loved most!

The joy was short-lived however. Passing 12,000 feet at 400 knots with the VSI (vertical speed indicator) still off the top of the dial, there was an adrenaline-charged bang. The engine dials suddenly read zero; warning lights indicating electrical and hydraulic power failures and the aircraft was rapidly losing speed. The engine had exploded and the Hunter had become uncontrollable.

It didn't take long to realise that escape from the aircraft was the only way to survive. After

hastily transmitting a Mayday call advising Wattisham of my perilous situation, and knowing I was over open Suffolk countryside, I jettisoned the hood and pulled the handle of the blind which protected the face from air blast and fired the Martin-Baker ejection seat.

There was a rush of air as I was shot out of the cockpit. The seat fell away below me as, thankfully, the automatic parachute opening functioned. In the distance I could see the aircraft diving away with smoke pouring from it until it hit the ground at high speed.

Hanging in the parachute seemed so tranquil and relaxing after the frantic activity of the few milliseconds earlier. But where was I? Where was I likely to land? From 10,000 feet I knew it would take about ten minutes to reach the ground.

Looking around, I recognised I was not far from Stowmarket. A soft landing in a field looked a good possibility. As I lost height the ground features became clearer. Was it my imagination or was I really drifting towards a line of high-tension cables? The prospect of 330,000 volts up my backside was not so relaxing. Nor was the sight of a nearby railway line with a steam train belting along it. Landing just in front of a train would not be my idea of fun. The light wind was clearly carrying me towards Stowmarket. Since it was around nine o'clock in the morning, the roads were busy with commuters and schoolchildren. Landing in front of a bus or car would be just as disastrous for me as a train.

By now I could see the anxious faces of people on the ground following my descent. It became increasingly obvious that I was going to land somewhere in the town. I searched frantically for an open space to head for. To my relief, I spotted a large garden that had a grass tennis court.

However, before I could work out which harness to pull to get the parachute travelling in the desired direction, there was a horrifying crash and I was jammed up to my waist in the roof of a terraced house. My flying boots had taken the impact and my legs were through the attic and into the bedroom below. What is more, a lovely (but elderly) woman was in bed with 'flu, somewhat alarmed by the unexpected intrusion.

The parachute draped itself down the side of the house, drawing my plight to the attention of the small crowd that had quickly gathered in the street below. While I was gingerly releasing myself from the harness, an enterprising local arrived with a ladder. At full extension, with his head just above the gutter, he politely offered a helping hand to get me down from the roof. It was pretty obvious to me, however, that sliding down the roof and getting safely on to the somewhat short ladder was going to be more hazardous than the ejection and parachute descent.

Not deterred by my rejection of his offer of assistance, he had the presence of mind to suggest I might find a drink useful while he sorted out a more agreeable solution. He clearly thought this would boost my morale—and he was not wrong—in full measure. For he shortly reappeared with a tumbler and a bottle of whisky.

So it happened that from driving a Hunter at 400 knots and 12,000 feet at one moment I found myself a few seconds later stuck on a rooftop drinking the finest-tasting whisky I have ever known.

Fortunately, before I got to the state of leading the audience down below to choruses of *Leaving Khartoum* and other well-known Air Force ditties, Stowmarket fire brigade turned up and my return to terra firma was safely completed.

The headlines in the London evening papers and BBC news bulletins made great play over my crashing through the roof into the bedroom with a bottle of Scotch, while the female occupant was still in bed. It led to a flood of messages arriving from my 'friends' on other fighter squadrons asserting that it was just another ruse, on my part, of getting into a lady's bedroom uninvited. I believe the repair patch on the roof of the house is still visible. I never did find the tennis court.

Tony Murkowski

VM, KZ, KW, ML Polish decorations

Pilot

147, 152, 257, 303, 309 and 316 Squadrons

Tony Murkowski, Poland, 1938

In readiness at Northolt, 1942

Ready for action at Friston on D-Day, 6 June 1944

"And I flew round like this..." Tony demonstrating what happened and how to a colleague on D-Day at Friston

Antoni Stephan Murkowski

'Tony' Murkowski has the distinction of having served in the Polish Air Force (in France) and the RAF. He trained as a fighter pilot and, in the RAF, was posted to 316 City of Warsaw Squadron, then later to 309 Squadron. After the war he joined 257 Burma Squadron (in time for the Korean War) then 147 Squadron, Transport Command, flying Sabres for NATO. He retired from the RAF in April 1975.

He was awarded several Polish decorations including the VM (the Polish equivalent of the Victoria Cross—the highest combat award—and given for his action in saving a Lancaster, the KZ (Cross for Valour), and two others: the KW and ML. Amongst his other awards are the British 1939-45 War Medal and Aircrew Europe Medal; he was also Mentioned in Despatches and earned several French decorations.

Story of a Polish airman

TONY Murkowski was born on 19 April 1920 in Poland. After the First World War he returned with his parents to Poland to the land and farm which had been taken from them by the Germans. The family moved to Czersk. Tony takes up the story:

After education at grammar school I began training as a pilot in Krosno. At the outbreak of war I was captured and became a prisoner of war but escaped from the Germans in Romania. I finally arrived in France where I joined the Polish Air Force. I remained there until France capitulated and was evacuated to Britain.

In July 1940 I began training as a fighter pilot on Battles and Spitfires. I was posted to 316 Squadron, City of Warsaw Squadron, at Hutton Cranswick in the East Riding of Yorkshire and later to Northolt, Middlesex.

There were many air battles but the one which stands out in my memory was in March 1943. The squadron had been re-equipped with the new Spitfire Mk IX. However, sometimes the engines 'conked out' and that happened to me and my Number 2... We came down through a thin layer of cloud right into a big formation of Focke-Wulfs! They must have thought that the whole RAF was attacking them for they scattered in all directions. They looked just like a shoal of little fish, glinting silver as they flicked and dived—and there were only the two of us! Our engines eventually restarted at a lower altitude.

Later in 1943, 316 Squadron was re-equipped with Mustang IIIs. After moving to Coltishall in Norfolk our role was now changed to strafing, escorting and diving on shipping.

When the flying bombs started, the squadron was transferred to West Maling in Kent. I had the luck to 'pip' all the high ranking gentlemen by shooting down the first flying bomb—the V1! Four weeks later on D-Day (6 June 1944) the squadron was moved to Friston in Sussex.

Tony Murkowski

A new squadron

MY next squadron was 309. It had just been re-formed as a fighter squadron at Peterhead in Scotland and our operation was to escort Beaufighters and Mosquitoes on their way to bomb German shipping in Norway. I didn't like that low level flying, especially in the fjords. It was ten minutes of hell but it didn't last long.

The squadron was moved south and we escorted bombers on long flights such as to Cologne and Swinemünde near the Polish-German border on the Baltic coast. The longest was to Berchtesgaden, Hitler's mountain-top retreat. It was most uncomfortable strapped into my pilot's seat for five hours.

In early April 1945 I was escorting Lancasters whose target was the shipyards in Hamburg. This was to prove to be the last battle of the war. After a fierce fight with the German jets (Me262) towards the end of a long battle, I noticed an ailing Lancaster bomber trying to escape from a posse of German fighters. By engaging them in a duel I managed to protect the Lancaster and it limped home.

My last operational flight was on 15 April 1945.

After the war

IN December 1948 I joined the RAF. After a refresher course I attended a conversion course on jets at RAF Bentwaters in East Anglia and was then posted to 257 Burma Squadron at Horsham St Faith in Norfolk where I was Number 3 in one of the first Meteor aerobatic formations.

In 1951 I was attached to 1 Operational Ferry Unit and was ferrying Meteors to the Australian 66 Squadron for the Korean War. I then went to 147 Squadron, Transport Command, which involved long range flying of Sabres (F86) from Canada for NATO.

On completion of operations I attended a course on air traffic control at Rufforth near York and enjoyed lots of Sabre flights at Linton-on-Ouse. On completing a course I became a test pilot for two years. That was followed by a further two years as Staff Pilot at Air Navigation School, Stradishall in Suffolk. My last posting was Operational Officer at Wattisham also in Suffolk.

First aerobatic team: Tony is second from the right

Lawrence Newton

George Medal

Flight Engineer

9, 12, 97 and 408 Squadrons

(Died 1995)

*Lawrie Newton shortly before he died in
1995*

Lawrence Newton

Lawrence Newton joined the RAF before the war as a fitter (engines). It was logical, therefore, that on the outbreak of war when he volunteered for aircrew, he became a flight engineer after training at RAF Halton. Subsequently, most of his flying was with 408 Squadron, RCAF, flying Lancasters from Linton-on-Ouse, Yorkshire. Lawrie left the RAF in the 1970s having reached the rank of Flight Lieutenant. After the war he became a 'Special' in the police force.

Early days

DURING Lawrie's early days in the RAF at one of his pre-war stations, a F/Sgt Discip. was very hot on airmen's appearance and cleanliness especially if they were going out of camp in the evening.

The F/Sgt would stand at the gate at the entrance to the camp and inspect them. On one very memorable occasion one airman was told,

"Go back and wash your hands, lad. I won't have it said that airmen from this station fondled village maidens' bosoms with dirty hands!"

(Thanks are due to Derek Eden for this story.)

Footnote

AT Lawrie's funeral, the clergyman, recounted Lawrie's occupation of his favourite seat and the fact that, whenever any strangers came into this small and somewhat remote pub, Lawrie would always greet them in a most friendly way. He would give them all sorts of most useful information whether they requested it or not: information such as where to find the 'Gents' or 'Ladies'. Thus the strangers would feel completely at home unless they should happen perchance to make some derogatory remark about England, the English people or the Crown. If they did so, then Lawrie's mood of affability would fade immediately and he would tell them in no uncertain terms,

"If you don't like this country, then why don't you just sod off!"

After the funeral service, a high ranking RAF officer remarked to the clergyman that he had never before heard the words 'Sod off' spoken from the pulpit. He suggested that the clergyman might have toned down the language a little bit.

"Oh, but I did!" said the clergyman.

We do not know when Lawrie was born but we rather suspect that instead of entering this world in the normal way, he might just have been hewn by the 'Almighty' out of a piece of solid English oak. Not only was Lawrie a very brave man and a patriot but he loved his fellow men, he was great company and, when he left the RAF, he continued to do his duty to others as a local councillor and as a special constable, among many other ways.

Lawrence Newton

THE following citation taken from the *London Gazette* relates to Lawrie Newton, a North West Essex and East Hertfordshire Branch Aircrew Association member who died on 22 December 1995.

In his memory, his friends in the branch have framed a copy of his citation and have had it hung in the Catherine Wheel pub, Albury, near Bishop's Stortford, above the seat that Lawrie regularly occupied.

The Queen has been graciously pleased to approve the award of the George Medal to the undermentioned: Flight Lieutenant Lawrence Cyril Newton (54969), Royal Air Force

On 21 November 1951 at 1520 hours, a Buckmaster aircraft from RAF Station, White Waltham, crashed just outside the boundary of Benson aerodrome. The impact caused the aircraft to break up and immediately to burst into flames. A group of officers and airmen, who had been playing football about 1,000 yards from the scene of the crash, set off before the impact to render assistance, under the leadership of Flight Lieutenant Newton who had observed the aircraft in difficulties.

 By the time they arrived, the cockpit section of the Buckmaster was a blazing mass, and shortly afterwards the first of the wing tanks exploded. Flight Lieutenant Newton directed a Warrant Officer to remove a casualty, who had already been extricated, to a safe distance from the burning wreckage, and then went straight to the forward end of the fiercely burning cockpit in an endeavour to remove the two remaining members of the crew who were seen in the midst of the flames. In the face of intense heat and with great difficulty, the nearest casualty, whose clothes were on fire, was extricated.

 Directing others to beat out the flames, Flight Lieutenant Newton returned to the wreckage, having seen movement by the member of the crew remaining in the flames. This time much greater difficulty was experienced and the Flight Lieutenant was obliged to call for further help.

 A second violent explosion then occurred forcing the newcomers to withdraw, but Flight Lieutenant Newton gallantly persevered in the face of this new hazard and finally extricated the third member of the crew. Unfortunately, on the arrival of the ambulance, the Medical Officer found that the last two casualties extricated were dead.

 Throughout this rescue attempt, Flight Lieutenant Newton displayed great leadership and set a fine example. Despite the apparent hopelessness of the situation on account of the intense heat to which the members of the crew had been subjected, Flight Lieutenant Newton persisted in his efforts, notwithstanding that but a slender hope of saving life remained. He displayed great courage and tenacity in the face of personal danger, not only from the original fire which was burning fiercely, but also from the bursting fuel tank which spread the flames over a far wider area. This officer suffered from severe burns to the hands as a result of his gallant rescue efforts.

Richard Ockendon

Pilot

37 Squadron

Richard Ockendon in 1946...

... and in October 1992 with the De Havilland Hornet Moth G-AELO (see story opposite)

Richard Ockendon

Richard Ockendon volunteered for the RAF in March 1942 but was placed on deferred service until October of that year. He reported to the Aircrew Reception Centre at St. John's Wood, London, and went on to train in Southern Rhodesia and gained his pilot's 'Wings' in September 1943. He was based in Egypt then moved to Italy in mid 1944. He served with 37 Squadron, 205 Group, near Foggia, Italy before being posted to Aden in February 1945. He returned to the UK a year later and worked at the Aircraft Torpedo Development Unit at Gosport from 1946-7. He was demobbed with the rank of Flying Officer in May 1947.

Renewing acquaintance with a Hornet

IT was just after the war that this story begins—although I didn't know it was the beginning of a story at the time. It was just an ordinary day and I wrote in my log book for 5 July 1946: *H(ornet) Moth. AW118. Pilot: self. 2nd pilot: S/Ldr King. Duty: To Wittering*

A few days before I'd flown a Beaufighter, a Firebrand, a Barracuda and a few days later an Anson, Tiger Moth and a Swordfish. It was nothing special—nothing out of the ordinary and I never gave it another thought until forty-six years later!

Duxford
In 1992 I was visiting the Imperial War Museum at Duxford and saw a De Havilland Hornet Moth, G-AELO, being worked on in a hangar. It was the same sort of aircraft that I had flown at the Aircraft Torpedo Unit in 1946 so, naturally, I was interested and got talking to one the chaps working on it.

"She shouldn't really be here at all," he told me, "she should have been at Little Gransden but had to divert because of bad weather."

I couldn't take my eyes off the Hornet Moth. There was something about her...

"I used to fly one of these," I said.

"Really? When?"

"Just after the war. My name's Richard Ockendon, by the way."

"Mark Miller," he introduced himself.

"How do you do?" I said. "Are you the owner of the plane?"

"No, she's owned by David Wells. He's not a pilot actually so I look after her and keep her in trim. You were saying about flying one like this just after the war?" he resumed the conversation.

"Yes. Her RAF service number was A118—or something like that." I felt slightly foolish. What if it wasn't that at all?

"You sure?" the man stopped what he was doing and looked at me curiously. "How come you remember?"

"I don't know," I said lamely. "I really don't."

And I didn't. Of all the aircraft I had flown before and since that Hornet Moth there was no reason for me to have remembered her number. Why on earth should I remember one aircraft's service number?

"Rings a bell. Come on," said Mark and together we walked across to Duxford's Reception Office. By this time I was quite excited. Could it be...? I waited a few minutes while records were consulted.

"Here we are, sir. G-AELO was once AW118."

"So this is the one I flew!"

159

"It would appear so, sir."

"I'll check surviving Hornet Moth serials when I get back," said Mark Miller, "just to make sure."

"And I'll check my logbook," I said. I could hardly wait to get home to find my old logbook and see if the two were one and the same.

I found the page headed 1946 and there, about a third of way down under 5 July, was AW118. It was unbelievable! Quite amazing! What were the odds on my finding an aircraft I had flown all those years ago? What if I hadn't been to Duxford? What if the weather had been good and AW118 had flown to Gransden as planned? What if I hadn't remembered her number? All those what ifs... If any one of those factors had been missing our paths would never have crossed.

Not the end of the story!

And that wasn't the end of the story! In October 1992, not long after seeing the Hornet Moth for the first time since 1946 I actually flew her again—the first time in forty-six years! I wasn't allowed to take off and land as I hadn't been in training but I flew her once we were airborne—for just over an hour—for about thirty-five miles. It was fantastic! Marvellous! I hadn't forgotten how to fly: it's like riding a bike—once you can do it you never forget.

And even *that* wasn't the end of the story! In early 1996 Mark Miller, the Hornet Moth's pilot, had contacted me,

"I've been invited to attend the eightieth anniversary flying display at RAF Wittering.

Want to come along in your old friend the Hornet Moth?"

I didn't need twice asking! In the event, the weather ruled out flying and so Mark and I drove to Wittering and spent the day as guests of the Station Commander. At lunch I mentioned how disappointing it was not to have been able to bring the aeroplane. Then I had an idea.

"I don't suppose we could have permission to fly it here at Wittering on Friday, could we? That's the 5 July. It'll be the exact fiftieth anniversary since I last flew the Hornet—and here at Wittering too."

The Station Commander smiled,

"That doesn't sound much of a problem. Of course you can! Be glad to see you again."

True to form the weather was bad but the clouds parted enough on the day for Mark and me to make our historic and nostalgic flight into Wittering.

The RAF did us proud. We (Mark and myself) and, of course, good old AW118, were guests of honour of the Station Commander, Group Captain Jerry Connolly and the Harrier pilots of Nos. 1 (F) and 20(R) Squadrons. Thus it was that Hornet Moth (AW118/G-AELO) and I celebrated our fiftieth anniversary at RAF Wittering—our destination all those years ago.

I enjoyed renewing acquaintance with the Hornet Moth enormously. As I look through my logbook again I'm just wondering... if anyone's got a Beaufighter (NV612 or KW285 or NV441) or a Swordfish (NR933) or a Barracuda (RJ948)... let me know, won't you?

Doug Page

Pilot

90 Squadron

Sgt Doug Page 1943

Doug at Cambridge in 1995

Doug Page

Doug Page joined the RAF Volunteer Reserve in November 1941 at Oxford. He trained as a pilot and was posted to 84 OTU and 1651 HCU, then 90 Squadron, Bomber Command. He flew Stirlings and Lancasters and completed thirty operations including three special supply drops and six 'gardening' (mine-laying) ops. His worst experience was losing his excellent flight engineer and his aircraft when flown by another crew. His 'best' experience was surviving the war.

The most highly qualified instructor in the RAF?

FOLLOWING the completion of my operational tour with 90 Squadron, Bomber Command, I was posted back to Stirling-equipped 1651 HCU at Wratting Common as a screened pilot.

This involved completing a flying course at 31 Base Instructors' School on the Stirling. Very soon after that I was posted to a course at No.3 Flying Instructors' School at Lulsgate Bottom (now Bristol airport) on Oxfords again. (Like many others I'd flown Tiger Moths and Oxfords whilst training.)

Almost immediately this course was followed by another instructors' course but this time on Lancasters at Finningley, Yorkshire. The powers-that-be must have known I was developing a taste for teaching and, by this time, I'd almost lost count of the number of instructors' courses I'd been on! I began to wonder if I was the most highly qualified instructor in the RAF!

I knew of several airmen who, after completing a tour were sent on instructors' courses but couldn't wait to get back to ops. As it happened, I enjoyed instructing and, after the Finningley course, I continued instructing until being demobilised in July 1946.

After joining Marshalls engineering company in 1952, I was lucky enough to have the chance to fly and eventually test-fly, many types of RAF aircraft. These included Spitfire, Mosquito, Vampire, Venom, Meteor, Brigand, Elizabethan, Viscount, Valiant and Canberra. There were also many civil aircraft that were not always such a pleasure to fly!

Finally, I got my hands on the Short's Belfast that we, as a company, managed to get through its civil Certificate of Airworthiness. This took me back to my old Stirling days as in some respects they were very similar.

I retired in 1984.

Bomb loads and targets

DURING my time on Stirlings with 90 Squadron the main task was to drop sea mines in the areas from the Frisians to the Bay of Biscay. Our load on these trips consisted of six mines, each weighing 1,500lbs. These were dropped from about 300 feet, usually in the approach to rivers and harbours.

A secondary task was to make air drops to supply the members of the French Resistance in rural France. These supplies were packed in long cylindrical steel containers with parachutes attached and dropped from a height of about 500 feet.

I completed nine missions of these types then changed to Lancasters. These were used by what was termed 'main force' operations and this was my role from now on.

On these missions we used a variety of ordnance depending on the type of target. On relatively small targets such as factories, railway junctions and troop concentrations we used a mix of 500lb and 1,000lb bombs. On oil refineries and large towns: a mix of 1,000-4,000lb high explosive bombs combined with canisters of small incendiary bombs, the idea being to blast the buildings then burn them. (On reflection, my mind is even now at times troubled about this.) Airfields called for a mix of 500 and 1,000lb bombs to cause maximum damage to runways and parked aircraft.

Bill Porter

Flight Engineer

156 Squadron

Bill Porter, flight engineer,
156 Squadron, 1943

Bill and fellow flight engineer from Warboys, Cambridgeshire, Basil Johnson, at the recent dedication of the stone outside Upwood airfield. From here in 1944-5 flew 139 Squadron (Mosquitos) and 156 Squadron (Lancasters) of No.8 Pathfinder Group 1944-5.

Bill Porter

Bill Porter joined the RAF Volunteer Reserve in May 1942 at Cardington, Bedfordshire. He trained as a flight engineer and was posted to 156 Squadron, Bomber Command, at Warboys Cambridgeshire, with Pathfinder Force flying Lancasters. He completed eleven operations—each one an experience! Sadly, his crew was killed in action in January 1944—Bill had been grounded the previous day.

A close-run thing

IT was 18 November 1943. My crew was down to fly our old pal and favourite, P-Peter (JA912 Lancaster III). We always had confidence in her and everything seemed right. Briefing informed us that the target for that night was 'The Big City'—Berlin—well named as it was thirty-three miles across: a long way, after dropping your bombs, to the relative safety of darker skies.

We drew our parachutes from the store. Printed on mine was 'Wing Commander Duigan'. I knew he had finished his second tour of ops. shortly after we started on ours. He was a tough Australian and a lucky one. I hoped his luck would be carried in his parachute. Was it some kind of omen? A lucky charm? It was a cheering thought.

Despite our confidence things quickly began to go wrong. The weather forecast was for clear skies over Germany but it proved to be 10/10ths cloud up to 12,000 feet and the forecast wind strength was way out. Either King, our navigator, didn't spot it or Doug, our wireless operator didn't pick up a broadcast of altered wind speed from Bomber Command HQ. Consequently, King said,

"Navigator to pilot: time to target is now—" he was rudely interrupted by a burst of anti-aircraft fire around us. Buffeted around in the hail of ack-ack fire and hearing the clangs of shrapnel hitting old P-Peter, I thought,

"We're for it now. They've got us on the hook with their radar-predicted flak." But, thanks to George, our skipper, jinking the Lanc. around we eventually got away.

Once clear George said,

"Pilot to navigator: where was that?"

"Brandenburg, skip," replied King.

From Brandenburg we were supposed to make a timed run to Berlin but, because of the wind strength, we were at the target already—ahead of everybody else!

At the briefing we had been told the time over the target would be sixteen minutes with twenty-seven aircraft bombing every minute. If we went round again we would be late and the anti-aircraft guns would have us on our own again.

"That options out," decided George much to our relief although to my surprise he then said, "Navigator: give me a reciprocal course back over Berlin." King did so and we swung round 180 degrees and back we went.

By this time the target was well alight. Our planes, silhouetted against this and the searchlights on the thick cloud beneath us, looked like strange insects crawling over a vast table top. Those that spotted us going the wrong way must have thought us very foolish, or that we had a duff navigator aboard. But we dropped our bombs and left, inwardly congratulating ourselves that we had got away with it and that the worst was over.

We had to fly south-west to pick up the main bomber stream heading home. Everything was remarkably quiet.

"Christ!" yelled George suddenly over the intercom as he sent P-Peter into a nose-dive.

"What the hell?"

There was a deafening bang and we plummeted like a broken lift. My feet left the floor. I hung on to the canvas back of my seat and saw my parachute pack apparently floating in mid air. After what seemed like an age, when I felt sure we would hit the ground and that would be it, George pulled P-Peter out of the dive.

"Everyone OK?" he asked over the intercom. Doug, regaining his composure at his wireless operator's panel, ignored the question and said,

"All the internal fuselage lights have come on. We'll look like a Christmas tree from outside. I want something to smash the bulbs."

"Use the hammer in my toolkit," I indicated to Doug as I was busy checking the engine gauges.

"All engines seem all right. Exhaust stub flames OK for colour, skip," I said.

"That's a relief," replied George. Doug's voice came again over the intercom,

"Just been down the back. Al's heading this way," he said referring to our rear gunner, "he's hurt his hands."

It turned out that in the nose-dive Al had thought we were going down for good and had taken off his gloves to open his turret doors to get his parachute in readiness for baling out. As he had held on to the metal to pull himself out, his hands had been severely frost-bitten and he had pulled all the skin off his palms and fingers. Doug installed him on the rest bed and he remained there holding his painful hands in the air for the rest of the trip home.

Doug borrowed my hammer and hit the light bulbs. (He took a kind of fiendish pleasure in smashing up Air Ministry property, he said later.) He had tried to man the rear turret but it was useless and would not rotate

at all. Fortunately, it was not needed for the trip back home was uneventful.

We joined the circuit over Warboys, were told to take our place in the queue and circle while waiting to land. My heart sank. The petrol gauges were showing almost empty now. Ten minutes later we were still circling and I had to tell George of my worries.

"Be safest to use the transfer cock and feed all engines from the starboard main tank—that's got most in," I said.

"OK, Bill, go ahead."

I held my breath and crossed my fingers (not literally) as I turned over the feed controls to that tank. The engines continued to purr without faltering but even so, I was desperately worried about the petrol. Five more minutes went by and we were still circling.

"I hope these gauges are accurate or else we're in real trouble," I told George. That spurred him into action and he called control to tell them. They insisted we wait and continue circling.

"We can't," I said, "we've no juice!"

George called control again,

"We are short of petrol and we're coming in."

He headed for the downwind leg of the runway watching for other planes landing as we were jumping the queue. I put the undercarriage down and checked the tyres with an Aldis lamp. We couldn't check whether the tail wheel was there or not.

"Bill, cut the throttles," said George. I did so and hung on for a rough landing but all was well and we taxied back to our pan, shut down the engines and all was quiet.

An ambulance whisked away our injured rear gunner for an MO's inspection. (He was later admitted to the RAF hospital in Ely.)

When I emerged from P-Peter the sergeant in charge of the ground crew was standing at the bottom of the ladder.

"All engines OK, chiefy," I told him confidently.

"Wanna bet? Come and have a look."

The side cowlings on both port engines had

been ripped off and the outer one had about eight feet of the flexible alloy air intake branch hanging down. The propeller blade tips on both airscrews were bent.

"Ignore my remark about the engines, chiefy," I said.

The next day as we surveyed P-Peter in daylight the ground crew told us that, on dipping the tanks there had been only thirty-five gallons of petrol left.

I went round to the rear turret. Al had been lucky that it (and he) hadn't been cut off entirely—even the ammunition belts were severed. He and our mid upper gunner had been fortunate in that the nine flak holes in the fuselage were between their positions. The astrodome had been sliced off—another foot or two further forward and I'd have had it—so too would George.

So, what exactly had happened? It seemed that we had collided with two aircraft: the one George saw to port when he had instinctively taken evasive action by shoving the control column forward and sending us into a dive but close enough for the other aircraft to wipe off the astrodome. In diving we had hit another aircraft but how the side cowlings came off remained a mystery.

It was extraordinary that a plane had been directly underneath us. It dawned on us that it could well have been an enemy fighter with upward slanting guns just ready to have a go at us when we fell out of the sky on top of him! We could well have written him off. It was a cheering thought out of such a close run thing.

It was then I thought about my parachute: had the tough Australian, Wing Commander Duigan, been watching over me last night?

A sad duty

ONE day I was down on orders to be Orderly Sergeant. After doing the normal duty around the airmen's mess at lunchtime and teatime bawling out, "Orderly Officer: any complaints?" and following him up and down the hall like a shadow, I had to meet him at the debriefing room at midnight.

By then it had been established which crews had not returned from ops. and were listed as 'missing' We would go to the NCO crew members' huts to clear their lockers, pick up their kitbags and take them to the adjutant's

office for safe keeping. Three crews were missing that night and so we must have cleared about ten lockers; we didn't clear officer crew members' kit.

It was a sad job to do and we packed away several photographs of girlfriends or wives. It was hard not to think of the awful shock that awaited them but you could not let your mind dwell on it, even so...

It was the worst duty I ever had to do in my entire RAF career. I suppose I was just unlucky to be on that duty when ops. were on.

Fireworks

ON a raid to southern Germany we were routed over Beachy Head near Brighton. It was dusk and our bomber stream was just south of London on its night's op. It collided (metaphorically speaking) with Jerry planes going north on their bombing op.

Naturally, our ack-ack guns opened fire on them. However, some of our lads, not knowing of the incoming enemy raid, thought the ack-

ack was aimed at them and immediately fired off the colours of the day. This, of course, gave the game away and Jerry took it up as well. There were Very cartridges being fired all over the place until the sky looked more like a Guy Fawkes' Night firework display than a bombing raid.

Good job they changed the colours every hour.

When Mae West didn't come to the rescue

ON ops. that involved flying over the sea we wore Mae Wests (inflatable life jackets) underneath our webbing parachute harness. Usually, this presented no problem but, as flight engineer, I was constantly having to check my gauges panel and log temperatures and pressures. In addition I had to heave weighty bundles of 'window' (silver foil to jam German radar) from behind the pilot's seat to throw out of the chute in the bomb aimer's compartment at the front of the aircraft. All this while the pilot continually corkscrewed the Lancaster to put a fighter pilot off his aim should our gunners not spot him coming in.

One time, in all this manoeuvring, I accidentally caught the inflating lever on my Mae West. My parachute harness fitted snugly and as, the Mae West began to inflate beneath it, there was nothing to 'give' except my chest!

The obvious answer would have been to release the pressure by deflating the Mae West or undo the parachute harness but there were still three hours before we would land back at base and that included a North Sea crossing.

I was gasping for breath as the Mae West and the parachute harness strangled me. It was a case of being between the devil and the deep blue sea—almost literally. Fighter attacks could happen anytime, anywhere—even over our own base—and so it wasn't advisable to strip off anything which contributed to your survival, even for a few minutes. I wasn't a strong swimmer and, had I deflated the lifejacket, there was no way I could have blown it up again had we ditched in the sea.

All I could do was adopt a stooping posture to ease the pressure. Unfortunately, such a position looked like I was asleep and so I moved from time to time to make sure the rest of the crew knew I was awake!

Medal ribbon

A rumour went around 156 Squadron about the issue of the then 1939-43 Star medal ribbon issued to aircrew who had completed one operation.

An order for a somewhat excessive amount of this ribbon was put in by Stores. Back came the reply,

"The medal ribbon is worn as a 3/8-inch strip above the left breast pocket, not as a scarf."

Arthur Power

DFC

Navigator

83 and 106 Squadrons

Arthur Power's crew prior to an air test before the night's op. on Rozitz, February 1945
Left to right: F/O Ted Brown DFC (Canadian) - pilot; F/Sgt Wally Woodhouse (Rhodesian) - mid
upper gunner; F/Sgt 'The Egg' Eglington - flight engineer; Arthur Power - navigator; F/Lt Dave
Davidson (Canadian) - wireless operator; F/Sgt Frank Watson DFM (Ireland) - bomb aimer;
F/O Fred Lindsay DFC (Jamaican) - rear gunner

Arthur today

Arthur Power

Arthur Power joined the RAF in January 1939 at Padgate, Warrington, and remustered in 1941. He trained in England and Canada before being awarded his navigator's brevet in February 1943. He joined 106 Squadron and later 83 Squadron Pathfinder Force, 5 Group, Bomber Command, flying Lancasters in both squadrons. He flew forty-six operations in all and was awarded the DFC. He was demobbed in April 1946.

In the beginning

I trained as a navigator trained in Canada at Rivers, Manitoba, from October 1942 until February 1943. I joined 106 Squadron based at Metheringham, Lincolnshire, in April 1944. My crew was a remarkable bunch. There was F/O Taylor, our pilot, ex-public school and a Surrey County Cricket Colt; he was known to all and sundry as 'Tolly' and F/O Terry Haycock, our wireless operator from Belfast, was something of a flyweight boxer.

These two had already flown a tour on Hampdens together and came back for a second bash. The rest of us had lost the pilot with whom we had survived OTU and HCU. He had developed mumps or some such malady. We were fortunate to link up with 'Tolly' who had a reputation as a very experienced 'airframe driver', and he was keen to get us—due largely to my 'above average' assessment—or so he said!

There was Sgt F.K. Watson, our bomb aimer, also from Northern Ireland, who claimed to be a Republican, and was known as 'Paddy'; Sgt Eric Hampson was the engineer and a Londoner; Sgt Wally Woodhouse, mid upper gunner, was from Rhodesia and Sgt Fred Lindsay, rear gunner, from Kingston, Jamaica, who described himself as three parts milk and two parts coffee! He was from an old Jamaican family and had left Harvard University to join the RAF. He was over six feet tall—probably the tallest 'arse-end' Charlie in the business.

So, there we were—a sprog crew ready for our first op. For me it was an inauspicious beginning for I returned from my first op. to find I had left my parachute pack at dispersal!

On ops.

ONE or two ops. stick in my mind—in particular, the long haul ones soon after I joined 106 Squadron in April 1944. There was Brunswick on the 22nd—that was six and a half hours. Two days later we 'visited' Munich when we were routed over northern Italy thus approaching the target through the back door as it were. We were airborne for just over ten hours—that was our longest trip.

Then on the night of the 26th there was Schweinfurt—even the name has a nasty ring to it. Flying time there was nine and a quarter hours. We returned one of the few aiming point photographs—a nice picture of the inaccurate marking which made this raid less of a success than it could have been. On the bombing run we were hit by flak which knocked out our starboard outer engine. Luckily, there was no fire and the engineer managed to feather the prop. We came home on three engines. For the first (and last) time I left the navigation compartment to look at the target!

Our next trip was Toulouse on 1 May, then Mailly-le-Camp on 3 May. Mailly was something of a relief as it was a mere hop and a skip after the clobbering we received at Schweinfurt. I was rather surprised to learn later that our photograph was plotted some 1,200 yards from the aiming point—obviously not one of bomb aimer Paddy's best nights!

Pathfinder Force

WE stayed together until Taylor and Haycock finished their tour. By that time Fred Lindsay and myself had been commissioned and found ourselves with Paddy Watson, Wally Woodhouse and Eric Hampson 'volunteering' for the Pathfinder Force. (In fact, we were 'head-hunted' by dear old 'Hamish' Mahaddie—crew selector for the Pathfinder Force.)

We were posted to 83 Squadron, a Pathfinder squadron recently detached from 8 Group to provide, with 97 Squadron, 5 Group's own Marker Force. Based at Coningsby, Lincolnshire, we acquired another pilot, P/O Ted Brown RCAF. We flew twenty-two operations with 83 Squadron from August 1944 to March 1945.

It was during this time that I was involved in the New Year's Eve 'party' over Oslo Fjord with Brown as my skipper leading a small force of marker aircraft from 83 Squadron. Following us were aircraft from 617 Squadron (the Dambusters) to do the actual bombing. One of their aircraft was piloted by Johnnie Fauquier.

We made a low level crossing of the North Sea, climbing to 8,000 feet at the Norwegian Coast. At precisely midnight we were fired on by a ship that we identified later as the *Köln*. It was near the northern end of the fjord and heading south at high speed. We released a string of flares and called up 617 Squadron who were to bomb the ship target. Air-to-air communications were never brilliant in 1944 but the voice that answered, "We're on our way, chaps!" didn't sound a bit like Johnnie Fauquier (unless he had been doing a crash course at Oxbridge between ops!) However, with the target belting along at some 30 knots it was a problem to keep it lit. Brown called in his marker force to back up our flares while we stayed close to the *Köln* which kept up a flak barrage enabling us to maintain a visual contact. At this point one of our marker force was shot down by a Ju88. With 617 still "on our way, chaps" we orbited the area and, as a last resort, as all flares finally burnt out, we fired off every Very cartridge in the place—but still no sign of 617.

Out of flares, Very cartridges and low on fuel we left them to it. Incidentally, during this time we did drop our one and only bomb—a 2,000lb armour piercing bomb. The squadron bombing leader, who came for the ride, claimed a hit on the bow section!

We never heard what happened or why we didn't see 617.

In Alan Cooper's book, *Beyond the dams to the Tirpitz: later operations of 617 Squadron* (London, Goodall, 1991) the author mentions that two cruisers (*Köln* and *Emden*) were in the fjord. I recall being briefed on only one, the *Köln*. I suppose it could be that while we of 83 Squadron were busy marking our target, 617 may have picked up the *Emden*. Or it could be

that, as someone suggested at the time, 617 were "in the wrong bloody fjord"!

Bomber Command Diary for 31 December 1944/1 January 1945 records: *Oslo Fjord. 28 Lancasters of 5 Group attacked cruisers in the fjord, but no direct hits scored. One Lancaster lost.*

I don't see how they get twenty-eight Lancasters. According to Cooper's book Fauquier led twelve from 617 and we (83 Squadron) were less than half squadron strength—I wonder who the other lot were! (Cooper says there were eight from 83 Squadron and eight from 97 Squadron. One bomb was seen to be "a near miss on a large ship" which "swung her 90 degrees to starboard and brought her to a standstill". Cooper says the attack took place between 0003 and 0051.)

Who bombed what and where?

IN 1995 I was in contact with Fritz Lamprecht who, in 1944, was a cadet officer on board the *Köln*. We exchanged correspondence and he sent me information including plans of the ship and her detailed war diaries which give a minute-by-minute account of her activities. In a letter he asked me to excuse his imperfect English which, he said, he had learned at school a long time ago—it seemed pretty good to me. He wrote:

...[at] the same time [31 December 1944] the cruiser Emden *was also deployed on the Oslofjord. Because the two ships were similar it is easy to understand why your bomber crews confused them.*

Reading your report about the raid on 31

December I am not sure you really attacked the Köln. *This night* Köln *was anchoring eastside Island Rauöy (Rauen) between the island and the landcoast. The wardiary of the* Köln *describes exactly the course of the raid. The estimated altitude of the attacking machines = 3000m. (9000 feet). During the whole attack the anti-aircraft-artillery of* Köln *was not in action. No bullet was fired. The captain only tried to evade the bombdroppings, with success, perhaps also with fortune ... My combatstation on* Köln *was the 88mm anti-aircraft-artillery. I stood free on deck and could observe all events.*

So, if the *Köln* didn't fire and wasn't moving, the mystery still remains: who bombed what and where?

John Robinson

AFC and Bar

Pilot

21, 44, 76, 100, 542 Squadrons, 228 OCU

F/Lt John Robinson in the spring of 1969 at Central Flying School, Little Rissington, Gloucestershire

John in 1996 at the Guild of Air Pilots and Air Navigators Trophies and Awards banquet where he received the Master's Commendation for the joint production of a paper entitled The future flight deck

John Robinson

John Robinson joined the RAF in 1952 and gained his pilot's 'Wings' the following year. He spent the next ten years flying Canberras, including A and H bomb trials in Australia and the Pacific, before becoming a flying instructor. He led two formation aerobatic teams, the Red Pelicans and the Poachers, while carrying out his instructional duties which culminated in instructing HRH the Prince of Wales. During his time in the RAF he was decorated with the Air Force Cross and Bar by HM the Queen and retired as a squadron leader at the end of 1974.

The start of it all

I was born in Westcliff-on-Sea, Essex, on 29 March 1934. The outbreak of World War II broke up my primary education as I attended five schools in under two years and finished up at Burnham-on-Crouch. I left secondary education at Maldon Grammar School after the fifth year having taken the School Certificate.

I then joined my father's dairy business but, with National Service looming, I thought flying was a good idea even though I had never been near an aircraft other than the wrecked ones around the farm during the war when I picked up the debris in my donkey cart. I tried to join Fleet Air Arm but was turned down because of hammer toes but I was accepted by the RAF.

I passed the aircrew selection at Hornchurch and much to my father's chagrin joined the RAF on 4 May 1952 reporting first to Cardington for induction. It was then on to No.3 Initial Training School at Cranwell for my first course that started out 160 strong with about fifty-fifty pilots/navigators but in the end only eighty passed out in September 1952.

Pilot training

My pilot training course at 3 Flying Training School at Feltwell, Norfolk, started with thirty, including four Burmese. I was the only car owner on the course—a 1934 Ford 8—that proved to be very useful and popular!

The training aircraft were Percival Prentices and North American Harvard IIs with the hours split 60/127. I managed my first solo after just over eight and a half hours dual.

Memories include the twin canals stretching north-east from Ely that proved useful for not getting lost and orientation for aerobatics; and runway circuits at Methwold, the relief landing ground, proved to be interesting due to the confines and hardness of a concrete runway as compared with the grass at Feltwell.

There was one incident when coming in to land at Feltwell on a solo flight on a Harvard when I bounced and rather than try to sort out the problem on the ground elected to go around again. The rapid power build up on the engine caught me unawares and the wing tip scraped the grass; fortunately, there was no more damage other than to my pride and the subsequent landing was successful.

During the last month of the Korean War fewer pilots were needed and consequently our half of our course were suspended but we graduated with our 'Wings' on 1 July 1953: eight British and three Burmese.

Advanced flying

My advanced flying course was at 209 Advanced Flying School, Weston Zoyland, near Bridgwater in Somerset, from July to December 1953. This was my introduction to what was affectionately known as the Royal Light Somerset Air Force (RLSAF)! We flew the Meteor T7 and F4 and I managed my first solo after five and a half hours dual.

The heating in the T7 was not at all good and a cross-country at 30,000 feet, unpressurised with only rudimentary oxygen systems, was no joke. The standard route was Weston Zoyland - Valley (Isle of Anglesey) - Worksop where the aircraft was refuelled and then a return direct to Weston Zoyland.

Worksop was a sister AFS whose students enjoyed the much more advanced Meteor F8 that was considered the 'dream machine' of Meteors. Low level cross-countries in Meteors were exhilarating, especially when my instructor got it wrong by going across Wincanton racecourse when a race meeting was taking place...

I had my first brush with officialdom during the night-flying phase when I flew east at high level and saw the lights of London. I carried on with the exercise of a high level let-down at Dunkeswell and on return to Weston Zoyland was regaling my fellow students about the flight when a big-eared instructor overheard the crew room conversation.

Apparently I should have not gone east and I had a one-way chat with the Station Commander. I flew my final handling test on 22 December 1953 having flown sixty-seven hours on the course.

The start of operations

My first operational tour was to be on Bomber Command Main Force flying Canberras—then a new aircraft for the Command but before starting at the Canberra Operational Conversion Unit I had to learn about the intracies of GeeH bombing at the Bomber Command Bombing School at Lindholm. At first this was on simulators and then flying in Varsities and Lincolns. (I also learnt about

playing poker in the evenings in the mess.)

In the early part of 1954 I took a Canberra bomber course at 231 OCU at Bassingbourn. The dual-controlled version was just about to enter service but initial flying was done on Meteor T7s. Such was the rush to train that on 1 and 2 March I flew seven sorties!

I was also the guinea pig student for the Canberra T4 as I did one sortie in this before going solo on a B2. I was crewed up with a sergeant navigator who was an ex-WOP/AG. Then followed general handling and navigation exercises and GeeH and visual bombing. On 8 April we dropped thirty-two practice bombs visually in one day which was almost unheard of. I completed the course with sixty-five flying hours in six weeks.

Postings

After training I was immediately posted to 100 Squadron at Wittering. However, I did not fly at all as the squadron was to become part of Bomber Command Development Unit and was to retain its Lincolns as well as the Canberras and I wasn't qualified on Lincolns.

On 26 May I was posted to 44 (Rhodesia) Squadron at Cottesmore, Leicestershire, where the Wing, consisting of 15, 44, 57 and 149 Squadrons, had just arrived from Coningsby having been flying Washingtons; we were now part of 3 Group.

In July the crew was joined by another navigator as the bombing expert. Flying on the squadron was mainly cross-country and bombing, both visual and GeeH, with the altitude gradually increasing to 38,000 ft for visual bombing.

One day when at the Chesil Bank bombing range I opened the bomb doors and increased power to maintain the speed. This action was promptly followed by a double flame-out at 38,000 feet. Fortunately, the Canberra was a good glider... I soon had Boscombe Down lined up but the engines relit at 15,000 feet— the maximum relighting height in those days.

On the move

FEBRUARY 1955 saw the Wing move to Honington so that Cottesmore's runway could be extended for V-force operations. 149 Squadron left the Wing and went to the RAF in Germany while 10 Squadron joined from Scampton; they were not happy about leaving 1 Group for 3 Group.

Several exercises were flown at command, group and station level but the fighters of the day couldn't reach altitudes that Canberras could; it was not unusual to see Meteors, Venoms, even Hunters and Swifts falling out of the sky in their attempts to intercept. When crews achieved their combat category they were entitled to 'Lone Ranger' (overseas experience) flights to Malta and Germany usually at weekends.

I carried out my first flying display on the Battle of Britain Day in 1955 at Little Rissington, Gloucestershire. This was my introduction to the 'field-on-the-hill' with a shorter runway than Bomber Command crews were used to but it went well.

Preparing for A and H bomb tests

In the autumn of 1955 volunteer crews were called for to take part in the A and H bomb trials to be undertaken in Australia and Christmas Island in the Pacific. The requirement was for all-bachelor crews and my crew helped me 'volunteer' for this task. This meant converting my four-year Short Service Commission to a twelve-year Direct Commission; both the posting and my renewed commission came within a day of one another.

In November 1955 I was posted to 76 Squadron, part of Task Force 308/5 forming at Weston Zoyland. Zoyland had now been taken over by Bomber Command and was well away from the normal Bomber Command 'patch'. This, of course, was my second time there and it was great to be back in the Royal Light Somerset Air Force!

The squadron's Canberras were the latest B6 with Avon 109 engines. They had been extensively modified, especially in the air conditioning system where powerful filters were built in. The task was to collect samples from A and H bomb clouds in specially adapted containers fitted over the wing tip tanks. The trials were to take place in the Monte Bellos islands off the west coast of Australia, and at Maralinga in Australia for the A bombs which were really triggers for the H bombs that were to be dropped from Valiants flying out of Christmas Island. It was mooted at one time that 'hot' (radio active contaminated) aircraft would be disposed off by flying them out to sea over the Australian coast then the pilot baling out but this never actually happened.

Navigation aids were very restricted and so a radio compass was installed. However, this equipment had a poor range and so navigators had to rely greatly on sun position lines with periscopic sextants.

Australia

The main part of the squadron left for Australia in February 1956 leaving behind two crews, one of which was mine, to ferry the back-up aircraft.

Eventually my aircraft, WT206, was delivered and I was the only pilot to fly it from May to July. Our work-up training consisted of long-range cross-countries using the limited aids which would be at our disposal Down Under. We also had to operate with primitive runway lighting and trained at night using a single line of gooseneck flares.

On 4 duly 1956, three aircraft, WT206, WT207 and WT208 set off for Australia flying via Idris, Habbaniya, Karachi, Negombo, Changi and Darwin to Pearce in Western Australia. (WT207 later blew up over Derbyshire at 57,000 feet when fitted with double Scorpion rocket motors.)

There were no restrictions on altitudes in those days and the aircraft were cruise-climbed up to 57,000 ft on some legs. At Idris on the first night stop our crews met up with a Hastings crew flying the same route. By the end of the trip they were really fed up with us for when they left in the morning our aircraft were still parked with covers on and, on reaching the destinations, the same aircraft were again on the ground and their crews in the bar!

On arrival at Darwin, WT207 (flown by a Wing Commander and crew from Binbrook) had become unserviceable. As rank had its privileges, he pinched my aircraft leaving me with the heap. Six days later we arrived at Pearce, Western Australia, to become part of Air Task Group Buffalo. Unfortunately, we had only a short time to settle into Western Australia as on 10 August the squadron transferred to Edinburgh Field, South Australia, just north of Adelaide.

The flying was fairly limited but what there was was spent on meterological recce flights over the Australia Bight, landing in outback airfields on practice diversions or carrying VIP passengers.

In mid April I flew to Christmas Island via Amberley and Nandi, Fiji, for Operation Grapple. The last leg was all water for over 2,000 miles and only sunshots for navigation. Rehearsals for the first H bomb test were flown from the beginning of May and I was tasked with flying as VHF radio link relay and target reconnaissance following the explosion. I had to be the first jet aircraft airborne and position mid-way between Christmas Island and the target, Malden Island in the south Pacific.

The take-off with maximum fuel from a 6,000 feet runway and temperature in the region of 32^0C meant that there was not much margin if an engine failed: we would then be shark fodder. The bomb was dropped by a Valiant aircraft of 49 Squadron and exploded about 8,000 feet above sea level. While the explosion took place our orbit was flown in the opposite direction to avoid the flash and its possible after-effects. I then had to fly low level over Malden Island to make an initial survey of the damage incurred.

On one rehearsal all the aircraft returned to find the airfield under a tropical storm and were talked down on ACR 7 radar by an ancient air traffic controller. All the aircraft landed safely but some sustained damage to flaps from the flooded runway. Such was our gratitude that the controller did not pay for a single drink in the bar that night! (It didn't cost us much though as gin was only twopence a shot, but the tonic was very pricey!)

More H Bomb tests

On 15 May 1957 the first British H bomb was tested. Following this I made two trips taking VIPs to Honolulu, our main diversion some 1,200 miles to the north.

Another task was to ferry an aircraft with fuel gauge problems that could only be fixed back in Australia. I flew via Canton Island to Nandi and 100 miles out encountered problems with the starboard engine which had to be shut down. I then had to carry out a single engine let-down on NDB (non-directional beacon) and landed in unpleasant weather. I handed the aircraft over to a relief crew from Australia and toured Fiji for a few days including a visit to the RNZAF Sunderland base at Lathala Bay. I later got a lift back from Nausori to Nandi in a RNZAF Bristol Freighter.

It was then back to Christmas Island in a Hastings loaded completely with booze but as I had a touch of Asian 'flu I couldn't enjoy it. There was a second test but I didn't take part in this: I was purely a spectator. The third and last H bomb for Operation Grapple was tested on 19 June and at the beginning of July the squadron returned to Australia. However, I was to spend another five days in Fiji with an unserviceable aircraft. Once back at Edinburgh Field I managed to visit New Zealand for the first time with a trip to Ohakea in mid July while preparing for Operation Antler, another

A bomb trial at Maralinga. We were now joined by Varsity aircraft for surveying and Aborigine searches and so I flew quite often as co-pilot when based at Maralinga.

It was while I was here that I saw the first Sputnik—the Russian artificial satellite.

Return to the UK

I flew through three more atomic clouds before the trial was completed in October 1957 and my tour with 76 Squadron came to an end. I returned to the UK as a co-pilot on a Varsity—twelve days via Alice Springs, Darwin, Biak, Zamboanga, Labuan, Changi, Mingaladon, Calcutta, Karachi, Bahrein, Habbaniya, Nicosia, El Adem, Idris, Istres and Tangmere to Hemswell.

On the leg from Karachi to Bahrein nearly all the crew had dropped off to sleep and I woke up to find the sun in a strange position relative to where it should have been. The navigator had a very rude awakening and we soon found out that the compass had become desynchronised and turned the auto-pilot through 90⁰ sending us towards the South Pole!

Following a month's leave in November I reported to the Bomber Command Holding Unit at Coningsby and in January 1958 was posted to 542 Squadron at Hemswell. This was a sister squadron to 76 but tasked with background sampling for nuclear fallout. This entailed flying the Squadron's Canberra B2s as high as 47,000 feet.

In April 1958 Val and I were married and settled down in married quarters at Hemswell but in July the squadron moved to Upwood. During August and September I carried out airtests and ferried a Canberra B6 for our C Flight which was on detachment in Australia. Middle East problems caused different routing to Australia this time: Luqa, Kano, Eastleigh, Khormaksar, Karachi then normal route to Laverton, Melbourne. On return we had to divert to Wyton from Upwood due to weather. At the end of October the Squadron was

renumbered 21 but three months later was disbanded. I was then posted as a co-pilot on V-force but with the squadron commander's blessing turned this down. Bomber Command then felt that it had had enough of me and I was posted to Fighter Command. I was not destined to fly the shiny new fighters of the day but Canberras.

New posting

I arrived at Leeming in North Yorkshire, which was the home of 228 OCU, a night fighter training unit, to find several Valetta T4s which had been adapted as navigator-radar trainers with airborne interception radar in a modified nose, and only one Canberra—a T4. Previous nav/rad training had been carried out on the Brigand. The Valetta was purely an interim measure until enough Canberra B2s could be modified as T11s with extended noses to house the Airborne Interceptor radar and navigators' compartment to accommodate the instructor and student.

As I was the most experienced Canberra pilot on the unit, the others being ex-night fighters, I had to conduct all the acceptance airtests for the new T11s and at same time be refamiliarised with Meteors as the unit had stripped-down versions of the NF14 for use as target aircraft.

I was also made the unofficial training pilot on the Canberra T4 for instrument flying practice for other unit pilots and the station commander. This proved to be the beginning of the rest of my flying and on 28 March 1960 I was made an Instrument Rating Examiner by the Central Flying School.

To Germany

One day in May 1961 I picked up the phone in the crew room and found it was a crossed line. Wing Commander Advanced Wing, O.C. Javelins, was talking to Personnel Staff at HQ Fighter Command who wanted to post a simulator instructor, who was not even qualified on Canberras, to RAF Germany as

John Robinson

Command Instrument Rating Examiner (CIRE). I hot-footed it round to his office and diplomatically mentioned that I understood that there was such a posting in the offing and I was due for one. I also suggested that as I was already an IRE on type I would fit the bill.

One telephone call and the question: could I be in Germany in three weeks? Could I?! My last flight at Leeming was on 1 June. I arrived at Wildenrath on the border with Holland on 15 June and made my first flight there five days later.

My official appointment was as RAF Germany's Canberra CIRE, answerable to HQ but to be based at Wildenrath. The units there were 17 Squadron flying Canberra PR7s in the role of low level reconnaissance day and night; 88 Squadron flying Canberra B(I)8s, with the main role of nuclear bomb attack and secondary interdictor with four 20mm gun pack and shallow dive bombing, and RAF Germany Communications Squadron with a VIP Valetta, Pembrokes, Devons and a Meteor T7 and NF14.

Kuwait

Within fifteen days of arrival I was invited to join 88 Squadron for the first Kuwait war as I had considerably more Canberra experience than most of their pilots, although not in the interdictor role. Half the squadron was deployed to Bahrein with remainder at Akrotiri. I made my way to Akrotiri by Beverley to Lyneham, then Britannia to do an instant conversion to the B(I)8.

First it was shallow dive bombing at Episcopi Bay. The first attack resulted in the bomb carrier being released and the two 25lb bombs colliding and exploding immediately under the wing—not very funny, especially as we were in a dive towards water at about 400 feet.

On the next sortie there were no problems as eight bombs were successfully dropped. However, on my first formation shallow dive bomb attack a bomb was accidently released into the middle of Episcopi village due to confusion of radio transmit and bomb release switches; my previous Canberras had their transmit buttons where the B(I)8 had its bomb release button.

The next day I was introduced to air-to-ground gunnery. The engineering chief said that normally only two guns at a time were armed for practice firing but he wanted to check out the gun pack on this aircraft so all four would be armed. When I first fired the guns I thought the whole aircraft was going to disintegrate and the range safety officer at Larnaca accused me of deliberately blowing his target to smithereens!

By 19 July I was declared fully operational by both day and night and informed that my planned target was the main post office in Baghdad.

By the third week in July the Iraqis had heard about me and withdrawn their threat. I returned to Wildenrath having had a few days R & R on the Cyprus beaches.

New duties

I settled into my office in Flying Wing HQ and was given tasks of Station Flight Safety Officer and Unit Test Pilot which was a chance to get my hands on all the aircraft on the station. These included the Army Air Corps Beavers also based at Wildenrath.

Some of the out-of-the ordinary tasks I had were trouble-shooting a Canberra B(I)8 which persistently side-slipped on LABS (Low Altitude Bombing System) bombing and this was solved by a trip to the British Aircraft Corporation at Warton where I was told *not* to watch the fix. I obeyed but heard a loud bang—it sounded like a sledge hammer hitting the top of the rudder! It did the trick though!

I assisted 17 Squadron with their work up on the NATO Exercise Royal Flush which was all low level at night. One night we flew to

Otterburn, Vlieland and Nordhorn ranges taking three hours and all of it below 500 feet in poor weather. We returned to base to discover all the other crews had been recalled due to the bad weather.

I spent a considerable time at Gutesloh checking out 20 Squadron Hunter pilots on the Meteor for towing duties and had the privilege of collecting two brand new Meteor F8s from Maintence Unit at Kemble for use as target towers.

Another duty was standing in for OC Flying at Gatow, Berlin. I was checked out again on Chipmunks for flights round East Germany but not East Berlin—it was most unnerving watching tank gun turrets follow one round the sky.

Instructing again

I finished my tour at Wildenrath in January 1964 when Central Flying School caught up with me and I was sent to the Qualified Instructors' course. This was carried out on Jet Provost T3s and T4s at Little Rissington, Gloucestershire. It was not a happy course due to personality clashes but I succeeded and at the beginning of July 1964 was posted to 7 FTS at Church Fenton as a B2 Qualified Flying Instructor (QFI).

In the first month I flew nearly fifty hours, almost all of it instructing. I was upgraded to B1 then recategorised to A2; I renewed my IRE authority in June 1965 and became a flight commander in November 1965.

We had our fair share of problem students among these were several Jordanians and an Air Chief Marshal's son. However, he thanked me for getting his son through the course by way of a Comet route trip to Singapore. There were, however, some good students and one of mine eventually became CO of The Queen's Flight.

In November 1966 7 FTS was closed and I was posted as a staff QFI to the Central Flying School at Little Rissington.

Aerobatics and the Red Pelicans

AT Little Rissington I was immediately introduced to formation aerobatics, reacquainted with the Varsity and checked out as captain. In August 1967 I gained my A1 QFI category and was asked to join Examining Wing as a 'trapper' (pilots' term for an examiner) but declined as I wanted to have a season of formation aerobatics with the Red Pelicans. However I did make several visits with Examining Wing to various flying training schools. In October 1967 I was detached for a week to the CFS helicopter station at Tern Hill, Shropshire, and got checked out on the Sioux T1. I have one-and-a-half hours solo on helicopters to my credit!

February 1968 saw the start of training for the Red Pelicans and I was given the No. 2 position. By the end of the month we had had an accident; a mid-air collision between the Leader and No 4. However, we were allowed to continue and flew a summer season of displays around the UK.

When I returned to base from two Battle of Britain displays that I received the news that my father had died.

The Red Pelicans were re-formed in January 1969 and I was appointed Leader for the year. June saw a visit of HM the Queen, Prince Philip, the Queen Mother and Prince Charles for a presentation of the CFS Colours. The Red Pelicans had to operate out of Kemble for their display in front of Their Majesties. Unfortunately, they were late returning from lunch which meant we were desperately short of fuel before we had finished.

In September I introduced the Jet Provost T5 into Training Command and the trials and early conversions took up considerable time. However, it did not stop the highlight of the Red Pelicans' season as we visited Munich in the October and the Oktoberfest. As well as flying with the Red Pelicans I was checked out on the Gnat and flew my first supersonic flight. I also undertook the evaluation of BAC Strikemaster, an upgraded version of the Jet Provost, and the Macchi 326G.

I was tasked with forming Training Flight to standardise the staff QFIs at CFS, no mean task when one is dealing with all A Category instructors. I also housed a rehabilitation unit for aircrew who had had psychological problems with flying and in this we had a 50 per cent success rate.

During this tour I was averaging around fifty hours flying a month mainly on standardisation flying but other tasks included air-to-air photography. One memorable trip was flying the late Arthur Gibson to take photos of Ray Hannah, of Red Arrows fame, in a Spitfire he was privately flying. All went well until it came to flying a formation loop when the power of the Spitfire left the Jet Provost alone in the sky!

While carrying out an air test on a Jet Provost T5 in May 1970 the engine flamed out during a high level manoeuvre. Once again I was flying a 'jet glider'. I put out a Mayday call on the Little Rissington frequency and was told to 'Standby'—not exactly what I wanted to hear but my attempt to re-light the engine was successful.

It was around this time that the RAF was looking for a replacement for the Gnat as an advanced trainer. In anticipation that the British Aircraft Corporation would win the contract with its P69 I was interviewed to join as project pilot. However, Hawker Siddeley with its Hawk won the contract and there was no position for me but I did take the opportunity to get my civil Commercial Pilot's Licence which I would have needed had I been appointed.

I was then shortlisted to join the Red Arrows but Bill Loverseed, of Farnborough Caribou fame, got his medical back and was selected.

Red Pelicans fly past Blackpool Tower in June 1969. Photo: British Aircraft Corporation

The Prince and the Poachers

IN August 1970 I was promoted to acting Squadron Leader and posted to the RAF College at Cranwell as OC Headquarters Squadron with responsibilities for the flying standards of all the staff and students, the Ground School, the College Air Staff Instructions and the Unit Flying Order Book and as Leader of the Poachers Aerobatic Team. In the December the Golden Eagle project to train HRH the Prince of Wales was being launched and I was tasked as the deputy QFI. I undertook the conversion training of the primary QFI, Dick Johns, who is now the Chief of Air Staff.

We had two Jet Provost T5s, specially built at Warton that each night were locked under guard in a hangar. We also had our own ground crew.

There was no such thing as 'ground tested and found serviceable' as any item that was put unserviceable in the Aircraft Technical Log had to be investigated and cleared.

On the acceptance air tests for the aircraft I had to flame out the engines, allow them to cold soak for a period and then relight them. I chose my days and position carefully for this. The work-up on the two aircraft, XW322 and 323, involved some 200 hours flying each. We also had to check out a navigator who would 'ghost' HRH on certain solo flights.

I first flew with HRH on 29 April 1971 and took my turn throughout his training which covered all aspects from the standard student pilot syllabus. HRH graduated on 20 August 1971.

John with HRH the Prince of Wales who learned to fly at the RAF College, Cranwell, 1971-2.
Photo reproduced by kind permission of the AOC and Commandant, RAF College, Cranwell.

We carried out several displays in Germany. One time No.2 aircraft went badly unserviceable at Cologne and required an overnight flight by two of the team to bring out spare parts. We always carried our ground crew with us and they had the aircraft repaired for the display on the next day.

Another time we did a tour of Germany taking in Gutesloh and Leipheim (with an exchange of flying in their G91s and much southern Germany low level flying by Training Command aircraft). Then it was on to Bremgarten where we met up with the Red Arrows and Patrouille de France. We retraced our steps to Munich for a visit to the Oktoberfest but got caught by fog in north Germany on the return to Cranwell. Eventually, we found Pferdsfeld was within range of Cranwell and so we refuelled there. All went well until crossing into the UK when we found that Cranwell had 'clamped' due to low cloud and fog and had to divert to Coltishall, Norfolk. We visited Lugano in Switzerland for the British week. Lugano has a very short runway and is surrounded by hills;

we flew out via Wildenrath and Zurich but three aircraft had to divert to Milan due bad weather. Eventually, all the aircraft arrived and we flew five displays in three days. We finished with a fly past of all the British aircraft at the show: a Harrier, HS125 and six Jet Provosts.

In September 1973 we flew the tightest show ever at Hopsten, Germany, where we were up against Phantoms and F104s making lots of noise and flying with apparently no restrictions; we managed our full display of loops and rolls inside a 2,200 feet cloudbase.

Other features of Cranwell flying were formations for each graduation in their course numbers. The trickiest was the '100'—getting the two zeros symmetrical was extremely difficult. I always chose to be 'whip' which involved getting the various aircraft to move into the right positions to create a neat number. The College Commandant, an Air Vice Marshal, would often ask to accompany me and I recall him taking control once when we were clear of the formation over the North Airfield and flying so low that it appeared to me we had passed between the rugby posts!

Final years

IN October 1972 HRH the Prince of Wales returned for refresher flying and this was to be my sole task. I had a one-way chat with the AOC-in-C on what was required and what I was *not* to do. The aircraft were brought out of storage and HRH's flying went well.

Alongside all this activity I was still carrying on with the duties for which I had been posted such as normal standards flying of checks and tests. At the end of my two years' tour in November 1972 I was posted supernumary Squadron Leader as Poacher Leader which allowed me the extra year with the team.

In the Queen's Birthday Honours List for 1973 I was awarded a Bar to my AFC.

At the beginning of 1974 Dominies/HSI25-2s arrived from the College of Air Warfare at Manby, Lincolnshire, and I flew one to

Gibraltar via St Mawgan and Porto returning via Istres. In June 1974 I volunteered for early retirement following a review of my future prospects by Air Secretary's Branch at Ministry of Defence. I then had to study seriously to convert my Commercial Pilot's Licence to an Airline Transport Pilot's Licence.

Soon after escorting the C-in-C of the Yugoslav Air Force at the Farnborough 1974 Airshow I met the Commandant of the Civil Aviation Flying Unit. He wanted me to join the Unit but there was then no vacancy. However, he found me an interim job as an Operations Officer at Civil Aviation Authority HQ Shellmex House. On 31 December 1974 I retired from the RAF and was dined out in College Hall at Cranwell almost completing a full circle. I had flown over 6,800 hours.

George Smith

Navigator

357 Squadron

China Bay, Ceylon, August 1945 after last and longest operation: twenty-two and a half hours in a B-24 Liberator.
Left to right: *Walt McDougald (air gunner); Les Powell (wireless operator/air gunner); Jack Stott (air gunner); Harry Smith (wireless operator/air gunner); Jack Tate (bomb aimer); Geoff Smith (captain); Ray Taylor (second pilot); George Smith (navigator)*

Sometime in the mid 1970s at Duxford with Liberator flown in from India (now at Cosford).
Left to right: *Reunion of Walt, Les, George and Geoff*

George Smith

George Smith was accepted for aircrew in July 1941 and trained as a navigator. He flew Wellingtons at 14 OTU and Stirlings at 1651 HCU in 1943. In 1944 he was posted to South East Asia Command as Liberator reinforcement and was with the air arm of 357 (Special Duties) Squadron, Special Operations Executive (SOE).

Just one of those days...

SOME dates stick in your memory, don't they? The 24 and 25 June 1943 stick in mine. I was at 1651 HCU at Waterbeach flying Stirlings. The 24th had begun innocuously enough—in fact, the whole day had been innocuous. It wasn't until the day was nearly over that it happened.

We'd been on a routine flight and were coming into land. It was dark and, my skipper said later, he could have sworn the runway just didn't seem as long as it had been when he'd taken off. Yes, you've guessed it—we ran out of runway, or, as we prefer to say: the aircraft overshot. That in itself might not have been too bad except there was this steamroller... The aircraft was a write-off... not sure about the roller.

We consoled ourselves by saying it could have happened to anyone but the powers-that-be didn't seem to see it that way. Oh well, we reckoned it would all blow over in a day or two.

The next day we'd been doing circuits and bumps for two hours—piece of cake. We were coming into land at Tempsford when there was a sickening bang and a tyre burst. Normally, we'd have coped with that but why did some idiot have to park a Halifax right in the way...

Score for two nights' flying: one aircraft written-off, two aircraft severely damaged and one steamroller—doubtful.

It was one of those times when it was questioned, in no uncertain terms, whether we really were an asset to the RAF.

However, things looked up for George and he was ultimately engaged on dangerous and secret work in the Far East...

Cloak and dagger stuff

AFTER the cessation of operations I was made to sign the Official Secrets Act in view of my work with 357 (SD) Squadron which had been concerned with dropping and supplying agents in India and Ceylon and flying operations to Burma, French-Indo-China, Thailand, Malaya and Singapore.

It had all been very secret and we were given to understand that we were bound by this Act for thirty years. We took this very seriously but there has never been any notification of release from this. The thirty years have long since come and gone and much has been published since so that there seems little likelihood of my ending up in the Tower of London if I tell of my part in it all. Anyway, it's seldom that anyone wants to know what went on 7,000 miles away fifty years ago!

357 Squadron, which consisted of three Flights of Lysanders, Dakotas and Liberators, was mainly engaged in dropping and supplying agents to Force 136 and Z Force in Japanese occupied territory. The Lysanders did the nearest drops and actually landed behind enemy lines. Medium distances were covered by the Dakotas and the Liberators did the long operations of up to twenty-four hours.

The crew with which I was navigator flew twenty-eight ops. lasting from nine to twenty-two hours but the longest ever was just over twenty-four hours flown from Ceylon by another crew. This endurance was achieved by stripping the aircraft of armour plate, cutting down on ammunition, removing the ventral ball turret and reducing the number of guns from ten to six. Three of the four bomb bays were fitted with extra tanks giving about 1,000 gallons of extra fuel. This grossly overloaded the aircraft so that it was virtually a flying petrol tank and made take-off a time of no little anxiety.

My longest op. was the last one and was twenty-two and a half hours duration. The route was China Bay, Ceylon, to the Nicobar Islands (Pygmalion Point), then to Diamond Point, Sumatra, and south down the Straits of Malacca to Roepat Island. Here we turned east into Jason Bay, north of Singapore, where we dropped the agents. (As it turned out, they were 'made redundant' as the atomic bombs were dropped a couple of weeks later.) Initially, we flew from Jessore and Cox's Bazaar in India but in the last few months were moved to China Bay to avoid the worst of the monsoon which made flying a bit unpleasant.

Eric Stone

DFC

Pilot

220 Squadron

Eric Stone (right) flying training Tiger Moths in 1938-9...

...and flying a desk in 1947 after leaving the RAF

Eric Stone

Eric Stone joined the RAF Volunteer Reserve in 1938 as a trainee pilot at Southampton. He was twenty years old. After Elementary Flying Training School he was posted to Little Rissington in Gloucestershire. Here he gained his 'Wings' on Avro Ansons and became a fully qualified sergeant pilot before being posted to 220 Squadron, Coastal Command, Thornaby, Yorkshire, flying Ansons then Hudsons. He applied for and was granted a permanent commission in the RAF with a substantive rank of Flight Lieutenant. However, he declined this for family reasons and left the RAF in 1946. Eric is now eighty years old but still attends the annual reunion of 220 Squadron with his wife. Most of what Eric writes is from memory as his two pilot log books, together with other memorabilia, were stolen soon after he left the RAF.

Volunteering—and afterwards

WHEN I joined the RAF Volunteer Reserve I lived at Eastleigh, five miles from Southampton. I attended lectures three nights a week and was paid half-a-crown an hour for this. We flew Tiger Moths once a month during Air Service Training at Hamble on The Solent and for this I earned five shillings an hour. After call-up I continued at Marshalls flying field at Cambridge, again on Tiger Moths.

Eventually, I was posted to 220 Squadron, Coastal Command, at Thornaby, Yorkshire, which flew Ansons. If I remember correctly I think my NCO number was 754615. Soon after my joining, the squadron converted to Hudsons and I was sent to Silloth, Cumberland, for a conversion course. On my return I was second pilot on a Hudson crew of four (two pilots and two wireless/air gunners)—the second pilot acted as navigator. From Thornaby we carried out low level recces up the Kattegat off Sweden and convoy escorts in the North Sea.

In 1940 the squadron moved to Wick, Caithness, in northern Scotland. Our duties were almost all recces off the Norwegian coast, low level shipping strikes and attacks on coastal aerodromes and factory installations.

These recces usually consisted of two Hudsons; on reaching the coast one aircraft would go north and the other south. All our missions were about 500 feet or lower to avoid detection. Enemy aircraft were Ju88, Me109 and Me110s. We evaded them by hiding in the clouds, for a solitary Hudson was no match for them.

It was our job to send back information about shipping numbers, course, position and so on. The squadron would then send an attacking strike force later in the day or early evening. We carried four 250lb SAP (Semi Armour Piercing) bombs with twenty-second delay action bombs.

Our losses were heavy—as you might expect.

Shipping attacks

VERY soon I was promoted and had my own crew. We carried out many shipping attacks. One time we flew really low. There was a bang. The aircraft shuddered but continued. It wasn't until we got back to base that one of the ground crew said,

"What the hell's this?" He pointed to what looked like part of a ship's mast sticking out of the aircraft. I looked and said,

"So that's what that bang was! I did wonder!"

"You must have been pretty well on the deck."

"We were."

On another occasion six Hudsons attacked ships at Aalesund in Norway at night.

We sank seven ships and bombed fish oil factories—the smell must have been pretty overpowering!

(An official account of the incident is given in Eric Stone's DFC citation below.)

```
                 ROYAL AIR FORCE AWARD

   The King has approved the following award in recognition of gallantry
   and devotion to duty in the execution of air operations against the
   enemy:-
   Distinguished Flying Cross. - Flight-Lieut. Eric Arthur Stone
   (130928) R.A.F.V.R., No.220 Squadron. Flight-Lieut. Stone has an
   excellent operational record. He has completed two tours of duty and
   has taken part in large numbers of anti-shipping, anti-submarine,
   convoy escort and air/sea rescue sorties. On two occasions, he has
   participated in attacks on [an] oil factory at Bergso in Norway and,
   during anti-shipping operations off the Norwegian coast he bombed two
   ships, obtaining hits on both. On one of these attacks, which was
   completed at mast height, the wing of his Hudson aircraft hit the
   mast. Flight-Lieut. Stone skilfully flew the aircraft back to base
   where he made a safe landing. On long-range anti-shipping duties,
   this officer has displayed the utmost endurance and skill.
```

A close-run thing

THE squadron sent a detachment of four aircraft to St. Eval, Cornwall, that were employed on cross-patrols over Brest watching the *Scharnhorst* and *Gneisenau*. Sometimes aircraft were damaged by anti-aircraft fire and had to be flown back to Wick. My crew and I were flying one of these when both engines packed up over Cardigan Bay, Wales. Somehow we just made the cliff tops and force-landed amongst the gorse bushes.

"Come on! Get out! Quick!" I shouted to the others, knowing how quickly the Hudson could catch fire. We were out of the aircraft and running like hares to put as much distance between ourselves and the aircraft that we thought was about to catch fire at any moment.

Suddenly we realised someone was missing.

"Hang on a mo! There's only three of us!" I had visions of one of the crew being trapped in the blazing aircraft. I glanced back to see our WOP/AG, F/Sgt Richardson, who already had the DFM, standing on the wing with a small fire extinguisher heroically pumping little squirts on a smoking engine.

"You hoping for another gong?" I called, relieved that he was OK and yet anxious in case the plane blew up, but the smoke subsided and the danger was over.

Flying Fortresses

OUR stay at Wick ended when 220 Squadron was scheduled to do long distance escorts in the Atlantic. I and another pilot were sent to Polebrook, a Bomber Command station, to convert to four-engined B-17C—the forerunner of the American B-17E—the Flying Fortress. The B-17Cs were supplied through American Lease-Lend Scheme but proved inadequate for Bomber Command. We took over these aircraft and 220 moved to Aldergrove, Northern Ireland. Here we converted other pilots and re-crewed nine in a crew, losing our old well-regarded Hudsons. The squadron was relieved of operations for the time being in order to convert properly to new duties.

The Americans, meantime, had developed the Flying Fortress and wished to let Britain have some on Lease-Lend. The Fortress had power-operated gun turrets front, rear and below, as well as free side guns. It was decided to send an operationally experienced crew to America to test this aircraft and my crew, augmented by F/Lt Edser, a flight commander on 220, were chosen to go. This was in early 1942, just after Pearl Harbor. We were, therefore, some of the very first RAF people to go to the USA in uniform.

We left Liverpool on a 9,000 ton cargo ship called SS *Strategist* in a 4-6 knot convoy via Iceland and Greenland. The other 'passengers' were four Merchant Navy captains going over to crew Liberty ships. The voyage seemed endless (it was actually about three and a half weeks) and I was scared stiff of being at sea!

We landed at Halifax, Nova Scotia. It was fantastic to see all the lights after the black-out back home. We went to Washington DC and after a week were sent on a train called the *Orange Blossom Special* to an American OTU at Sebring in Florida. It think it took two days and two nights. Whilst at Sebring we were divided amongst trainee crews to pass on our experiences. Our stay lasted about three months and we then flew a Fortress back to England via Montreal and Gander, Newfoundland, before landing at Prestwick, Scotland. To the best of my knowledge this was the first Flying Fortress to come to Britain. The flight took about eleven hours.

I rejoined 220 Squadron which then moved to Ballykelly and was gradually equipped with 'Forts'. However, America's entry into the war and the success of the Lancaster bomber prevented many other Coastal Command squadrons being equipped with 'Forts' but I think about two squadrons were using them eventually. The 'Fort' was a superb aircraft and I fell in love with it.

Dangerous game

ONE night I was lucky(?) to be first on 'the scene' during an op. and for a moment it didn't dawn on me just where we were or what we had got ourselves into. Then the penny dropped.

"Recognise those aircraft?" I asked the crew.

"Ju88s?" came the doubting reply.

"Can't be…"

"They are!"

This called for some quick thinking.

"Pretend we're one of them!" I said.

"What!"

"We'll fly circuits with them. Switch on all navigation lights!" This we did and joined in their circuit. So good was our deception that we were even give a green light! Then we played our joker. We dropped our bombs from about fifty feet and beat a hasty retreat. Not a shot was fired at us!

The crews who followed us weren't so lucky—our bluff had been called but we had got away with it. Fortunately, though, there were no losses. You can imagine what I was called in the sergeants' mess afterwards!

Wales—and whales

I was promoted to Warrant Officer and, after much persuasion, took a commission going straight to the rank of Flying Officer. It was shortly after this that 220 Squadron moved to Benbecula in the Outer Hebrides. Here our worst enemy was the weather which could be horrendous. Several times we had to land in Iceland as we could not make base. We continued our long distance flights—all of them 1,000 feet or below and most averaged ten hours or so.

The squadron was on the move again and left Benbecula a short time after I was awarded the DFC and the Air Efficiency Award. We went to St. David's in Wales where we flew Liberators as well as 'Forts'. The Liberators had Leigh searchlights on the wings. At St. David's we practised low level, depth charge attacks at night with the Navy using radar—a bit hair-raising at 100 feet above the sea! We must have

been OK as 220 Squadron was sent operational on twelve-hour, all-night, anti-submarine Leigh light patrols from Lagens in the Azores and Gibraltar. At first, these night attacks provided us with a surprise.

"What the hell's that down there?" asked the radar operator.

"Looks pretty big."

"A sub already?" My heart came into my mouth. Was the radar to be believed? After the same thing had happened a time or two we realised that our 'submarines' were, in fact, whales! I reckon many a whale got a sleepless night after we picked it up on radar thinking it was a German sub!

When we spotted something (not a whale!) the radar operator had to be spot on because switching on the light gave us away and, if we did not see the sub first, he undoubtedly saw us!

Back home

ON our return to England the Liberators were converted to carry thirty-two passengers. The squadron was were based at Waterbeach, Cambridgeshire, and we used to fly from there to Karachi (now in Pakistan). Karachi was a collecting point for some Far

East personnel and we used to pick up service people and civil servants coming home on leave or retirement. We used to go via Castelbenito, Tripoli, Lydda in Palestine and Shaibar, Persia, about every three weeks each trip lasting about ten days.

Bob Taylor

DSM

Telegraphist air gunner

818 and 849 Squadrons (Fleet Air Arm)

Bob Taylor during his training in 1941

Bob at Yeovilton in 1997 with Royal Navy
Historic Flight's Fairey Swordfish

Bob Taylor

Alfred Newton Taylor (better known as 'Bob') was born on 13 March 1923 in Easingwold, North Yorkshire, and joined the Fleet Air Arm branch of the Royal Navy in August 1941. After training as a telegraphist/air gunner he served in 818 Squadron equipped with Fairey Swordfish until September 1944 and, thereafter, with 849 Squadron equipped with Grumman Avengers. 818 Squadron was based on the aircraft carrier HMS Unicorn and for a short time in 1944 on the escort carrier, HMS Atheling. 849 Squadron was based on the aircraft carrier HMS Victorious which, from November 1944, became part of the British Pacific Fleet. Bob was demobilised in December 1945 and released from Naval Service in February 1946. He was awarded the 1939-45 Star, the War Medal (1939-45), Atlantic Star, Burma Star with Pacific Clasp and the Defence Medal. His Distinguished Service Medal (1 May 1945) was awarded for action in the Palembang (Sumatra) air strikes.

Currently Bob is a member of the Telegraphist Air Gunners Association; HMS Victorious (1941-5) Reunion Association; Aircrew Association; the Royal Navy Historic Flight Support Group (incorporating the Swordfish Heritage Trust) and Goldfish Club. (He 'ditched' off the west coast of Sumatra in the Indian Ocean after attacking a Japanese-held oil refinery at Palembang on the east coast of the island. Because of damage to his aircraft two attempted landings on Victorious were aborted and during the third landing circuit the aircraft ran out of fuel. His ditching, therefore, was not of the conventional 'tail down' variety but more of an ignominious flop into the water! He and his crew were rescued by a destroyer, HMS Whelp.)

Diary of an naval airman

As a teenager I joined the Home Guard and served with the 6th North Riding of Yorkshire Battalion from June 1940 to August 1941.

Living in that part of Yorkshire and whilst on Home Guard duties I often saw battle-damaged Whitley bombers limping back to their airfields after raids in Europe. This did not diminish my keenness to fly but I hoped to do so in a wider geographical theatre. Combining flying and being a sailor as well seemed a good idea so...

1941

March: Volunteered for air crew duties in the Royal Navy, Fleet Air Arm Branch.

13 August: Entered service as Naval Airman 2nd Class at HMS *Royal Arthur* (formerly Butlin's holiday camp, Skegness) for a month's initial induction and basic naval training.

Much emphasis was placed on knots—the rope sort, not speed—it turned out that I never tied another knot in my entire Fleet Air Arm career!

We also had to learn to row a ship's whaler—a clinker-built, general purpose boat which, at *Royal Arthur* was secured by four hawsers, one to each corner of the children's paddling pool!! The oars had one-inch holes bored in them and rowing nowhere equipped with these did prompt the question, "What on earth have I let myself in for?"

18 September: Commenced two-months' training (31 Course) as Telegraphist Air Gunner (the Navy equivalent of the RAF's WOP/AG) at HMS *St. Vincent,* Gosport.

15 November: Initial air experience and commenced in-flight training as a Telegraphist air gunner at HMS *Kestrel,* Worthy Down, near Winchester.

Bob Taylor

1942

14 August: Commenced gunnery course at HMS *Curlew*, St Merryn, Cornwall.
28 August: Start of operational training at HMS *Landrail*, Machrihanish, Scotland
18 October: At HMS *Daedalus*, Lee-on-Solent, Hampshire, joined 818 Squadron equipped with Fairey Swordfish, initially for operational training at naval air stations in Scotland and Northern Ireland.

1943

23 March: With 818 Squadron joined the newly commissioned aircraft carrier, HMS *Unicorn* which was then engaged, primarily, on convoy protection duties in the Atlantic, Mediterranean and Indian Oceans with the squadron flying anti-submarine patrols.
September: As part of Force V *Unicorn* involved in Operation Avalanche—the landings at Salerno, Italy.

1944

During the first seven months of 1944 HMS *Unicorn* was based in Ceylon (Sri Lanka). 818 Squadron flew from the ship and also from shore bases on that island.
23 August: 818 Squadron embarked on the escort carrier HMS *Atheling* in Ceylon, to provide anti-submarine patrols for a return convoy to South Africa.
11 October: Left 818 Squadron and, with 818 crew, undertook a conversion course from Fairey Swordfish to Grumman Avengers with 756 Squadron at HMS *Ukussa,* Katakurunda, Ceylon. (These American purpose-built carrier aircraft represented to us, a considerable transition from the old Swordfish. They were sturdy, reliable, comfortable and proved later that they could absorb a lot of punishment and still remain in the air.)
19 December: Joined 849 Squadron and embarked on HMS *Victorious* which had become part of the British Pacific Fleet; this later became known in US parlance as 'Task Force 57'.

1945

January to June 849 Squadron was involved from *Victorious* in the following operations: Operation Meridian (January) air strikes against enemy oil refineries at Palembang, Sumatra (Indian Ocean) and Operations Iceberg 1 and 2 (March to May) air strikes against enemy airfields in the Sakashima Gunto island group (Pacific) in support of the invasion of Okinawa by US forces, and Operation Iceberg Oolong: air strikes against airfields and docks on Formosa—now Taiwan.

From time to time in the Pacific we were subjected to the much-publicised kamikaze raids. The thick armour plating on British fleet carrier flight decks provided much greater protection against these attacks than the US counterparts fitted with wooden flight decks. For them, a single direct hit could reduce the vessel to an inferno. *Victorious* suffered one direct hit (which did not disrupt operations) and a number of near-misses; we were luckier than one or two of our sister ships— particularly HMS *Formidable.*

My most unnerving personal 'kamikaze experience' was sitting in our aircraft early one morning, 'bombed up' and waiting to take off, only to be told that an attack was imminent and that we should sit tight until the 'all clear'!! Fortunately, the attack did not develop.
22 June: Left 849 Squadron when HMS *Victorious* returned to Sydney, Australia. After six weeks 'in transit' left Sydney on the cruiser HMS *Devonshire* for the UK.
14 December: Demobilised from HMS *Daedalus,* Lee-on-Solent.

1946

15 February: Class A: release from service. Except for occasional experiences my service with the Fleet Air Arm was enjoyable and rewarding. At an early age I saw a large slice of the world and was fortunate to enjoy good luck which was denied to some of my contemporaries. I value the many friendships made during the war years particularly those that have endured to this day.

Fred Taylor

Pilot

111 Squadron

....Fred now with Concorde in the background

Fred Taylor

Fred Taylor joined the RAF in September 1940 at Cardington, Bedfordshire. He trained as a civilian in California before America entered the war and was awarded his pilot's brevet in December 1941 just at the time of Pearl Harbor. A fighter pilot on Hurricanes and Spitfires, Fred served with 111 Squadron in the UK, North Africa, Italy, Corsica and the south of France. He completed two tours and, after returning to the UK in October 1944, was "condemned to take a Flying Instructors' course at Upavon on Oxfords."

Not-so-friendly fire

IN June 1942 I joined 111 Squadron at Debden, Essex, then part of 11 Group. We were engaged in operations over northern France and were part of the escort for the first raid on Europe by the American Eighth Air Force's Flying Fortresses attacking the marshalling yards at Rouen. From where we were, it looked as though the Norden bomb sight wasn't needed that day! However, it was a different matter a couple of days later for on 19 August 1942 was the first major, and ill-fated, combined operation—the raid on Dieppe.

My first outing was something of a baptism of fire for I caught a shell from a FW190 but, fortunately, sustained no serious damage. On my next trip I was attacking a Dornier 217 when suddenly there was total silence. I thought my engine had been hit and, as I was too low to bale out, I would have to ditch. I decided to put down by a big ship, thinking that there would be plenty of hospitality on board! Alas, when I tried to jettison the hood it didn't come off and so ditching wasn't an option.

On checking throttle movement my instruments told me the engine was still working but I could not hear it. I headed for base and found I had no flaps or brakes but I did have a very large hole in the wing! Instead of approaching at 90mph, I came in at 120mph! Apart from the hole in the wing, the engine had lost all its oil and the aircraft was riddled with shrapnel everywhere except the cockpit. On examination of the shrapnel it was reported to have come from the Royal Navy...

I was suffering temporary deafness due to the noise—which was why I couldn't hear my aircraft's engine!

North Africa

SHORTLY after this we were taken off ops. and prepared to embark for Operation Torch, the invasion of French North Africa. During this campaign we operated about ten miles behind the front, from a landing strip scraped out by a bulldozer. We gave close support to the Army and escorted bombers attacking Tunis and Bizerta. We had to maintain a standing patrol over our airfield for it was often attacked by German fighter bombers. It was not much fun being ground-strafed!

While we were equipped with Spitfire Vs, with an enormous sand filter which knocked 30mph off our speed, the Germans had FW190s and the latest mark of Me109s—the Gustav—which was much faster than our Spitfire.

When Rommel was retreating from the Eighth Army he came across American troops defending Kasserine Pass in Tunisia. He attacked them with the idea of pushing north to the Mediterranean, thus cutting off the British First Army from the bases in Algeria. This battle was too far away for us with our normal fuel load and so we had to carry extra fuel tanks, fly down to the battle area and shoot up anything that moved. We kept this up until the Army had control.

On one of these 'outings' I was flying back to base, out of ammo and not a lot of fuel left when I looked behind me and saw three aircraft coming up astern of me. I thought they were Hurricanes then suddenly realised that there *were* no Hurricanes around there! I whipped round pretty smartly as the three Me109s sped by with guns blazing!

I had another stoke of good fortune a little later. We were in full squadron strength and deep into enemy territory when my No.2 developed an internal glycol leak. He was pouring out clouds of white smoke for all to see. I had to take him back home.

We were going quite gently for his engine was struggling to cope when I saw four Me109s. Unfortunately, they saw us. They circled above us. While I waited for their attack, I was desperately thinking of how I could defend my No.2. The German fighters circled us four or five times—then just flew away! (I have always wished I knew why they departed but have always been glad they did!)

Italy

THE Eighth Army and First Army duly met up and, eventually, brought the battle for North Africa to an end. I was then 'tour expired' and took a 'rest'. Six months later the battle had moved to Italy and I with it. I asked to rejoin 111 Squadron and my wish was granted. The squadron was based north of Naples, just a few miles south of Monte Cassino. We had Spitfire IXs that were vastly superior to the Vs and gave us some advantages over the enemy aircraft such as height, speed, climb and manoeuverability.

The Anzio bridgehead was in a delicate state and we spent much of our time providing air cover for ground troops.

Early one morning we were proceeding to the bridgehead in full squadron strength, the CO was leading one flight of six and I was leading the other flight of six. Soon after take-off we got the message from Ops. that German aircraft were forming up north of Rome. First it was twenty plus, then forty plus, then sixty plus and, as we neared Anzio, it was a hundred plus—and they were going to get there at the same time as us!

We were on patrol going west towards the sea when I saw them and turned in to attack them. I told the CO where they were and expected him to join me but he didn't. We continued our attack until well north of Rome when I decided it was time to call a halt. We were short of ammo by now and had used a lot of petrol in going flat out. This was the time when the Germans would turn around and attack us—when we were ill-prepared for it. Five of us reformed at the mouth of the Tiber and we set off for base. Half way home we heard our No.6 aircraft calling, "Mayday! Mayday!" but there was nothing we could do. Day-long searches failed to find any trace of him and nor was he reported as a prisoner of war.

At this time we were having a little trouble in that, for no apparent reason, an engine would just stop working! One or two pilots had force landed, some had baled out and some had just made it to the airstrip at Anzio.

One day, a little to the south of Rome my engine stopped and, for the second time, I experienced the strange sound of silence but it was not my hearing this time. Fortunately, I was able to reach Anzio only to be greeted by a few shells from a 'Big Bertha' in the Frascati hills—not an uncommon occurrence when the Germans spotted any activity on the airstrip.

I couldn't get away until my aircraft was fixed and so spent the night with some Americans in their tent. Their hospitality was terrific and we had an excellent meal before retiring. However, at about three o'clock in the morning there was panic! Huge German Tiger tanks were reported only a hundred yards away—and I was in the tent alone! I scrambled out into the pitch-black night and listened. I strained my ears for any sound. Nothing. I couldn't hear any tanks and so, after a few minutes, I went back to bed and no Tiger tanks appeared.

In May 1944 Rome was liberated and the front line moved north. We moved up too, always as close to the front as possible. We spent our time escorting bombers and shooting up any 'interesting' targets. The enemy didn't like this; their ack-ack was very good and led to a number of casualties.

When we had reached as far north as Elba we were moved to Calvi in Corsica in preparation for the invasion of the south of France. This was something of a non-event. The Germans retreated without any resistance and there wasn't a single German aircraft to be seen. Our task was to seek out the German convoys and destroy them. As the Germans were using horses to draw their supply wagons, many of the horses were, alas, killed. The stench of rotting carcasses permeated the whole of the Rhone Valley.

When the army from the south joined up with the army from the north we were sent back to Italy. I had completed my tour and an extension and was sent to Naples. On return to base I was told there was a five-month wait for

a troopship back to the UK. I organised my own transport and arrived in Croydon forty-eight hours later!

Not-so-happy ending

ALL stories should have happy endings but mine didn't. I was posted to Upavon to take a flying instructors course on Oxfords... This was something of a let-down, to say the least, for, after operational flying overseas, Training Command in England was very, very dreary.

By now the war in Europe had ended. I applied for a posting back on ops. in the Far East—they had Spitfire VIIIs there. I was still waiting when the Americans dropped the atom bomb on Japan and so the next event was my de-mob.

Douglas Thornton

Pilot

**500 Squadron Mediterranean Coastal Air Force
Communication Flight (Khartoum)**

Douglas Thornton at Taffaroui,
near Oran, North Africa, 1943/4...

... Douglas fifty-five years later

Douglas Thornton

Douglas Thornton joined the RAF in June 1941 after beginning his service career in the Territorial Army in April 1939. He trained as a pilot in Canada and was awarded his 'Wings' and a commission in February 1942. Amongst the aircraft he flew his favourite was the Hudson. He served in 500 Squadron, Coastal Command and the Communications Flight (Khartoum), Mediterranean Coastal Air Force.

Early days

FOLLOWING the Battle of Britain there was a shortage of aircrew and volunteers were welcomed. Although my experience of aeroplanes was limited to a ride at Sir Alan Cobham's Flying Circus in 1930, I applied for the job. I was interviewed at Cardington, Bedfordshire. During the interview I was shown a number of triangles,

"Can you name these triangles, Thornton?"

My mind was in turmoil. I mixed up obtuse and scalene as I pointed to one,

"This is an obscene triangle, sir."

There was much laughter which relieved the tension a bit! Despite that gaffe I was accepted.

It was much later on, at Swift Current, in the heart of the Canadian prairies, that hands-on flying training began. No.32 Elementary Flying Training School was equipped with De Havilland Tiger Moths DH 82c. I learned how to handle the plane in the air and on the ground—and how to get from the one to the other safely. I went solo after nine hours. My instructor was an American, from Texas, a great guy. On one occasion he took me in a Tiger Moth. Below us his girlfriend was wielding a camera.

"Hold tight," he said to me, "she's taking our picture! This'll make a good photo!"

Whereupon he suddenly swooped over the hedge then dived sharply under the telephone wires. I thought I was going to be decapitated! I don't know how the photo came out.

The next move was to No. 34 Service Flying Training School at Medicine Hat and flying the Harvard II that, to a newcomer, was an enormous, unfriendly monster—and the rumours weren't encouraging,

"Dangerous things those Harvards."

"You can't get them out of a spin—well, not easily."

"They swerve on take-off" and so on.

It was, therefore, reassuring when another rumour later went round that these first rumours applied only to the Harvard I. Whether any of this was true or not I don't know, but at least it made us treat the machine with respect and keep our concentration and when someone told us,

"If you make a mistake it could be your last" it was a sobering thought. In spite of early misgivings, the Harvard became a pleasure to fly.

During the latter part of the course I was pleased to be offered one of only six places allotted to Coastal Command.

All at sea

No.31 General Reconnaissance School, Charlottetown, was an intensive ten-week course in operating over the sea in co-operation with the Royal Navy and others. Here I learned to get lost over the sea (instead of over the land) and how to recognise various foreign naval units that were supposedly wandering around the ocean in large numbers—and in World War I formations. Ship recognition was quite difficult: models about three inches long were placed on a blue-painted board on the floor and we had to recognise them from about ten feet away. If we could not manage the names at least we were expected to know if they were British, German, Italian or Japanese and whether they were battleships, cruisers or whatever.

We were also introduced to navigating, as distinct from learning about it, and the further complications of star-gazing and astro-navigation.

The team...

The next stage was at No.31 Operational Training Unit, Debert, Nova Scotia. Here we were put together as crews: a pilot, navigator and two wireless operators/air gunners. It was important to operate with a crew one trusted and got on with and, although this seemed to have been arranged in a haphazard manner, I was fortunate with my team comprising a Welsh navigator and two Canadian WOP/AGs and we flew together for almost two years.

... the plane

The plane we flew was the Hudson. I must put in a plug for this excellent machine because no one else seems to. Few people today have heard of it, and even at the RAF Museum at Hendon there is only a passenger version tucked away in a corner. It was developed from the Lockheed 14, a 1937 passenger plane, and was used as a civil airliner in UK. It took Mr. Chamberlain, the then Prime Minister, to Munich in 1938 to obtain his famous but sadly worthless, piece of paper from Hitler offering 'peace in our time'.

Hudson flown by Douglas while escorting convoys.

(Douglas cannot resist the temptation to add, for the benefit of those who think that the war was won solely by Spitfires and Lancasters, that on 8 October 1939 a Hudson from 224 Squadron sighted a Dornier flying boat, attacked and sank it. This is reputed to be the first enemy plane shot down in the Second World War. The Hudson's crew were a chivalrous lot and directed a nearby Danish fishing boat to the scene to pick up the Germans from their dinghy. Unfortunately(!) they were all repatriated to Germany and lived to fight another day—this was reported by Lord Haw-Haw in one of his radio broadcasts from Germany.)

Overseas

West Africa

I had reached the exalted rank of Pilot Officer when I arrived in Freetown Harbour, Sierra Leone, on New Year's Day 1943. After about three weeks we were allocated our planes for a flight to Casablanca. The city was full of people, planes and rumours of a top brass gathering. It was the now famous conference between Churchill and Roosevelt and their staffs at which the Allied demand for the unconditional surrender of Germany, Italy and Japan was issued—we didn't know that at the time, of course.

After the war Churchill described the lavish arrangements made for them in a large hotel with conference rooms and plenty of comfortable villas. However, after our long day toddling up the West Africa coast at 120 knots *we* could find nowhere to sleep. It was already after sunset and so two of us slept on the floor in a hangar and two slept in the plane.

The next stop was Gibraltar with its extraordinary runway built out into the harbour and having The Rock in the middle of the circuit.

From there we went east to Blida, Algeria, where I joined 500 Squadron 27 January 1943.

North Africa

500 Squadron had been involved in the North Africa landings (Operation Torch) in November 1942, and by the time I arrived in January 1943 relationships between the Allied forces, the Free and the Vichy French seemed to have stabilised. However, during the months of November and December it was reckoned that there had been twenty-five U-boats in the western Mediterranean. During November alone five were sunk, three by 500 Squadron. The mess was full of stories.

"Did you hear about the attack on a U-boat with a depth charge? Direct hit—ripped open the conning tower."

"Any damage to the plane?"

"Rudders, elevator and trimming tabs shot up. Wings bent up six feet!"

"How about the pilot?"

"Managed to fly and maintain control for fifteen minutes or so. Gained a bit of height by using the crew as moveable ballast."

"What happened?"

"Over Algiers one engine cut and the crew were forced to bale out at about 1,500 feet. The pilot and one of the gunners were picked up in Algiers harbour."

"The other two were killed," and the conversation ceased.

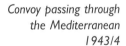

Convoy passing through the Mediterranean 1943/4

On patrol

SORTIES of six or seven hours consisted of convoy escort, anti-submarine sweeps and searches for dinghies and other objects. Some convoys were quite large—over sixty ships with their escorts—these would be the slower ones; the faster ones comprised a few liners with escorts. Not only were the convoys company for us, they were the reason we were there. Knowing that gave a greater sense of responsibility with so many lives at stake than when flying over the empty sea playing hide-and-seek with a U-boat.

It was on one such sweep—our forty-ninth sortie and after 270 hours of flying over apparently empty seas—that I noticed something.

"What's that down there?"

"Where?"

"Port side." It was dusk and it took a few seconds for us to make out the shape.

"It's a U-boat!"

The W/OP sent out a first sighting report. The navigator selected the depth charges and worked out where we were. I circled the plane so that I could see the target against the light hoping he would not see me before I began my run in.

He saw us, fired and began submerging. I turned steeply passing a few feet over the conning tower and dropped the depth charges. The W/OP's voice was excited as he sent his 'high priority' message—everyone else had to get off the line.

"No response from our base," he said disappointed.

"Nothing?" I asked.

"No. Just a minute—" he made contact and relayed the message. "Liverpool picked it up," he said relieved. "They've re-transmitted it for us."

In the intelligence report the attack was noted, as was the fact that the plane had been hit in the tail—the only convincing evidence that we had not dreamed the whole thing up! A later report indicated that the submarine was damaged and had returned to base.

Sad times

MY first night solo in a Hudson was shared with a New Zealander, Lloyd Trigg, who a year or so later attacked a U-boat which fired back at him. His Liberator caught fire but he pressed on and crashed on the U-boat and sunk it. On the recommendation of the U-boat commander, who was one of the few rescued, Trigg was posthumously awarded the Victoria Cross. (This was recently sold in London for £138,000.)

As a crew we sometimes had the job of judging low level bombing. We would sit in a cabin in sand dunes at the end of a lake near Oran and assess the accuracy of our colleagues as they came round at about fifty feet and dropped practice bombs or markers on a dummy submarine. Once I had left the other three to carry on their task, which was not too unpleasant lying out in the sun, while I went into Oran to visit the stores.

On the way back I met an ambulance and was informed that one of the planes had turned too near the ground and crashed and the pilot, a particular friend with whom I had trained, was killed. I felt badly about not being there but there was nothing that I could have done.

On another occasion I was O/C night flying and had just seen a crew go out to their plane and was preparing myself for a quiet snooze. I was almost asleep when I heard the plane take off—then there was silence. I thought: "That can't be right" but could not at first think why. I rushed outside and there was a column of flames and smoke about a mile off the end of the runway. I didn't sleep much that night.

Navy

RELATIONS with the Navy were always important—they were known then as the Silent Service—and we sometimes wished they were not quite so silent, like when we homed in by radar on what turned out to be a French battleship, of whose whereabouts we had not been informed. Not unnaturally the ship resented the intrusion and showed it. We quickly backed off—if a plane can be said to do such a thing.

There was a real attempt to get together and the RAF took up naval officers as passengers so that they could see our problems, and the Navy took us out on their patrols so that we could see what it was like from their end. I think this went down quite well and I enjoyed the Navy's hospitality for two or three days in the Mediterranean, diving overboard from time to time and having a swim.

Moving on

WE moved as a crew to the Mediterranean and Middle East Communication Flight based at Capodichino near Naples. The army had reached halfway between Naples and Rome and it was on 4 June 1944 that Rome fell.

Three months earlier the volcano overlooking Naples, Vesuvius, had erupted. Even in Sicily the visibility along the north coast was drastically reduced. Operations at Naples were severely affected but by the time we arrived Vesuvius had simmered down. We flew round and looked at the boiling liquid inside the crater. We also visited Pompeii, which was buried in volcanic ash in AD 79 but over the last 200 years has been excavated, exposing life there as it was centuries ago.

The time came for us as a crew to split up. We had been together for a long time and there was inevitable sadness in now going our separate ways. The friendship and teamwork of a crew has to be experienced to be really appreciated and I was extremely fortunate. I would not say we never disagreed but we worked well together and I am still in touch with one of the Canadian WOP/AGs after fifty-three years.

We often forget the debt we owe to the ground staff. Much of our maintenance was done in the blazing sun but I never had any

mechanical failure and only once or twice an instrument or electrical problem. It says much for the quality and thoroughness of the work of those to whom we entrusted our lives.

My posting to the Middle East was a surprise. In Egypt I stayed in the transit camp at Heliopolis then on to Khartoum—shades of Gordon and Kitchener—and just about the end of the world to me.

On the Communication Flight that I joined in September were two Hudsons and two Ansons. One feature (probably not found on a Lancaster!) is that when visiting a remote airfield where there were no facilities, the engines of the Anson could be wound up with a starting handle. This was fine for the pilot but not so good for the winder when the temperature was about 100°F. The Anson's reputation had been well summed up by the adaptation of an old saying "Anson is as Anson does"…

Generally, we carried enough fuel to cover the return journey or on to a place where fuel was available. Some of the small airstrips we visited were remote and it was not unusual for refuelling to be carried out by a team of Sudanese who put their spears aside and stood on the wing pouring the stuff in through filter funnels from four-gallon tins—a somewhat distinctive 'native' bowser!

Social life

SWIMMING appealed enormously but was best done in a pool. Once we had flown a District Officer back to his home some way up the Blue Nile and were staying the night with him before going on elsewhere. It was hot and we asked about swimming in the river.

"You can if you want but watch out for crocodiles. It's all right if you splash around a bit," he added casually.

It didn't sound very promising but, having asked the question, we felt we could not let the RAF down and so had a very quick dip. Trying to swim keeping our legs as near to our chests as possible was difficult!

Music was another relaxation and I was fortunate in that my navigator was a professional cellist. I was a very amateur pianist and with one or two others we were involved in making music together in places as far apart as the governor general's palace and the sergeants' mess.

On one occasion we took the cello with the intention of giving a 'concert' at an isolated RAF unit. When we arrived we found that the CO had just died in tragic circumstances and obviously our 'concert' had to be abandoned.

When we returned to Khartoum our colleagues' sympathy was with the deceased,

"It was the prospect of having to listen to you lot that did him in!"

Finale

THE last time I flew was on 24 November 1945 to Malakal and Juba and returned to Khartoum in a Anson AX403. The home journey was by air to Cairo, then on to Alexandria, by boat to Marseilles, train across France and then to England and Wilmslow where I was demobbed in time for Christmas 1945. I had never flown in England, having spent all but three months of my four-and-a-half years' RAF service overseas.

I began in the army in 1939 with two stripes on my arm and ended in the RAF in 1945 with two on my shoulder—not exactly a meteoric rise to glory. I have omitted the difficult times, the anxiety, loneliness, errors of judgement, the heat, the boredom, the longing to see an end to it all and be back at home.

There were so many plusses: many wonderful friends, learning about people, working in a team, looking for the best in everyone, accepting responsibility, flying an aeroplane, and in it all finding my Christian faith strengthened. I served in or visited over twenty countries, all full of interest and unforgettable experiences. Looking back I had a comparatively easy war—more like a Mediterranean holiday some would say—but it did not seem that way at the time.

The greatest 'plus' was meeting Betty, my wife, in 1940. We corresponded regularly for six years and got to know each other through writing of our hopes and thoughts, of friends and family.

It was a long time to be apart and we had not spent more than three weeks together, adding up the odd days, between our first meeting and getting married. We have made up for it since in our fifty-two years together since.

Ralph Tyrrell

MBE

Bomb aimer

44 and 207 Squadrons

*Ralph Tyrrell as a cadet at No. 9 Initial Training Wing,
Stratford-upon-Avon, October 1942...*

*... and in front of the Lancaster at East Kirkby
during the 207 Squadron reunion 30 April
1995*

Ralph Tyrrell

Ralph Tyrrell joined the Air Training Corps as a cadet at 276 (Chelmsford) Squadron in January 1941 and volunteered for RAF aircrew that December. He trained in Canada as an air observer and served with 207 and 44 Squadrons, Bomber Command. He later trained for Tiger Force operating in the Far East. He spent some time in India and has flown in Wellingtons, Stirling, Lancasters, Dakotas, Harvards and Varisties amongst others. In 1960 he was CO of 276 (Chelmsford) Squadron Air Training Corps. He has devoted much time to the ATC and for his services was awarded the MBE in December 1993. He is currently President of 276 ATC, President of the RAF Association (Chelmsford branch) and Deputy Chairman of East Essex Wing ATC.

A telegram from Monty... and other snippets

LIFE was good to me. I started in Canada on the PNB (Pilots/Navigators/Bomb aimers) scheme, although I got off to a somewhat inauspicious start whilst at 31 Bombing and Gunnery School, RCAF Picton, Ontario, (near enough to Toronto to go for weekends and enjoy Canadian hospitality!)

I was flying in a Bolingbroke (Canadian version of the Blenheim) in December 1943 with a F/O Swaddling. We had just taken off and were at about 1,000 feet when the port engine burst into flames. We landed pretty sharply and were met by fire engines. Flying time: 20 minutes; DNCO (Duty not carried out)...

In January 1944 whilst at No. 7 Air Observers School, Portage La Prairie, near Winnipeg, I was in an Anson piloted by a Sgt. Stewart on a night navigation exercise. The Anson took 147 turns to wind up the undercarriage and I had just recovered from doing that when we encountered a snowstorm and 'white-out' and were immediately recalled to base. After another 147 turns we only just managed to land safely. DPCO (Duty partly carried out)...

Back in England the following October whilst at 1660 HCU, Swinderby, flying Stirlings, I was sent as part of a complete crew on a bombing exercise. The weather clamped down but we pressed on and completed the details. *Bomber Command (5 Group) News* published our story:

1660 Conversion Unit ... reports an example of perseverance on the part of F/O Howard and crew who were detailed to drop twelve practice bombs in indifferent weather conditions. The exercise took four hours to complete and two Category A results were obtained.

We got a 48-hour pass for that! Incidentally, I'm still in touch with my skipper, John Howard.

On 13 February 1945 we took off at 1800 for Dresden—a ten-hour op. We were in the first wave. Another air cadet, Doug Bannister, from Chelmsford who had joined the ATC with me and became a W/OP was on the same trip. Regretfully, he never came back. To us, it was just another trip. We could not refuse for to do so would risk being labelled a coward and considered LMF—lacking moral fibre.

On 16 March, en route for Wurzburg, we had just taken off when the Lanc. in front of us blew up, disappeared completely and almost turned us on our back.

Ralph Tyrrell

We bombed Wesel on 25 March to assist Montgomery crossing the Rhine. When we got back a telegram from the great man awaited us, congratulating us on the accuracy of our bombing (5 Group, that is, not me personally!)

A 'hairy' time was on 14 April 1945 coming back from an op. The flight engineer said he didn't think he had enough fuel to get back to base and so we lobbed into Manston with the gauges showing 'empty'. Just as we reached the end of the runway all the engines stopped—no wonder—a large lump of flak had embedded itself in the starboard underwing had caused a fuel leak.

I was also on Operation Dodge (bringing troops back from Italy) and Operation Manna taking food to occupied Europe).

At the end of the war I, like many others, became redundant aircrew. Eventually, I got a ground job on the north-west frontier of India where they forgot me for three months...

Looking back, I was one of the lucky ones to survive on an operational station and I will always remember all those who did not make it back.

Derek Waterman

DFC

Pilot

96 and158 Squadrons

(Died 1989)

Derek Waterman flew several ops. in Halifax Friday the 13th. *As a tribute to 'Hallybags' this one was 're-created' and rolled out in September 1995 at the Yorkshire Air Museum, Elvington, near York. Photo: Anne Grimshaw*

Derek Waterman

Derek Waterman was one of the three founder members of the North West Essex and East Hertfordshire Branch of the Aircrew Association and became its first branch secretary. Apart from having won a DFC, Derek's other claim to fame was that he flew some ops. on a Halifax named Friday the 13th. This aircraft survived well over 100 ops. Unfortunately, like all other Halifaxes, it was scrapped at the end of the war. However, the Yorkshire Air Museum at Elvington near York has gathered parts from various Halifaxes all over the world and rebuilt an almost complete one. In honour of the original aircraft, the Yorkshire Hallybag has also been named Friday the 13th. This branch of the ACA has prepared a framed collage showing the aircraft and photographs of Derek and his crew. This was presented to the Yorkshire Air Museum and has pride of place in the main hangar. Derek also wrote some of his experiences in Friday the 13th in a booklet entitled Have a good time, chaps and this is reproduced here.

Daylight raids on Duisburg

"TRANSPORT will pick you up in half an hour, breakfast at 3.30." The corporal who gently shook me and awakened me from a little more than four hours' sleep delivered these words in a somewhat sympathetic and apologetic tone. It was Saturday morning of 14 September 1944 on a large and dispersed aerodrome a few miles south of Bridlington, Yorkshire. RAF Lissett was the home of No. 158 Squadron, 4 Group, Bomber Command, flying Halifaxes.

The intruder had already switched on the electric light that showed the cold interior of a barely furnished wooden hut, shared between Fred (who wasn't one of my crew) and myself. It showed too the disgusted expression on Fred's face at being so politely told to rise at such an early hour on this cold autumn morning.

"Half an hour—well it's no use going to sleep again—just time for a cigarette before our batman brings in some hot water. No need to shave as we'll be back again by mid-day at the latest. Anyway we shall have tonight free," I said.

Such thoughts were merely a consolation as I puffed at the last of the cigarette and emerged from the warmth of my bed and hurriedly reached for my clothes draped untidily over a bedside chair. The water was refreshing and enabled me to realise more clearly the reason for being in a vertical attitude so soon after going to bed.

"Wonder where the target is Fred?"

"Happy Valley, I suppose," said he in his customary matter-of-fact tone between puffs at an ancient briar that constantly decorated his countenance. (Did Fred ever feel scared?) This thought often passed through my mind at times such as this. I felt extremely weak at the knees but Fred might easily have been dressing for a routine morning parade. One couldn't help being fond of him, he was a personable soul and, except for his refusal to hurry at any time, made a pleasant room-mate.

"Hurry up, Fred. Transport outside. I'll carry on. See you later but for God's sake get mobile."

I left him slowly donning his pants and

223

ventured out into the cold morning air and boarded the American-type bus, which by this time held a dozen or so odd-looking, semi-conscious beings. Conversation was limited to hasty 'good mornings' from my own particular crew and perhaps the odd few seated around the door.

At such early hours, tempers are varied. Jack, my mid-upper gunner, usually managed to awake cheerfully and I could hear his cheery voice above the quiet hubbub of the crowd. Some were talking but the majority wishing they had taken the CO's advice and not visited Bridlington the previous evening where liquid refreshment, at most times, ran freely. The latter showed their regret with half-closed eyes and by their obvious disapproval of the comparative gaiety of their brighter-eyed colleagues. After all, the CO had told us that there was the likelihood of an early morning show and advised us to drink with moderation and to get to bed early.

Fortunately, I had taken his good advice and was very glad. I felt a little tired but otherwise reasonably fit. An impatient driver soon appeared and asked whether there were any more to come. A quick check by crews' captains found Fred (alas, a captain himself) the only one absent.

This discovery brought forth in chorus, raucous shouts of: "Come on, Fred. Pull your finger out" and many other impolite requests for him to join the not-so-merry throng, or to ruddy well walk. The mess, being nearly two miles away, was perhaps the only reason why Fred with pipe smoking furiously, boarded the vehicle with the ease and grace of an early arrival and shouted "OK" to the driver. This caused a considerable amount of good humoured leg-pulling, which Fred took rather seriously.

"Couldn't find my matches" he explained, this being a good reason for twenty-four men being ten minutes late for breakfast. The driver started up and turned from our site and on to the main road. This led, with dangerously narrow curves, first to the sergeants' mess, where the NCOs left us, then to the main entrance of the officers' mess where the rest of us alighted hurriedly, anxious for a cup of tea to perform its usual wonders of reviving the half-dead.

An early start

Bacon and eggs are, I think, a delicious breakfast but somehow, at this unearthly hour, they seemed utterly out of place. Surely breakfast was best appreciated between the hours of eight and ten o'clock. However, after a cup of tea I tackled the food and even enjoyed it.

By now, most early morning tempers had mellowed and eyes began to open. The one thought and topic was the 'trip'. Where were we going?

"Just hope it's a nice easy French target," said Wilf, my navigator. Reg, the bomb aimer exclaimed that he wanted "an op'—not a ruddy joy ride"—contemptibly interrupted him! Surprisingly, these words were sincere; ex-London policeman, Reg, was a bomber pilot's dream. He would do all those little jobs you yourself would forget in the rush and panic. He could make a joke of tragedy and, above all, could effect wonders in keeping a cool and cheery atmosphere amongst the rest of the crew. At twenty-nine, he was six years older than the average in our 'team'. That was one reason, but the answer was not in his age but in his unquestionable supply of guts. A grand type for whom I was extremely grateful on numerous occasions—in fact, every time our wheels left the ground.

There were more cigarettes until it was time to report for briefing. Within five minutes we would know where we were going. Again we boarded the bus and moved down the hill towards the aerodrome with its huge hangars silhouetted against a sky already showing signs of a typical autumn dawn.

Somehow, the crowd had changed: the carefree atmosphere that existed over the breakfast table had now gone. Faces were serious, thoughts of wives, mothers and even young children were only partially concealed and obvious. I wondered whether I would do this journey again or enjoy the thrill of catching the train to King's Cross and the fourteen days' leave that would follow. I even thought of telegrams and my mother's dread of such impersonal scraps of paper. Perhaps that was the worst part of all this: the ones at home—their bravery is genuine for the mystery of action is not with them.

Happy Valley

"OK, blokes! Ten to one on Happy Valley!" The would-be turf accountant would have shown good returns had bets been made to the contrary. The bright red tapes pinned at various points on the large-scale map of Europe at the top end of the briefing room came to an abrupt halt at Duisburg. This large inland port in the Ruhr spread its arms of heavy industry and oil refineries to either side of the Rhine.

My knees suddenly weakened. We disliked and feared the Ruhr, known throughout Bomber Command as 'Happy Valley'. Its defences were strong and its gunners accurate and enduring. They would fire until the last aircraft had weaved its way through their dangerous barrage. Ten thousand tons of bombs would not halt their incredible efforts to shoot us from the sky.

Our first job was to empty our pockets of all odds and ends with the exception of identity cards. The rest of our pocket contents were put into a small envelope and labelled with one's name and locked in a safe until we would return.

We were all then issued with escape kits: silk maps, compasses concealed in buttons or collar studs, concentrated chocolate, benzedrine tablets and one or two other forms of food and drugs to be consumed or used in the case of emergency. The WAAF who provided us with these ingenious boxes of tricks smiled as she did so—with that smile seemed to go the hope that the need for using them would not occur.

Briefing

We took up our seats at our usual tables and awaited the arrival of the Station and Squadron Commanders. Meanwhile, everyone talked of the target, route, bomb loads and guessed at the approximate time of take-off. As it was now almost five o'clock we presumed the latter would be around seven.

The chatter ceased suddenly when the Group Captain and Wing Commander followed by Officers-in-Charge other sections entered the crowded room. The atmosphere was tense and smoky as we all stood respectfully to attention.

"Good morning, chaps. Sit down, please." The words came from a tall, heavily built man sporting a handlebar moustache—the Group Captain, our Station Commander.

Chairs moved noisily as the crews again made themselves comfortable. The Wing Commander, a man in his early thirties, was, to my mind, the ideal Squadron Commander. He lived to fly, was liked and highly respected by all and was extremely annoyed because as CO he was allowed to operate only twice a month. When he did fly, he chose the toughest targets; he could so easily have done otherwise. We liked him for this, followed him loyally and were grateful for his sound advice.

"Well, gentlemen, as you see, the target is once again in the 'Valley'. We are putting up twenty-six aircraft this morning. The main force will be 1,200 strong."

There were sighs of relief from us all. We preferred to operate in large numbers, the defences would be heavy but we knew they could do much more harm to a smaller force. Besides it was comforting to think of so many others on the same journey.

"Zero hour is 0930. We are in the first wave and our bombing time is zero plus two [0932]. You are to bomb at 21,000 feet and your run in will be on a heading of 087°. I don't think it is necessary to mention defences as most of you are already acquainted with them in this area.

225

Take-off time of first aircraft 0630. Set course over base 0700. Climb to reach the English coast at 14,000 feet. You will be fortunate in having an escort of Spitfires and Mustangs provided by our old and trusted friends, 11 Group. They will rendezvous over Beachy Head where they will join you. Keep in close and give the fighter boys a chance to afford cover to the stream. Pathfinders will be marking the target with red and yellow target indicators from zero minus two onwards. Master Bomber will use the code name 'Clever Boy' and your code name as the main force will be 'Samson'.

"Please remember this, any engine trouble, turn round, jettison your load and return to base. Death-or-glory stunts are unnecessary and will be frowned upon, your job is bomb the target and return your aircraft and crews safely. Have a good run, boys, and very good luck to you all." The last words were said with unquestionable sincerity.

Weather report

There followed a brief outline of the weather we were expected to encounter en route to the target and return from the Meteorological Officer, a small, thin man who seemed to be able to make a description of a cloud formation sound absurdly humorous. He struck one as being much more suitable for ENSA rather than the chart studying Met. Officer. Weather can, of course, make a considerable difference to the success of any bombing mission and can make flying either very pleasant or uncomfortably dangerous. We listened intently.

"There's a possibility of early morning mist but this should not interfere to any great extent with take-off. Very little cloud over England—perhaps 3/10ths cirrus at 25,000 feet. Target clear—no icing—winds at bombing height, ten to fifteen miles an hour. On your return the mist will have dispersed. The weather should be the least of your troubles."

A few words from the Wireless and Gunnery Leaders on radio procedure and defence areas brought general briefing to an end. The Group Captain then took the stand and with his customary words, "Have a good time, chaps" he brushed his handlebar moustache and closed the meeting.

All navigators, meanwhile, had been attending their own special briefing and when I walked into their sanctuary, Wilf was methodically drawing in tracks on his chart and making out his flight plan.

"Everything OK?" I asked him.

"Just bang on," he replied. He gave me a captain's map—a small-scale map of Europe on which he had also drawn the tracks representing our route. At each turning point he had inserted the estimated arrival time. Should he have the misfortune to be injured, this important piece of paper would help me in navigating the aircraft myself.

I then made for the Flight Commander's office to sign the flight authorisation book that, as its name suggests, authorised the particular flight and was signed by the flight commander.

Pilots briefing was in ten minutes and so I quickly strode over to the crew room where I drew my parachute and donned a Mae West, parachute harness, flying boots, an old brown scarf and gathered up helmet and oxygen mask. Then, together with Jock, our engineer, made for the pilots' briefing room where the Wing Commander discussed with us petrol load, recommended cruising speeds and taxi out times. Our machine with the identification letter F (and hence named *Friday the 13th*) meant that we were to be No.6 to move off in alphabetical order round the perimeter track into take-off position.

Time was now 0545 and transport was already waiting outside. Most crew had already collected flying rations and were sitting waiting in the buses. The squadron padre was making his rounds, wishing good luck to all. Although a well-intended gesture, his presence always struck me as being rather morbid. Climbing into the bus was always rather a complex business. One would trip over parachutes or become entangled with oxygen tubes and suchlike and I could never quite understand why navigators' bags were so full and bulky. They took up a mighty lot of room.

Despite the numerous obstacles we somehow all managed to squeeze in. A quick glance round assured me that my six pals were all safely on board. I only hoped they'd remembered everything. It was a damned nuisance if we got out to the aircraft and found someone had left his oxygen mask or something equally important behind.

Our bus carried crews for aircraft E, F and G—twenty-one of us. We soon arrived at E-Easy and dropped Tommy, a jovial New Zealander, with his mixed crew of fellow countrymen and Australians, a wild bunch but grand types.

"Have a good trip, Tommy. See you at lunch time!" My last remark was a superstition. I said it to everyone getting out before us and to everyone left in, as we gathered our kit and alighted. I never missed saying those words or something similar. I thought they passed unnoticed until one day Reg pulled my leg about it. I still continued with my silly habit even after that although I felt a little embarrassed and always avoided Reg's smiling eyes.

Six o'clock: ten minutes for a smoke and then the start of another adventure.

Preparing for take-off

I always allowed twenty minutes from boarding the aircraft until taxi-out time. Starting, warming and testing the four engines, checking control movements, cockpit lights, oxygen flow, compass and gyro instruments and other lesser but vitally important details, usually could be managed in fifteen minutes. The margin of five minutes left time to get settled in and to make oneself comfortable and, in the case of minor mechanical faults,

gave the ground crew a possible opportunity of putting things right.

Fortunately, at all times everything was 100 per cent perfect and I don't think I could possibly say more to stress the keenness and efficiency of the ground crew: Tom, the sergeant, and his five underlings. They slaved over and nursed the aircraft as a mother would her child. Already our four-engined friend had made eighty-nine visits to enemy territory without one single mechanical fault not attributable to ack-ack or belligerent fighters. We all proudly boasted this great record.

The last few drags at my cigarette were definite and full of appreciation for its apparent stimulation. I smoked heavily and knew it would be about five hours before I would enjoy another.

"OK, chaps, pile in. It's ten past six."

Cigarettes were reluctantly thrown away and there were good wishes from Tom and the other lads. Jock, our engineer, had a look at the tyres, flaps and so on. Again, everything was fine. He quickly followed the other five into the machine whilst I said my usual prayer, followed by a rubbing of my right foot over the ground—another ridiculous superstition.

I gained this peculiar idea from an instructor at Heavy Conversion Unit. He had told us of an injury he had received on an operational flight. He had always rubbed his foot into the ground before boarding his aircraft but that night he had forgotten to do so.

I made up my mind there and then that when I got to a squadron I would do it before each take-off. I would try not to forget. I never did. It all sounds so very stupid now but it was then a vital part of my routine.

Once inside the aircraft, nervousness seemed to disappear. This, of course, was not true: it only meant that the concentration on starting the motors and having much to think about overcame inner feelings. Already, as I climbed into my seat, the others had settled in and had completed their pre-take-off drills.

I began mine by opening the side window

and shouting to Tom that I was ready for starting up. Thumbs up from him and the boys showed that all was ready.

Port outer, starboard outer, port inner, starboard inner—in turn the powerful motors roared into operation drowning all other sounds. Having allowed them to warm up, I pushed open the throttles fully in turn, both magnetos on each engine checked, propeller pitch operation OK, oil temperatures normal.

"Good old ground crew," I thought as I set the four throttles to keep the engines running at idling speed but not too slowly to prevent oiling up of plugs.

A-Able was now taxying on to the perimeter track.

"Are we all set?"

"Yes, I think I've remembered and checked everything. Too late now anyhow."

"OK, Reg, Brian, Wilf?" The latter two—the wireless operator and the navigator—then walked (or climbed) back to the fuselage rest position for take-off to lighten the weight in the nose. Reg followed, took up his seat beside me and helped fasten my safety straps. Oxygen mask fastened over my mouth he said over the intercom,

"All set to go."

"OK." I waved to ground crew for 'chocks away'. The large wooden blocks were drawn out from their position in front of the great wheels and we were waved an 'OK'. Tom and the ground crew all stood in line. We knew they were wishing us luck and a safe return.

Take-off

I opened up the throttles and started the machine rolling. B-Baker, C-Charlie, D-Dog, E-Easy: we followed the latter and took up our position in the procession round to the take-off point.

Met. had been right: there was a slight ground mist but nothing to worry about. The entire squadron seemed to be there to see us off. I was elated. Fears were still hidden—we'd get back OK—nothing could happen to us—

but I think all must have felt that way.

We followed closely behind E-Easy and halted about twenty yards from his tail as he came to a standstill to await his turn to take off.

Brakes on—throttles fully open to clear engines—propeller pitch set fully fine for take-off—flaps 20° down. We rolled forward and as we received our green light, I released the brakes and swung on to the runway heading east and into a slowly rising sun.

"OK, chaps—here we go."

Take-off was always a hazardous affair—an engine cutting on becoming airborne would not be a pleasant experience. Some 10,000lbs of high explosive could make a nasty mess. With a full load, the Halifax Mark III had a strong swing to the right on take-off and so, as I rolled forward, I applied full left rudder and opened up the starboard motors just slightly ahead of the port. This assured a straight start but once momentum had been gained I neutralised rudders and pushed throttles fully open—so far, so good.

I felt Reg's hand behind mine as I held the throttles at maximum boost as I needed both hands for the actual 'lift-off. I told Reg to hold them there and lock. As I grasped the wheel with both hands, Reg pulled over a small lever on the side of the throttle quadrant that held the four levers in position and made it impossible for vibration to alter their settings. We rapidly gained speed: 95, 100, 110 miles an hour. Stick slowly back—we were airborne—fifty feet.

"2,400 revs, please, Reg," I said referring to the propeller speed. He reduced the revs. The roar of the engines was less deafening and became a more evenly synchronised hum. At 400 feet, I throttled back and raised the flaps. There was a slight drop in height and an alteration of pressure on the stick. This necessitated a slight change of trim. When properly trimmed, an aircraft should theoretically fly 'hands and feet off', but in practice didn't quite work in that way.

Nevertheless, trimming lessened the work of the pilot considerably.

We now were climbing at 160 mph. Jock informed me that all pressures and temperatures were normal. With his broad Glasgow accent, he was sometimes difficult to understand. This, plus the inevitable crackling of the intercom, always caused trouble and discords resulted. 1,000 feet—everything was running smoothly although I sweated considerably.

"Switch on the oxygen, please, Reg, and you can all take up your respective positions." Three weighty individuals taking up their positions in the nose made it again necessary to adjust the trim. I asked Ken, the rear gunner, and the youngest of our crew, whether his oxygen was coming through all right. He said it was and, in turn, the others told me they were also receiving their supply.

Wilf requested me to climb over Bridlington and out to sea on a course of 092° for seven minutes. This would just bring us back over base at 0700 hours to set course with the other twenty-five aircraft of the squadron. As I peered over the side, I saw Bridlington partially enveloped in the morning mist but was able to pick out June's house on the outskirts.

""See you tonight," I thought hopefully as I banked slowly and headed seawards.

Wilf came through and in his usual quiet manner told me to be at 4,000 feet over base and to set course on a heading of 225° degrees. I set this course on the compass grid ring in readiness and steered by the directional gyro indicator that was synchronised with the magnetic compass.

Over the sea

We were now approaching base. The rest of the squadron all appeared miraculously at the same time and we closed in and formed a loose formation. I counted twenty-five aircraft—everyone had got off without mishap. The aerodrome below looked empty and deserted.

As we turned on to our first course Jock told me quite casually that the starboard outer cylinder head temperature was running high.

"OK, Jock, thanks. Keep your eye on it and let me know if she gets any higher, will you?"

On reaching Goole, only a short distance from base and our first turning point, we turned port and headed east towards the coast. I secretly envied the few people below—some walking, others cycling along the winding country roads. They seemed insignificant and appeared as pinheads. The mist was clearing rapidly showing the countryside in its thousand and one colours—so wonderfully peaceful it was difficult to believe that within two hours we should be a target for unfriendly gunners.

Now our twenty-six aircraft, still close together formed only a small part of a long procession. I didn't attempt to count the black specks that covered the entire sky. 1,200 bombers, each with a sting of 10,000lbs. Surely the German population would collapse soon? In addition to this saturation bombing, our armies were meeting with success in all sectors. The American Air Force was even penetrating the Reich as far as Berlin in daylight. The tired people of the English cities were enjoying long-deserved peace in the absence of German raiders and rockets. Once again my thoughts were interrupted by Jock's voice.

"All temperatures normal now and everything bang on."

Wilf informed me that we were dead on track and on time over Beachy Head. I could now see numerous squadrons of fighters circling a few thousand feet above us—just small dots in the sky. It gave one a grand sense of security—they were there to protect us—the hazard of enemy fighters would be lessened considerably.

E-Easy was now flying thirty yards or so on my port beam—we kept together and climbed on slowly towards the Dutch coast. Slowly gaining altitude made it necessary for me to increase boost periodically, as the air became thinner with height, to maintain a steady climb more power was needed.

Enemy coast ahead

The Dutch coast gradually became clear and Reg was checking his map carefully to give Wilf a crossing pinpoint. Our route did not take us over any large coastal towns. Experience told us that such places were very heavily defended. Naturally, it was almost impossible to miss some of the inland towns. One of these was Tilberg and clusters of black puffs were already welcoming the leaders of the stream. From a distance they looked surprisingly harmless but as we neared the town, I realised they could be, and were, horribly unpleasant. One or two bursts appeared rather too near to be healthy so I made a slight climbing turn to the right to skirt the town.

E-Easy remained on course. I couldn't help thinking him rather foolish. It was unnecessary and asking for trouble—trouble that could be avoided. Most of the stream in front of us had crept round to the right of the town's defences just as we had. I watched until he emerged from the cloak of lingering black smoke puffs into the comparative safety of the clear blue sky on the other side of Tilberg.

We slowly turned to port again to regain our track. I couldn't catch E-Easy as he must have been a few hundred yards ahead. He had become lost from view and added to the forerunners of the stream. Other squadron aircraft were now mixed with us as we ambled onward towards the German border.

Wilf told me that the slight deviation from track had put us a minute behind schedule and asked me to increase speed. I explained that we were now at 20,000 feet and would climb the remaining 1,000 feet to bombing height, then would increase air speed to 175.

At 21,000 feet, I levelled out and trimmed her to fly straight and level. The engines were behaving magnificently and the occasional OK from Jock assured me that all instruments were showing normal readings. Only another fifteen minutes to zero hour. Soon we would reach our destination and my apprehension had returned. My clothes were moist with nervous perspiration. My jaws ached through chewing gum from the very moment I had entered the aircraft. Another habit, but it did serve the dual purpose of clearing one's ears, which occasionally cracked due to the change in pressure at various altitudes was also a substitute for smoking.

Reg was now giving Wilf frequent pinpoints that he plotted on his chart. The bombsight was ready.

On target

I could see the Rhine winding its way through the large industrial towns of the Ruhr Valley. One of these, Reg identified as Duisburg.

"0925," said Wilf as he instructed me to alter course to 087°. This was our bombing direction and, theoretically, should bring us over the target. The Pathfinders were now being fired at. The sky filled with black bursts. It was difficult to differentiate between the leading aircraft and the lethal puffs, most of which indicated spent 88 millimetre shells.

"There are the first target indicators," Reg shouted excitedly as I observed massive red cascades of fire bursting on the thickly built-up area forming the target. Brian, the wireless operator, took command of the intercom and asked me to switch on the receiver to Channel D, the radio frequency for this particular mission. As the set warmed up, I was deafened by the atmospherics through the headphones and also the attempts by the Hun at jamming.

These were usually unsuccessful for we always managed to receive the Master Bomber's instructions. (Master Bomber was the name given to a few hand-picked Pathfinder pilots and crews who went into the target with the flare-dropping aircraft. They were without exception veterans of numerous operations and their task was to decide the accuracy of the target indicators and to subsequently transmit instructions to the main force.)

We were now in Reg's hands. He could see his target and it was his job to give me the necessary alterations to course to bring us steadily up to the target.

"Hello, Samson, hello Samson, this is Clever Boy. Bomb the north side of the red TIs—bomb the north side of the red TIs," came the instructions referring to the target indicators.

"Bomb doors open," requested Reg as we ran up with two minutes to go. I could now see stick after stick of bombs falling from the leading aircraft. It was an impressive sight. The town was already covered by thick grey smoke against which brilliant red flares burned marking the target.

"OK, Reg. Bomb doors open."

No longer were voices calm and steady. We now shouted. We were tense and tempers were short.

"Five degrees starboard," yelled Reg. "OK, OK, keep her there—left, left, bit more, left, left, steady, steady."

It was now a struggle to keep the aircraft on an even keel. The slipstream from those in front tossed us about and made it difficult to fly straight and level. The flak was intense and I could smell cordite. Its unpleasantly pungent smell meant that the bursts were dangerously close. There was a loud bang then a noise like hail rattling on a corrugated iron roof. We had been hit but how badly, I did not know. The aircraft still responded to the controls and that was the main thing.

"Bombs gone—keep her steady, we want a good photo." A red light flashed in the cockpit which meant that as the bombs were released, the camera had automatically taken a photo of the area over which our bombs were dropping.

Fifteen seconds later a further two flashes of the red light indicated that the photo had been taken. Those fifteen seconds seemed like an hour. I had to fly as straight and as level as possible to get a good photo. It was important not only for Reg's satisfaction whose job was

judged by this, but was also instrumental to intelligence in assessing the damage caused by the massed assault.

"Bomb doors closed." We were now through the worst of the flak as I dived sharply to port building up speed to 250 miles an hour. We had descended to 17,000 feet as I straightened out and turned onto the course Wilf had given me for our first leg on the homeward journey. I asked Jock to check the bomb bays—by lifting small panels he could see whether all the bombs had released or not.

We were out of the range of the gunfire and could still see the rest of the stream going in amidst a heavy curtain of flak. By now the target was almost completely covered by spirals of smoke that blanketed the whole town. It looked like hell. I saw a Halifax receive a direct hit from a shell and burst into a thousand pieces. No parachutes emerged. I didn't think it was one of our squadron for they should have all bombed by now.

"All bombs have gone," reported Jock after I had asked Wilf to log the time and position of the aircraft that was hit.

I felt safer now. We were on our way home. I would see June tonight—perhaps go to the pictures. It seemed such a contrast to the hell we had just left in our wake.

We still could not determine where we had been hit but everything seemed OK—probably a few holes in the fuselage. We maintained 17,000 feet; our cruising speed should have been 175 but we flew at 200 miles an hour. Everyone hurried home; to be among the first to land was everyone's aim. This annoyed Flying Control for to have about ten aircraft all requesting landing instructions at the same time was not easy but we couldn't, or wouldn't, see their point at the time—we wanted to land and that was that.

Homeward bound

"Everyone OK?" I asked. Everyone was—and very excited too. "How about some rations, Jock—come on, you ruddy foreigner, give the driver some chocolate, I'm hungry."

Jock duly passed round a bar of chocolate cream which, after unhooking my oxygen mask, I quickly ate. Oxygen always created an awful taste in my mouth and the chocolate was wonderful.

On crossing the Dutch coast, I again put the nose down in a gradual descent endeavouring to be at the English Coast at 10,000 feet, at which height we would fly over England. The sun was now shining brightly—a heavenly morning—the sea looked bluer than ever before—the foam of folding waves glistened like sequins on an evening gown.

We were safe now—life was precious. I wondered if any of our squadron had been shot down. We'd had a lucky run lately. This was our thirty-fourth trip—maybe one or two more to do—would we make it OK?

We reached 10,000 feet a little before we got to the English coast so I levelled out and asked Jock for a cup of coffee. At the best of times, hours-old coffee from a flask tastes like anything but coffee—this was no exception but then it tasted divine. At 10,000 feet it was safe to discontinue the use of the oxygen so Jock took a cup to each of the crew. I felt refreshed after this and my mind was on Bridlington that evening.

A little over four hours ago the countryside had looked unreal, possibly because I loved its green fields and lanes so much that I was scared of the possibility of never seeing them again. Now they belonged to me once more and looked even more beautiful with the sun tracing its shadows over a green and yellow carpet of English farmland. Here and there small groups of houses and scattered farms formed villages. Large towns with their tall chimneys belching smoke—the industrial areas of the North Country, contrasting with their German counterparts we had left behind—a blazing mass of sheer destruction.

By this time I was beginning to feel uncomfortable. I was cramped from sitting in the same position for so long and Hull was a

welcome sight—just twenty minutes back to base. I eased forward on the stick and increased slightly the throttle settings that gave us around 220 mph and a descent of 500 feet per minute to bring us in at about 1,000 feet, the height at which we made the airfield circuit. Three or four other aircraft were in front but I couldn't distinguish their markings and so didn't know whether or not they belonged to our squadron. We hadn't done so badly.

"Hello Stepin, Hello Stepin, F-Fox approaching base at 3,000 ft, permission to join circuit please. Over."

"Hello F-Fox, Hello F-Fox, this is Stepin, you are No.3 to land, landing is to the east, over. Stepin from Fox, Roger, out."

The flying control WAAF whose voice I heard sounded wonderfully feminine and could have been a personal welcome.

"OK, chaps, climb into the rest position."

Back came Wilf, a satisfied grin on his face. Yes, he'd navigated us well, his job for today at least, was finished. Brian passed me next, he too was smiling. He lived, ate and slept radio—he knew his job 100 per cent and we all had the utmost faith in him. If ever we were lost or not sure of our position, by contacting various stations, Brian would be able to give Wilf a fix that he could plot and so determine our whereabouts.

"Good trip," said he as he ambled by. Then Reg once again, the seat by my side was clicked home into position and he jumped into it to assist me in the landing.

"Stepin from Fox, downwind, wheels, wheels." This was a safety check to make sure one didn't forget to lower the undercarriage! Many a landing had been made with wheels still in the retracted position.

"Quarter flap, please, Reg. Fox to Stepin, flaps, flaps, over".

"Stepin to Fox, Roger, out."

B-Baker was landing as we turned onto the base leg. One more had landed before him so we were third back—not too bad out of twenty-six.

"Stepin to Fox, you are number one to land. Out." We now turned gently on to the final approach at 800 feet.

"Pitch fully fine and half flap, please, Reg."

I slowly eased back the throttle as we approached at 125 mph. I was slightly overshooting so asked Reg for 3/4 flap to give us a quicker rate of descent without having to cut down the power. Heavy aircraft drop like stones if power is reduced too much. We came over the airfield boundary nicely.

"OK, Reg, cut throttles."

This he did whilst I checked our descent into a very shallow dive and then slowly eased back on the stick to stall the aircraft at about five feet from the ground. She landed with a slight bump but in one piece.

"Stepin to Fox, turn right at intersection."

"Fox to Stepin Wilco. Out."

As we started to lose speed I gently applied the brakes and taxied slowly to the intersection and made for our dispersal point.

Safely home

Tom and the ground crew boys were waiting—they were genuinely pleased to see us. I swung the aircraft into position at dispersal and before switching off, once more checked all engines, magnetos, flap operation and so on. Everything was OK—we couldn't have been hit very badly. It was very quiet when the engines stopped and how lovely it was to get out of that seat and stretch my legs. Before I could get out of the cockpit, Tom appeared in the fuselage and asked whether everything was all right. He sounded more serious than usual.

"Yes, Tom, she's fine, but why the harassed look and the panic?"

He excitedly informed me that the aircraft was needed again that night—another twenty-six were needed again that evening. This shook me to the core. Normally, at the most, we did only one trip a day—usually one every other day. I consoled myself with the thought that another crew would take her tonight. We'd never been asked to do two in a day—one

Ruhr trip would last me for two or three days.

Ken and Jack, the gunners, had been the first out and had immediately rushed around looking for damage. They found five holes in the fuselage and beamed proudly as they told the rest of us as we jumped out. Wilf was carrying a jagged piece of iron fragment that he found lodged in one of the holes.

"A good souvenir!" he said.

The bus was already waiting for us. Two crews already aboard shouted to us to hurry for they were anxious to get their cup of tea and get the job of debriefing over. We bade farewell to Tom and the boys and quickly climbed into the bus. The crews met us with questions as to how well our trip went and told us that they too had been hit but not seriously. One had sprung an oil leak in the port inner engine but it had functioned well enough to keep running all the way home.

On arriving at the briefing room the words 'All back' written boldly in chalk across the blackboard were a cheerful welcome—our run of good luck was continuing. As we handed in our escape kits and drew out our personal belongings. A WAAF officer handed us welcome cups of tea and biscuits that we took with us to the debriefing.

F/Lt 'Chalky' White smiled in his usual way as we sat down. He was glad to see us—he seemed to like us all and took a personal interest in every individual on the Squadron.

"What was the trip like?" he asked as we took our seats and helped ourselves to the free cigarettes. Perhaps it was because they were free they tasted grand and I chain-smoked throughout his informal questioning. I told him that we'd had a good trip although comparatively uneventful and proceeded to give him details of bombing height and defences encountered. From his log Wilf then gave positions of aircraft shot down.

Target for tonight

I had a slight headache and felt even worse when I saw my name included in the list for the night's trip. I could hardly believe it. Tom had been right—there was another show on and, what was more, *we* were participating. My dreams of a quiet evening were dashed. I felt tired and depressed and even more despondent when I learned that the captain of the crew that should have taken our aircraft had gone sick.

Having changed my flying kit and deposited Mae West and parachute, I ran over to the Flight Commander's office to sign the flight authorisation book, indicating a completed trip. I looked up at the record of sorties. Our crew had two more to do to complete one tour, after which we would enjoy at least six months' rest. The only consoling thought at the time was the fact that another trip tonight would leave only one to do. I was anxious and ready for a rest. With the exception of Reg, I knew my crew were ready for this rest too. Reg could have gone on indefinitely, thirty-four penetrations into Germany and occupied Europe had affected him no more than would the equivalent number of runs down to the English coast. He loved danger but accepted and talked about it quietly and didn't shoot a line.

The bus that ran us up to the mess was a hubbub of voices: crews exchanging experiences and the terrific pasting they had given the Rhineland town.

I felt dirty and my head ached severely as I jumped from the bus and made for the mess cloakroom. A wash and brush-up revived me and I strolled into the small bar. The Wing Commander, in the middle of a crowd, was apologetically referring to the night's trip.

I washed down three Aspro tablets with a small beer then went in search of food. Our ex-hotel chef was a popular fellow and he cooked extraordinarily well. Today was no exception: soup, roast beef and Yorkshire pudding, followed by jam tart. We ate well, talked of the trip and afterwards took our coffee into the anteroom securing two comfortable armchairs in front of the open log fire. I still didn't feel

too good despite the Aspros and a good lunch. After only a casual glance at one of the daily papers I became drowsy and subsequently fell asleep. I must have slept for three hours or so for, when I woke, the room was practically empty and most of the boys had gone back to their beds to snatch a few hours' rest before they were needed again.

Tea would be ready within half an hour and so I decided to stay put in front of the fire. I felt lazy although the Aspro had started to take effect and my head ached less. I dozed again but was soon awakened by the crowd—the call of tea had caused most of them to leave their beds. Once again the anteroom became alive. One or two were standing around, cups in hand obviously almost ready to catch a bus into town for the evening.

They were shaved and their buttons glistened—I envied them. As a night operation was pending, the incoming phone calls would be cut—June would not be able to get through. If I didn't call at her home before six o'clock, she would guess I was otherwise engaged.

Three hot cups of tea removed the last traces of my headache and I began to wish away the hours. I slept again until someone tapped me on the shoulder and told me that food was to be had. I didn't feel hungry but struggled through a plate of bacon, eggs and chips, punctuated frequently by sips of hot, milky coffee.

Off again
Again we waited for the transport—the early morning procedure would be repeated.

The rest of my crew, at this time all NCO's, had been collected separately from the sergeants' mess and it was not until I arrived at the briefing room that I saw them for the first time since we had departed at lunch time.

Various guesses had been made at the target but it came as a surprise to see the red tapes still forming the same shape as they had earlier: Duisburg. I felt easier and thought of the chaos that the second air armada within fifteen hours would bring to the German civil defence squads, to say nothing of the misery of the wretched inhabitants of this unfortunate city. I didn't feel sorry for them but felt that the end of the war was surely close. After all, they had bombed our cities and had shown no mercy. Many of my colleagues must have inwardly shared similar thoughts, especially perhaps the Londoners, for they realised the effect bombing could have on helpless citizens lacking the powers of retaliation.

The briefing was similar. Once again we were to form up with other squadrons to make a bombing force of 1,200 machines. The target was any part of industrial Duisburg that showed lack of attention from the morning's effort. Zero hour 02.30. Our bombing time zero plus five.

At 23.14 I waved "Chocs away!" and swung onto the perimeter track. I kept a safe distance behind the aircraft in front as we taxied slowly round to the west side of the field. His tail light made the outline of his rear gunner visible—a strange, ghost-like sight in his two flying suits and tight-fitting helmet. The rear turrets were bitterly cold and gunners had to dress themselves in the warmest clothes possible. Some lucky ones sported electrically heated suits but even with these the cold at heights of four miles high could make them most uncomfortable. The rest of the crew were more fortunate: hot air from the engines was circulated throughout and around the cockpit and, except in the case of extremely cold conditions, all but gunners would be reasonably free from the biting cold outside temperatures.

A green flash from an Aldis lamp was our cue to line up on the runway. I opened up the motors and rolled her into position, a long narrowing avenue of lights made up the flare path which was to guide us on our take-off run into the dark night. As I gently opened up the throttles, the four engines roared responsively into action and once again took us rapidly down the lighted path and lifted our twenty-seven ton monster into the air.

Once I had left the ground the lights of the airfield formed their regular pattern below and gradually faded into the still dark night as we climbed on a steady course seawards. Wilf said we had time to fly on a course to Scarborough and back before setting course proper on the first leg of our run.

We could see a faint coastline and distant rings of lights as we climbed steadily on a course to Scarborough. These lights were other airfields and appeared very close to each other. They were the boundary lights that formed a circle round an entire aerodrome making identification of a landing ground simpler but also to assist pilots in keeping on a close circuit in bad weather.

I could now see moving lights all round me: the green and red wing-tip lights of other aircraft contrasted with the ceiling of stars above us—a wonderful sight. I enjoyed flying at night for the air was smoother without the turbulence often experienced during the day.

Our route was exactly the same as the morning and, as we climbed towards the coast having set course over base at midnight, I thought of the people I had envied early that morning—they were now awake in their homes listening to the roar of our stream overhead.

After crossing the English coast, there was only starlight—all wing lights were switched off. How could so many aircraft maintain the same route without some of them colliding? Fortunately, however, this rarely happened, thank God.

Enemy coast ahead—again

Once again as we crossed the Dutch coast we were greeted with familiar starbursts that abruptly trailed into puffs of grey smoke and floated past our wing tips. Again we were fired upon, a couple of searchlight beams added their doubtful beauty to the official welcome.

I told Wilf I was altering course temporarily

200° to starboard to evade the far-reaching beams of those dangerous lights. To be coned in half a dozen merging streams of lights was blinding and made it extremely difficult to read the instruments on which one relied so desperately at night.

We managed by this slight alteration of course to dodge their beams and subsequently turned back onto course. Far in the distance was a red glow. I checked our position with Wilf who told me that we were 150 miles from Duisburg. But it was the target, still burning furiously from the morning's attack. As we flew on, the fire became a carpet of flame against a dim horizon, gradually increasing in area until the winding Rhine showed its shape separating the two sections of the town.

Already the town was outlined by a ring of searchlights whose beams slowly waved up and down in helpless indication of their feeble efforts to embrace the leading bombers that had already entered the target area. I felt very safe, gunfire was heavy but inaccurate. As we lined up on our bombing run I looked down into a hell of burning ruins. For the first time I pitied the people below. For the first time I realised fully the misery and utter destruction that air bombardment could create.

Wilf, giving me our bombing run course, interrupted my thoughts. Tonight we were going in on a heading of 065°. I slowly banked and straightened out on the given course. The fires below turned night into day and there was little trouble seeing the massed aircraft slowly rolling in towards the inferno that only a little more than half a day ago had been Duisburg, a large and important inland port. Tomorrow it would be a graveyard. The outgoing roads would be crowded with thousands of homeless people. Yes, for a few moments, I did again feel sorry for those people but my sympathy was only short-lived. They had tried, without success, to obliterate our cities.

I thought how the tables had changed from the summer of 1941 when 'The Few' knocked the Hun out of the skies and saved us all by their spirit and unparalleled guts in the air.

Reg asked me to turn on to 070—he had already picked out his target, a group of factories on the south side of the river. The flak was now a little more accurate but did not compare with the intense barrage of the morning's run. As we bombed, new fires started in previously untouched patches of the town—the inferno grew and as we turned and dived away from the target having collected our photo, a huge curtain of dark grey smoke ballooned over the town.

Still the bombers were going in and still more fires started. Two aircraft went down in the target area which I asked Wilf to log—I was sure they were bombers. I looked away, blazing aircraft falling from the sky were unpleasant sights—and their crews might be our friends.

Homeward bound

Yet again *Friday the 13th* was behaving magnificently. I was now glad we had made this second trip—it left us with one only to do. I felt proud and elated at the thought of completing a tour and shooting a line as an instructor at some training establishment. We flew on fast towards the coast. On either side, a few flak bursts appeared reminding us that we were not alone on our way westward. Here and there searchlights swung across the sky. Somehow, once again we managed to evade their reach and still diving slightly, crossed the Dutch Coast at just a little over 10,000 feet.

It was very easy at times like this to consider the trip complete and disregard the possible menace of fighters. They had a nasty habit of tailing bombers out over the North Sea and then opening up. I'd seen it happen to a Halifax one night. I reminded myself of this and also my gunners, telling them to report anything that looked in any way suspicious. However, we crossed the English coast and still could boast an uneventful trip—a very easy one compared with previous night visits to the Ruhr.

A few minutes later, Jock reminded us all that it was coffee time and within a few minutes appeared with a cup of greyish brown liquid. Tonight it tasted even better than ever. The crew were bantering over the intercom. I reminded them, in a polite way, to shut up. They too felt good but it was still not too late for a fighter attack and we were not going to be caught now. If the intercom was used for chatter, it was difficult to hear the gunners should they spot a fighter on our tail. The boys realised this and lapsed into silence. The only noise was the drone of the engines.

Diversion

At 0440 Brian received a diversionary message over the radio. For reasons unknown, we were not to land at base. Normally, this meant bad weather at base but the weather was so perfect I could not imagine it changing to any great degree over the remaining eighty-odd miles. Wilf deciphered the coded message and informed me that we were to land at Catfoss, a training aerodrome only a few miles from our own aerodrome. This proved that the reason for the diversion was not due to adverse weather conditions or at least made it very unlikely.

At 0505 we circled Catfoss and touched down ten minutes later. Within half an hour twenty-five Halifax crews were informed that back at our home base of Lissett F/Lt Macadam had had an engine cut on his take-off run, had retracted his undercarriage and slithered to a standstill just short of the boundary fence at the far end. Fortunately, the rest of the squadron was already airborne. He and his crew had made a hasty retreat from a partially damaged aircraft containing 10,000lbs of high explosives. The bombs eventually exploded one and a half hours after the crash and fortunately caused no damage except a few broken windows on the drome and surrounding farmhouses. The aircraft itself was splattered in little pieces for hundreds of yards around the airfield. The runway was littered with jagged scraps of metal, a danger to the tyres of any aircraft landing—hence our landing at Catfoss.

Dawn was now breaking but before the sun appeared we were on our way by road to Lissett, our base. I was exhausted when, at ten o'clock, I pulled back my bedclothes and climbed into their cooling depths. I remembered little more than Fred reluctantly placing his pipe on the chair beside his bed and climbing likewise into his bed. Fred was tired too!

It was five o'clock when our batman quietly awakened us and poured boiling water into our respective washbasins for washing and shaving. He'd even cleaned our buttons and polished our shoes. We both showered then proceeded rapidly into Bridlington where we parted and went our various ways.

My way led me to a pleasant detached house on the outskirts of the town where I arrived in time for tea with June. We listened to the six o'clock news that gave a detailed account of the raids. They could not describe those sights I had witnessed a few hours earlier—that blazing hell. Could people like June, her mother, father and small brother, imagine what it was really like? No—they couldn't and I would not want them to. We didn't go to the pictures after all. Instead we sat around the fire and talked. The war seemed so far away and we talked of everything else.

Reproduced from Have a good time, chaps. *No publisher is stated and so we were unable to obtain permission to republish here. Apologies for lack of acknowledgement.*

Allan Weller

Wireless Operator/Air Gunner

40 Squadron

Allan Weller before one of two daylight trips over Yugoslavia, November 1944. Standing by aircraft 'R' in which he did five trips in succession.

Allan at home near Bath in 1997

Allan Weller

Allan Weller volunteered for the RAF in November 1941 and trained as a wireless operator/air gunner. He served with training units in Palestine and Egypt both as a trainee and later as an instructor. He joined 40 Squadron in Italy and completed forty operations flying Wellingtons.

A piece of cake but no crumpet!

I was sixteen a fortnight after war was declared and was due to return to Saffron Walden Grammar School where I had attended as a boarder since 1932. I took what was then the School Certificate at the end of the autumn term and obtained the necessary passes. I persuaded my parents to let me leave school and start my chosen career in agriculture whilst awaiting the then unforeseen war events to happen.

As the war came to life in the spring of 1940, I decided that when I had to go in the forces I would try for the RAF. Meanwhile, the rule was that training for aircrew would not start before the age of eighteen and, being engaged in what was considered essential war work and enjoying it, I did not volunteer for aircrew until November 1941.

Having been accepted as WOP/AG I did not receive my call-up until August 1942 when I proceeded to Padgate, Warrington, and on to Blackpool for initial square-bashing and wireless training to weed out those who could not reach the required Morse standard—and there were quite a few.

Having finished at Blackpool, I was sent to Madley (No. 4 Radio School) in Herefordshire, arriving in time for my first Christmas in the RAF—and pretty lousy it was too. Thereafter I progressed through the ground W/OP course and on to the air W/OPs training. After thirteen months in RAF blue I finally sat in an aircraft—a De Havilland Dominie—to do air exercises with the old General Purpose transmitter and receiving sets. These were T1180 and R1181 if I remember rightly as used in Battles, Blenheims, etc. until the more modern Marconi T1154/R1155 sets became available in the Percival Proctors to which we progressed for solo exercises.

In December 1943, having qualified for the new signallers' brevet and been made sergeant, I was sent on Christmas leave prior to going overseas.

Allan Weller

Going abroad

IN mid January 1944 I was on board the *Stirling Castle* sailing from Liverpool via the Straits of Gibraltar into the Mediterranean, it having by now been opened again for through passage to the Suez Canal.

We disembarked at Port Said, thence to Heliopolis aircrew holding centre before proceeding in batches to El Ballah on the banks of the Suez Canal for the gunnery course. We had our first taste of tent life in the sand. It was a novel experience to open the tent flap, look outside and see huge ships apparently sailing across the desert.

From El Ballah we went to another holding centre in Jerusalem for about a month before going to one of three OTUs in the then Palestine. Two were for bombers and one for coastal training. Whilst at OTU we heard of the Normandy invasion on D-Day (6 June 1944) and wondered if we would ever get operational.

By August 1944 we were finished at OTU and were sent almost immediately to Italy by air, where, after a short while at a holding centre in Naples, crews were sent by rail in cattle trucks to Foggia to be distributed between the six Wellington squadrons based on and around Foggia.

Three crews from my OTU course were dropped off at 40 Squadron and we were allotted a tent recently occupied by a crew lost over Rumanian oil targets. During the time of our first six ops. we had no beds or furniture of any kind in the tent. Eventually, we constructed or scrounged makeshift beds and a wash basin. Fortunately, the weather remained good during this settling-in period. Sadly, one of the two crews who trained with me at OTU were lost on only their second op. I subsequently learned there were no survivors.

At this stage of the war our targets ranged from Salonica to Szehesfehervar, Hungary, plus many in northern Italy: Milan, Bologna, Brescia, Verona and so on. Mining of the River Danube had been a regular part of the Group's work during April to October 1944. We took part in the last of these on 4 October by the light of a brilliant harvest moon—low level all the way. It was a spectacular trip but resulted in the loss of an experienced crew over the river. The Germans by

Allan's Wellington taken from a Liberator on the way to a bridge target in northern Italy. Take-off was in the afternoon (daylight) to arrive over the target after dark. Late December 1944.

Foggia, Italy. 40 Squadron's living quarters for the winter of 1944.

now were evacuating Greece and we did two trips to Athens airfields without Pathfinders but dropping our own flares to harass the night evacuation by Ju52s from these airfields. November 1944 saw the Group doing a number of supply-dropping trips to Tito and his partisans in various areas of Yugoslavia. This was interspersed with bombing of troop concentrations, sometimes involving two sorties in twenty-four hours in increasingly worsening weather conditions.

The Wellington squadrons were gradually converted to Liberators. Having flown together as a crew since OTU we were tour-expired in January 1945. I never did hear from the bomb aimer, navigator or rear gunner again but met my pilot in transit camp in Cairo after returning to OTU as a screen W/OP until Japan surrendered. I was then made redundant and chose to train as a Met.

Observer (Ground) and spent the next year in the Western Desert at El Adam, a staging post on the trooping route to the Middle and Far East.

A feature of my operational and subsequent service in the RAF was the total absence of female company both on the squadron and at El Adam. Having been an A/C Plonk for most of my time training in Britain, what few WAAFs there were on training camps were severely rationed. I consequently arrived home just before my twenty-third birthday almost as innocent and certainly as shy of the fair sex as at the start of the war!

Having read many war books and heard many aircrew stories, my own tour of ops. was, in retrospect, a 'piece of cake'. Nevertheless, of the three crews that joined 40 Squadron on the same day in August 1944, ours was the only one to survive the forty ops. required.

Looking back

IT'S always struck me just how much a part chance played in whether we survived or not. For example, I first met my longest known friend in the RAF, Harold, at Madley on a ground wireless course. We remained in the same class through that and then the air training course; we were on embarkation leave together and posted to the same training units overseas. We ended up on sister squadrons in Foggia, Italy, sharing the same airfield.

I finished my forty ops. a week or two ahead of Harold and whilst I was on leave I heard that he and all his crew had crashed in fog just before his last trip. His twin brother, who trained at the same time but with different units, did not get sent abroad but completed his tour of ops. in the UK.

It was a standing joke in any billet or mess

when writing up the record of our latest dicey trip the optimistic would say,

"That'll be something to tell our grandchildren!" whereas the more pragmatic would reply,

"Just guarantee me children—that's all I ask!"

As one of the lucky ones with children and grandchildren my gratitude for life is profound. My generation was brought up by parents or guardians who had had first-hand experience of the Great War (1914-18) and were appalled at the thought of their offspring having to go through it all again with the inevitable loss of young.

The finest measure of the sacrifices that the likes of Harold and his comrades made is, to my mind, that our children and grandchildren have not been asked to do the same.

Eddie Wheeler

DFC

Wireless Operator/Air Gunner

97, 150 and 214 Squadrons

*AC2 Eddie Wheeler at
Cardington, December 1939*

*Eddie in 1996 ... with Bomber Command Chief,
Sir Arthur Harris*

Eddie Wheeler

Eddie Wheeler joined the RAF as a six-year regular serviceman in 1939. He became a wireless operator/air gunner in 1940 and served with 150, 214 and 97 Squadrons in Bomber Command flying Battles, Wellingtons, Manchesters and Lancasters. He was appointed 517 Squadron Intelligence Officer, Coastal Command in 1944 and was awarded the DFC in 1943. He completed sixty-nine operations of which three were aborted including three one-thousand bomber raids as well as twenty-seven ops. in the Pathfinder Force. He has published a book about his RAF experiences entitled Just to get a bed *from which this extract is taken.*

On being commissioned...

JUST a week after the D-Day landings [6 June 1944] I was summoned to the B Flight CO S/Ldr S. C. Jolly, and my thoughts were on the possibility of another posting. This was rather perplexing in the light of my living-out plans. [Allan was now married to Mollie]. It didn't seem possible that I would be posted back to operations again. On entering the CO's office, I was beckoned to a chair and S/Ldr Jolly ran over my career to date and asked if I had any future ambitions.

My reply was that my only plans were to survive the war. He went on to say that with my experience I should have at least achieved by now the position of Signals Leader with the relevant rank. After telling him of my previous interview for possible commissioning and my own reluctance at that time, he said that he was recommending me to attend Group Headquarters at Bawtry, Yorkshire, for further consideration, emphasising the benefits and advantages of being commissioned. The immediate financial aspects were not attractive as the pay of a Pilot Officer would not be very different to that of a Warrant Officer. However, the on-going rewards would of course be beneficial. After further persuasion, I agreed but registered that I would not be greatly disappointed if I was rejected at the interview. The consensus of opinion back at the sergeants' mess, discussing it with my instructor friends, was that I should accept a commission if offered so long as it never went to my head and meant that I ignored them thereafter!

So, resplendent in my 'best blue', the transport whipped me off to Bawtry and I entered the old mansion which housed the Group Headquarters staff. I felt completely relaxed as I joined five other candidates in the waiting room. The first interviewee, an AC2 wearing a white flash in his forage cap, indicating that he was an aircrew trainee, went in first and reappeared twenty minutes later without any visible signs of how he had fared.

A flight lieutenant then signalled me and opened the door announcing,

"Warrant Officer Edwin Wheeler DFC."

At a table sat four uniformed officers of varying ranks and I was addressed initially by an Air Commodore. To his question,

"Why did you join the RAF prior to the war?" I felt that I couldn't truthfully respond with, "Because I wanted a bed!" [Sleeping accommodation in Allan's young days had been in short supply and that was one reason why he had joined the RAF!] After some thought I replied,

"I wanted a career in radio and communications and thought this could be

247

better achieved within the Services."

To the question,

"Why did you volunteer for air crew duties?"

I just had to be truthful and say,

"I didn't volunteer, my name together with most of the others on the course was volunteered!" (Crews were so desperately needed that no one was allowed to fail the medical!)

This brought one or two smiles from the interviewing board. There followed a quiz session on my operational career that they found impressive and said so. I think that my speech had improved quite considerably since my previous interview when it had had a distinct Cockney accent, and certainly I had greater confidence. I was not asked any stupid questions as before such as about the arts, opera and so on of which I had absolutely no knowledge as I had never had the opportunity to learn about them.

In a very relaxed atmosphere I was informed that I would be recommended for a commission and was congratulated on my contribution to the RAF in a comparatively short period of five years. I had to wait another couple of hours whilst the other interviewees took their turn before the waiting transport returned to base. There were conflicting views of how the interviews had gone, some chaps having written themselves off completely and others expressing the view that it had been a 'piece of cake'. It appeared that I alone had been told that I was being definitely recommended. I told Mollie the news and she was happy and excited for me.

The next step was to await confirmation before going off to Gieves, the tailors, for kitting out.

My commissioning was announced in the *London Gazette* on 25 August 1944 and I was a Pilot Officer in the Reserve of Air Force Officers (RAFRO) with a new service number of 56118. The entry into the esteemed RAFRO was based on the fact that I had joined as a regular before the outbreak of war.

Although in the lowest commissioned rank of Pilot Officer, my five-figured service number immediately distinguished me as being a pre-war entry and I couldn't be mistaken for a 'rookie' P/O.

My first bank account had been opened at Glyn Mills to receive my monthly pay and I received a kitting-out allowance that seemed very generous at the time. My pay had risen from 13/9d (69p) a day as a Warrant Officer to 14/6d (72p) a day as P/O but my family allowance increased from 28 shillings (£1.40) a week to 40/6d (£2.02) a week. Total resources at about £7 per week might seem insignificant today but I thought I was doing very well just then!

I moved into the officers' mess and felt suddenly strange in that no-longer could I sprawl in the armchairs as we did in the sergeants' mess. We had to observe all the niceties and listen to the boring conversations of senior officers at the bar where we had to sign for our drinks and pay the mess bill promptly at the end of the month. Now, of course, in addition to continuing my instructional flying duties, I had to perform various extra duties like Orderly Officer. Imagine my embarrassment when, entering the airmens' mess at lunchtime listening to the Orderly Sergeant bellowing, "Any complaints?" and being relieved when there were none! On the odd occasion some bright spark would drum up a trivial complaint just for the hell of it.

On 28 August Mollie entered Eaton Hall hospital in Retford for the birth of our first baby. I remember being very nervous as perhaps most fathers are at this event. Since Mollie's earlier miscarriage I was keeping my fingers crossed that she would not have any further problems.

The next day, 29 August 1944, we were blessed with the birth of a lovely daughter, and I felt so proud and happy that all had gone well. We decided to name her Valerie Anne. When we went back to Ordsall Road in

Retford Mr and Mrs Truswell, our landlords, welcomed us warmly and treated Valerie as one of their own, fussing over her and making our world complete. We were so delighted with our good fortune, I was determined that we would have another child, hopefully a boy, but that was not all-important, another girl would be equally welcome and would receive all our love.

My flying instructional duties with No. 18 OTU continued through the year without too much excitement except for one incident involving an abortive take-off. Pounding down the runway at about 100mph and seeing the perimeter track approaching fast and the aircraft still not lifting can be rather perplexing. Tearing through the boundary hedge and finishing in a canal tends to make one think that flying is only for the birds.

... and on being awarded the DFC

WE were to remain at Bourn in Cambridgeshire for a further three weeks before learning of our postings, but two of these were spent on leave. It was whilst I was at home on leave that I discovered from the *Islington Gazette* that I had been awarded the DFC, it having being announced in the *London Gazette* on 19 October 1943.

My joy was complete, I had survived sixty-six operations (three others didn't count due to aborts albeit over enemy territory) I had been decorated, my official Permanent Pathfinder Certificate had arrived and many new aircrews were arriving daily to take up the challenge where I left off. Now I could more hopefully expect to see the end of the war and carry on with my happily married life.

During this leave, I was invited to visit the company I had worked for prior to the war—Herbert and Sons Ltd., at their Edmonton premises. The reception was overwhelming. The entire workforce were assembled and after a speech by my old friend, Stan Kitchen, I

stepped forward to receive from the Scale Shop Foreman, Fred Pennell, a beautiful barometer suitably inscribed: *To mark the occasion on the award of a DFC.*

I was choked for words. My world was complete, the good Lord had looked kindly on me and protected me through four hard years of war during which so many thousands had died. Proudly wearing the mauve and white ribbon alongside that of the 1939-43 Star, I returned to Bourn to receive the congratulations of the rest of the crew.

I was delighted to find that Johnny and Hitch [crew mates] had also been decorated but was saddened then to hear the news that Paul Carlyon, with whom I had flown in 1940-1, had been shot down and killed over the Bay of Biscay in a raid on Lorient some months earlier. News filtered through fast at this time and I learned that Fred Denman, my friend and front gunner on Wellingtons, had been decorated with the DFM out in the Middle East where he completed his second tour—again on Wellingtons.

Headquarters,
Path Finder Force,
Royal Air Force.

1st August, 1943.

To:-

647193 Flight Sergeant Wheeler, E.

AWARD OF PATH FINDER FORCE BADGE.

You have today qualified for the
award of the Path Finder Force Badge and
are entitled to wear the Badge as long as
you remain in the Path Finder Force.

2.   You will not be entitled to wear
the Badge after you leave the Path Finder
Force without a further written authority
from me entitling you to do so.

Air Commodore, Commanding
Path Finder Force.

Eddie's award of Pathfinder Force badge

Tom Winup

Bomb Aimer

159 and 358 Squadrons

Tom Winup after leaving
Air Crew Reception Centre,
July 1942

Tom on a Caribbean-Panama Canal
cruise in 1997

Aircraft B-24 Liberator EW-287 'R' known as Rogues' Retreat
at Jessore, India, April 1945

Back row left to right: *Frank Flynn (navigator); Chuck King (air gunner);
Paddy Drummond (skipper); Tom Winup (bomb aimer) wearing service
cap; Tubby Salway (air gunner); Alan Dickson (air gunner)*

Front row left to right: *Johnny Lyons (wireless operator/air gunner);
Harry Copeland (air gunner); Clem Johnston (wireless operator/air gunner)
2nd pilot was Keith Tunbridge (he's taking the photo)*

Our crew was known as Drummond's Drips!

Tom Winup

Tom Winup enrolled in the RAF Volunteer Reserve in December 1941 in London but his service was deferred until July 1942. He trained in Torquay at No.5 Initial Training Wing before going to Canada to attend No.4 Bombing and Gunnery School at Fingal, Ontario, and No.1 Air Observer School in Toronto in the summer of 1943. He was awarded his air bomber's brevet in February 1944.

Having had a lifetime's fascination with India, he was delighted when the RAF posted him to 1673 Heavy Conversion Unit at Kolar, India. In November 1944 it was formed into 358 Squadron (Special Duties)—dropping agents and supplies into enemy-occupied territory for Special Operations Executive's (SOE) resistance groups. He was later posted to 159 Squadron. He served with 231 Group, South East Asia Command, flying B-24 Liberators. His regular aircraft was a Liberator (EW 287/R) called Rogues' Retreat whose nose art featured a scantily clad, buxom girl standing invitingly by an open door with a red light above it!

Shortly before the end of war in the Far East Tom took a bombing leaders' course and returned to 358 Squadron as Bombing Leader. He was based at Digri, Jessore and Salboni (Bengal), Kunming (China) and Pegu (Burma). He is now an active member of his local branch of the Burma Star Association.

Two reasons why I'm still here—or the whim of fate

IF it hadn't been for a whim of fate (or something) I wouldn't be here now. It was while at HCU on Kolar in southern India, 150 miles west of Madras, that we were formed into crews. We didn't have a choice: staff officers just put our names down. I was put with an Australian pilot, F/Sgt Porter, who struck me as a decent, dependable sort. I liked him from the word go and felt happy to fly with him. But then it was all changed and I was put down to fly with an Irish pilot, Paddy Drummond, who had a reputation for being drunk most of the time when not flying. I was hardly reassured and not at all keen. However, he proved to be a very good pilot.

As it turned out, Porter's crew crashed doing circuits and bumps. Had the change not been made I wouldn't be here to tell the tale...

The second reason occurred when, as part of our special duties (more of which later) three of us were given the task of a daylight drop on the coast of French Indo-China at a village called Moncay. The weather was awful—we never saw the ground for eight hours because of cloud—but we *had* to get there.

As we approached the area to do the drop of supplies to the French by parachute, all our powers of navigation and the pilot's flying skills were needed.

"Begin descent. Fifteen minutes to ETA," said our navigator. We dropped through the cloud hoping we were more or less in the right place.

"Any idea where we are?" asked our skipper hopefully. "Over land? Over sea? Hazard a guess, navigator!"

"No idea," came the not-very-reassuring reply. At 100 feet we broke cloud. "Over the sea, skip," said the navigator confidently noting the water below us.

"It's not what's below us I'm worried about," replied the skipper, "it's what's around us."

On all sides of us, towering towards the sky with their tops shrouded in cloud were dozens of small volcanic islands like skittles in a skittle alley. They were not marked on our maps and we'd no idea they were there. Somehow we had threaded our way between them. It was sheer good fortune (and the whim of fate again perhaps) that we had not collided with one of them.

Having established how I come to be here at all, I'll go back a little. My squadron, 358, was formed from 1673 HCU in southern India in November 1944. We were trained as a bomber squadron to do daylight formation bombing and despatched to bomb Fort Mandalay in Burma. (As you can imagine, there was much singing of *On the road to Mandalay*!) The fort's location prevented heavy artillery from reaching it, hence the need for bombing. We had also undertaken a jungle survival course—that was worse than beings on ops. but everyone survived—some better than others!

As it turned out it was our one and only bombing raid, for after that, we were retrained for special duties and moved to an isolated base about eighty miles east of Calcutta called Jessore (now in Bangladesh). We took over houses in the town (about six miles from the airfield) for our accommodation and almost became part of the local community. We played endless football matches against local teams which, as they got knocked out in the preliminary rounds, simply transferred their best players to the next village team to play us until, in the final, we were up against the best in the area. We lost.

Special Duties

SOE's Special Duties for my squadron and the sister squadron (357) included dropping agents—Eurasians, British and Americans—by parachute into French Indo-China, Thailand and Burma. We didn't know who they were or anything about them. The only time we saw them was when we picked them up before the drop and that was usually at night. We also dropped supplies packed in canisters.

Distances out there were so great and trips took many hours in the air, sometimes up to twenty-four. This involved stripping the aircraft down to a minimum and using overflow fuel tanks. Our casualties were actually higher than on regular bomber squadrons as we had no radar aids—it was all done by dead reckoning navigation—and some of that was based on travellers' records made in 1870! Hardly the most up-to-date information.

Consequently, there were many times when we hadn't a clue where we were—all those little islands didn't help either. Neither did the weather for the cloud base was often only just above the sea—or so it seemed. We'd often fly really low to try and find a landmark of some sort and could see peasants with cone-shaped hats running around. Sometimes we were so low that the map was no help—we were too close.

One time we spotted a river with an odd-shaped bend that helped pinpoint our position and from there we could head for the dropping zone—a football field. Right in the middle of the circle was a French officer—riding breeches, boots, the lot—we had to pull up to 200 feet, almost back into the clouds in order to drop the canisters, otherwise they'd have been damaged and probably hit him too! We made three runs like this—avoiding islands, groping our way through cloud, finding the football pitch and dropping our canisters. Each time we could see the Japanese but, fortunately, they didn't cause us any trouble.

That night in the mess one of the other two pilots on the same drop wrote, "We broke cloud at sea level and climbed to five feet!"

There had been three aircraft on those drops. They were hazardous runs, to say the least. The two officer pilots were awarded the Croix de Guerre but my skipper, Paddy Drummond, wasn't. He was 'only' a warrant officer…

Mid-air collision

I was on a bombing leaders' course at Amarda Road camp in the Indian state of Orissa. Six of us were to fly in close formation on a fighter affiliation exercise with American Thunderbolts.

A New Zealander who had served in my squadron (358) had a reputation for being the worst pilot in the world for keeping in formation. He had just been commissioned and sent to the unit as a staff pilot. My first thought was,

"Right, I'm not flying with you, chum!" However, I didn't have much choice and I was Number 4 with my aircraft's nose right under the leading aircraft which had our New Zealand friend as co-pilot. (He had, however, redeemed himself before he came to us by having plenty of guts and being awarded the DFC as a warrant officer—even so, his reputation stuck.)

The weather was bad—it was the monsoon—but all was going well, even the New Zealander out in front was holding course. Suddenly, the aircraft to port hit the leader. With all four engines screaming the New Zealander's aircraft, minus its tail unit, went down into a paddy field whilst the other aircraft lost a wing and also crashed.

Debris flew all over the place. I was waiting for something to hit us. Would we too follow him into the paddy field? However, a smart diving curve got us out of the way and, apart from superficial strikes by debris, we were unscathed.

All the crew of the lead aircraft, including the New Zealander, were killed. In total fourteen men were lost in this incident.

(In 1998 I was on holiday in Madras and took a taxi to visit the military cemetery where I found the graves of all fourteen. I remembered most of the names and it struck me how young we all were—twenty was the youngest but the oldest was only twenty-six.)

There's a follow-up to that story. About two or three years ago, quite by chance, at the RAF memorial at Runnymede, I met the daughter of one of the fourteen crew members who had been killed. She told me that her family had never spoken of her father's death but she had been researching it. Her name was Yvonne and she was the daughter of F/O Peter Ettlinger—a father she never knew. We are still in touch.

The official account of the accident from the Ministry of Defence as sent to Yvonne stated that:

At approximately 0945 hrs the formation, which had been encountering medium to bad weather, approached a heavy bank of cloud. The leader, Sqn Ldr Heynert, commenced to lose height in an attempt to fly underneath this, but reached the cloud before he was quite low enough and the formation entered the cloud. Number 6 by this time was some little way behind the formation. On entering the cloud visibility was reduced to nil and numbers 2 and 5 in the formation altered course starboard and number 4 altered course port. On coming out of the cloud aircraft number 1 (EW225 F/O Ettlinger) and aircraft number 3 (EW247) captained by P/O Herbert, were seen to be in close proximity, and number 3 was then seen to pull up and collide with number 1. The tail unit of number 1 was torn off and the aircraft crashed out of control, and one wing (which one not established) of number 3 was torn off, causing the aircraft to crash. Once the crash occurred neither pilot had any chance to execute a

reasonable forced landing, nor was there sufficient time for any member of the crew to make a parachute descent, the aircraft being at 1,000 feet and 2,000 feet at the time of the collision.

When the char wallah lost a leg

WHEN our squadron moved to Jessore it took one and a half days to shift everyone and everything by train. For some reason I had fallen foul of the CO and had been lumbered, along with a couple of other officers, with the job of being in charge of the troop train taking us to Jessore.

As well as RAF personnel we were accompanied by a group of char wallahs—'freelance' tea sellers who accompanied squadrons or army units wherever they went. They weren't officially attached to us but always came with us. Prior to 'joining' the RAF they had been with a Scottish army regiment and acquired Glaswegian accents on top of their Punjabi pidgin English! They looked after themselves pretty well and, I'm glad to say, were not my responsibility. Apart from RAF personnel who *were* my responsibility, I was also detailed to guard a locked tin trunk of secret records and documents.

We stopped at the railway junction at Kharagpur, about eighty miles south-west of Calcutta. There wasn't time for we three officers to take it in turns to supervise the tin trunk *and* get something to eat and, quite contrary to orders, I got a flight sergeant to guard it while the three of us went for a meal.

In the middle of our meal someone came running in in a state of high excitement saying a man had had an accident and his leg had been severed. My heart came in my mouth. I should have been out there keeping an eye on things, supervising the men. I was supposed to be in charge. There'd be an inquiry and maybe a court martial… My imagination ran riot.

I tore outside dreading the worst. Although I shouldn't say it, the relief flooded over me when I discovered that the accident victim was not an RAF chap but one of our char wallahs.

"What happened?" I said.

"He was trying to get water from the train's boiler to make the tea, you see. He slipped and fell and another train coming the other way ran over his leg, sir." (I won't try to write this in Glaswegian Punjabi!)

"See, his leg is here, sir!" The char wallah's son held up his father's severed limb for me. I blanched a little.

"You keep it," I said.

"Can you get it sewn back on, sir?" the son asked me. (He was well ahead of his time, for surgery then did not run to such skills.)

"No," I said and hastily organised an ambulance to take the man to hospital.

The next time I saw our char wallah he was hopping around quite spryly with a peg leg.